GRAHAM KERR'S SMART COOKING

GRAHAM KERR'S
SMART COOKING

Doubleday

LONDON · NEW YORK · TORONTO · SYDNEY · AUCKLAND

TRANSWORLD PUBLISHERS LTD
61-63 Uxbridge Road, London W5 5SA

TRANSWORLD PUBLISHERS (AUSTRALIA) PTY LTD
15-23 Helles Avenue, Moorebank, NSW 2170

TRANSWORLD PUBLISHERS (NZ) LTD
Cnr Moselle and Waipareira Aves,
Henderson, Auckland

DOUBLEDAY CANADA LTD
105 Bond Street, Toronto, Ontario, M5B 1Y3

Published 1991 by Doubleday
a division of Transworld Publishers Ltd

A catalogue record for this book is
available from the British Library.

ISBN 0385 40249X

Typeset by Falcon Graphic Art Ltd,
Wallington, Surrey
Printed in Great Britain by
Richard Clay Ltd, Bungay.

Acknowledgements

$\mathcal{N}$atural bookbirth isn't done alone – it is a team effort and I want to record my thanks, appreciation and affection for everyone who has contributed so much:

Robert Prince and Cynthia Morse, my food associates; Christine Rylko and Brenda Bryant for computer analysis and overall systems management; John McLean for his 'eagle eye'; Allyson Gofton for photographic foodstyling; Alan Gillard for photography; Sandy Silverthorne for the whimsical drawings; Connie Lunde for laying out each and every page; John McEwen for tenacity; Natalie Hall, my wonderful secretary; Judith Kern, wielder of the mighty editorial pencil at Doubleday; every one of our special friends at KING TV in Seattle, who tasted every dish. To my much loved son, Andy, for making my time go further and my beloved wife, lifelong friend and producer, Treena, to whom I now dedicate this book. Eat and be well!

Graham Kerr
September 1991

Table of Contents

Introduction

This book is about celebration and about being truly happy because we care enough to make some changes in the way we eat.

I'm a food man from way back. My parents were hoteliers; my earliest friends were chefs and waiters. My business was, and is, to please. For 26 years I did this by thinking of food only as it contributed to our sensual pleasure. 'After all,' I reasoned, 'if it doesn't look, smell, taste and feel fantastic, it won't bring them back for a second visit.'

For years I made 'good business' by applying this principle of sensual enhancement. *The senses were everything, the only thing!* From time to time I did get one or two letters pleading 'Don't you use a little too much butter and cream?' My serious answer to that was 'Madam, you could get run over by a bus and just think what you would have missed!'

And then came the jolt. My wife, Treena, suddenly had serious heart problems. She hadn't been run over by a bus but she had been buttered and creamed by the way we had been eating!

I began to develop a whole new approach to food. I became preoccupied with what food did to us rather than how it looked and satisfied.

I was obsessed with using less fat, less sugar, less alcohol, less salt, less artificial colour and flavour, less processing, less restructuring. More whole grains, fresh fruits and vegetables . . . all biodynamically organic! What had been smooth and succulent became grainy; what had been soft and velvety became thin.

Inviting aromas disappeared. Colours faded to earthtones, the less to encourage a lust attack! So overwhelming was the evidence of risk that science outsmarted the senses and, as Julie Child puts it, 'food became medicine'.

This couldn't continue; my entire family observed that 'food used to be so much fun but now all the joy of eating has gone'. Having successfully removed everything that looked even remotely risky, I was faced with creating at least a partial return of the sensual enhancement. It was either fix it up or eat alone!

I took time to make these changes so that what we ate would delight and not destroy. My first task was to consider the senses and their individual roles in our enjoyment of food.

We enjoy food with our senses: sight, smell, taste, touch and even sound. No wonder food preferences are so hard to change. I broke taste down into six basic groups: salt, sweet, sour, bitter, piquante (spice-hot) and mouthroundfulness – the sensation of fat/smooth.

I saw that salt, sweet and fat/smooth could be hard to change because each seemed to say 'Please Sir, I demand some more', whereas sour, bitter and spice-hot appeared to be self-limiting and less risky for most people.

The big question was, could I minimize the intrinsic desire for salt, sweet and fat by maximizing the sour,

1

bitter and spice-hot categories and enhancing those flavours with warm aromas, vivid colours and varied textures?

In short, could I create a sensual smoke-screen that would allow me to remove the excessive use of salt, sugar and fat without a loss of overall enjoyment? This was a terrific challenge!

I eventually shortened this idea to the one word *MINIMAX*. By combining the abbreviations *MINI* and *MAX*, I was able to say that healthy alternative styles of cooking need both risk reduction and flavour enhancement, and that this should always be considered one integrated activity to 'minimize risk, maximize flavour'.

I applied the Minimax concept to the moderate-to-high risk recipes of my past and gradually developed a kind of framework that allowed me total freedom to create *within* its limitations.

My goals were as follows:

■ To serve portions of a wider variety of fresh foods, and to achieve this by increasing aromas, colours and textures to offset taste and volume changes.

■ To reduce refined carbohydrates and to increase complex carbohydrates; that is, to eat fewer refined flour and sugar products, especially filled bakery items, and more fruit, vegetables, whole grains, peas, beans and lentils.

■ To eat less meat, fish and poultry (no more than a total of 6 oz/170 g per day) and more peas, beans, lentils, whole grains, low-fat dairy products, seeds and pasta.

■ To use less oil/fat in salads and sauces, especially for pasta, and to eat only small amounts of polyunsaturated margarines on bread and muffins.

■ To use fewer whole eggs (3–4 egg yolks a week for healthy folk) and less saturated fat from all animal protein and from tropical oils (palm, coconut, etc.).

■ To moderate the use of alcohol by substituting fruit juices or new de-alcoholized wines and by adding soda to ordinary table wines.

■ To decrease the use of sodium by eating fewer packaged and prepared foods that are high in sodium, by removing salt from the table, and by increasing the use of citrus juices, fresh herbs and spices, which I call 'bright notes'.

■ To read nutrition labels and ingredients lists on food packages and to look for those that use less fat, saturated fat, cholesterol and sodium.

■ To allow the proper atmosphere for digestion by eating fewer 'fast food' meals and enjoying more time with friends and family at the table.

■ To find ways we can benefit the less fortunate by changing our eating habits. For example, simply eating less food and sharing the money we save with someone who is hungry makes good sense, and is what my family and many of our friends have done for years. (Our own non-profit, educational corporation can provide you with information

on how to begin the process yourself. If interested, please contact
Creative Lifestyle International, PO Box 504, Tacoma,
Washington 98401).

All of these goals have been applied to every single recipe in this book, and
each apparent restriction has forced me to think differently about how and
even why I cook.

By examining ideas, techniques and recipes, one can get the measure of
how they taste and look, and rework them to retain what is 'good' while
applying Minimax standards to reduce their potential risk.

The occasional Fettucini Alfredo or chocolate cake isn't going to cause an
immediate disaster, but a semi-regular diet of these high-risk foods has a
cumulative effect. You will not learn to enjoy the aromas, colours and
textures of healthy foods, and could face a serious health risk.

Food is fun. It gives pleasure to the senses. By placing limits on that
pleasure, one invites rebellion. We tend to do ourselves damage just to
declare ourselves free! What I discovered within my own family is that a clear
understanding of the issues brings about not only acquiescence but an
extraordinary enthusiasm and desire to pass on the benefits to others. This is
why it is important to me that you think of these Minimax suggestions as
issues and ideas, not absolutes. Each idea is an option, an alternative, a
choice that you can make only when
you understand why so that you can
explain your decision to yourself and to
others.

Our whole family chose to understand
before we changed and, as a result, the
changes have meant lower food costs, smaller portions, fresher food, weight
loss and consistent energy. We've also grown to enjoy the clean, crisp tastes
that rely more on aroma, colour and texture than fats, salts and sugars. In fact,
we now prefer them to our velvet memories!

The most important first step in any decision is to know your own special
circumstances – those you inherit in your physical makeup from your
parents, and those you acquire from the way you were brought up to eat.

Your doctor will be able to assess your present exposure to
inherited risk and, by inquiring about your parents and siblings,
will form a reasonably accurate profile accompanied by some
sensible recommendations. However, only you will know about
your traditional eating habits.

Have your doctor give you a thorough physical exam. Discuss
your family health problems and ask him questions about
appropriate measures to adopt. Show him this book and ask
which of the Minimax numbers that accompany each recipe
should be your maximum level . . . for example, how many fat grams to
consume each day? What percentage of calories from fat?

Write a list of all your favourite comfort foods, the ones that bring to mind
some warm memories of the past. From this list you will see where your
'traditions' may need some modification!

The problem with permanent change is that we replace the known with the unknown. This is especially hard if we really like a soft, creamy wine sauce and don't like the sound of non-fat yogurt and cornflour taking its place! Please hold on to your culture and especially your sense and style of hospitality as principles, but break the mould into which these wonderful attributes are often poured. Every comfort food recipe has its emotional attachments. You might list yours and try to separate the tradition from the ingredients. A perfect example is the Swiss Fondue, where the idea of stirring the pot with friends is great but the recipe is loaded with fat. Please keep the tradition, but innovate with the ingredients. I've done this dozens of times in this book.

AROMA

*I*t is the aroma that fills the space between the plate and your head. In this apparent emptiness wafts most of the real art of cooking. Just hold your nose and eat and you'll see how vital aromas are!

Volatile oils, esters and essences are the perfumes of the plate and come from many sources, but none so concentrated and complex as herbs and spices. As with any 'perfume', these special aromas will fade in time, and this is especially so when some herbs are dried and some spices are ground. If it is possible for you to grow your own herbs, then please, please do it! The second best alternative is to purchase fresh herbs from your fruit and vegetable department. If you buy them dried, put the purchase date on the lid. Keep them in a closed cupboard and check them for aroma after six months. If they seem to have lost their essential pungency, you had better replace them rather than risk spoiling a relatively expensive recipe with a few pence worth of 'chaff'.

Spices work the same way. If pre-ground they too will rapidly deteriorate. This is why pepper is freshly ground by waiters in

restaurants where the food matters. I use a small high-speed electric 'chopping mill' to powder my spices when I need them. This works very well for the garam masala 'warming spices' that are added to Indian dishes just before serving and the popular creole seasonings that add warmth and depth. Essentially these little 'mills' work like the old pestle and mortar but in a fraction of the time, and they are well worth the investment.

DE-ALCOHOLIZED WINES

$\mathcal{D}$e-alcoholized wine is made the way wine is usually made, after which the alcohol is removed.

Until recently, the alcohol was extracted by heating the wine and evaporating the alcohol; however, this changed the way the wines tasted, in part because it changed their aroma. Now there is a new invention, rather like the desalinization system that removes salt from seawater. This reverse osmosis 'pump' removes all the odourless water and alcohol. The water is then replaced and the characteristic flavours of the grapes remain substantially the same.

De-alcoholized wine is different from wines with alcohol. The warm bite that alcohol brings, together with its ability to age a wine, makes it a unique and living thing that I enjoyed from my youth through my gourmet days. I admire and celebrate the skills of competent wine makers and have no wish to denigrate their ability or to ban their products; however, I do want to find creative alternatives for those who are at risk.

I use good de-alcoholized wines, especially those bottled in the Napa Valley of Northern California, because I won't cook with a wine that I wouldn't drink with pleasure, other than those especially concentrated and seasoned for recipe use. De-alcoholized wine provides aroma and colour and is, in my opinion, indispensable. I am often asked 'What if I haven't got a de-alcoholized wine? Can I use an ordinary white or red?' My answer is always the same: 'De-alcoholized wines are *my* personal choice. Please make your own decision. Good wines with alcohol will work just as well, and in any event, within a few minutes most of the alcohol will evaporate.'

MEAT IN THE MINOR KEY

$\mathcal{A}$ great deal of risk and added expense comes from the amount of meat we eat. Meat comes complete with both saturated fat and cholesterol, and while it is an excellent source of protein, we simply do not have to consume it in such pioneer portions!

In the 'old days' I would suggest 2 lb/900 g of raw meat for a four-portion casserole (8 oz/225 g per head). I first reduced this to 6 oz/170 g, then to 4 oz/113 g, and every now and then down to 2 oz/56 g. This puts meat 'in the minor key'. Obviously there is an immediate visual change. Where meat was the centre of attraction, it now becomes either the co-star or the understudy.

In order to fill the plate, other foods will become the stars; foods that have shape, size, texture and the natural bulk to satisfy visually as well as to provide energy. This, of course, will mean more vegetables, more beans, whole grains and pasta, all of which need to be beautifully cooked.

FRESH AND BEST IN SEASON

*W*herever you live, the chances are that vegetables and fruits also grow. When they reach prime season in your area, they are not only less expensive but they taste great! Whenever you add good fresh fruit and good fresh vegetables to your menu, you add good health and good taste at lower cost.

The following list includes all the popular vegetables in their proper main season. All vegetables are in 3½ oz/100 g portions and fresh prior to being cooked. Please use the chart as a guide to your selection.

READING LABELS

*A*lmost every processed or packaged food has a label that carries nutritional information. The problem is that few people know how to apply the information to their lives.

The first thing you should learn to assess is the fat content. When you read the label make a note of three numbers: the fat in grams, the total calories and the portion size.

Be sure that their portion is your portion! If they list a 3 oz/85 g serving of ice-cream and you eat 6 oz/170 g, you must double their figures. 3 oz/85 g is a single scoop! If the calories for 3 oz/85 g are 150 and you eat two scoops (6 oz/170 g), the result is $2 \times 150 = 300$ calories.

Each gram of fat is 9 calories, therefore, multiply the number of fat grams in the portion you have chosen by 9. This will give you the number of calories from fat. Divide the fat calories by the total calories and you will have the percentage of calories from fat. For example, in the above serving of ice-cream, if the fat listed is 8 grams, then:

$$8 \times 9 = 72 \text{ calories} \qquad \frac{72}{150} = 0.48 \text{ or } 48\%$$

The American Heart Association has suggested that no more than 30% of our calories should come from fat and that less than one-third of those should come from saturated fats. This 30% is for a healthy individual and is not recommended for someone with known risks.

Only your personal physician will know what your percentage should be, and you really must discover how your system works and the needs of your family.

Keeping track of saturated fats isn't so easy. On many ice-cream labels the amount of saturated fat isn't shown. You may write to the manufacturer or ask a registered dietitian, since each brand will vary.

You will note that I have listed percentages for every recipe. You need to know that the average percentage in this book is 24%. If you exceed

30% on one dish it's not the end of the world, providing you compensate with very low fat food for the rest of the day.

EAT UP YOUR OXYGEN

𝒥t would certainly be remiss of me if I did not add a brief word about exercise. The fact is that if you are going to make changes, you will be eating less and this will cause you to lose weight. But what weight? For the most part, your body is comprised of water, lean muscle, fats and bone. When you reduce carbohydrates the body needs less water and you can drop as much as 5 lb/2.27 kg in one day from water alone. Of course, the moment you eat any carbohydrates, the body conveniently holds up the waterworks and bingo . . . you gain back your 'weight loss' overnight!

In the Minimax concept our consumption of fat goes down, and refined carbohydrates (sugars, cakes, biscuits) are replaced by more complex carbohydrates (whole grains, pulses). So there isn't much water loss.

move it and lose it . .

If you simply ate less fat and overall calories and lay quite still in bed, your body would draw upon both lean muscle and fat for energy. If you move around actively you build your muscles, and their action appears to massage the fat that infiltrates them. In this squeezed state the fat is more available as fuel and is used for energy. You now firm up by building muscle and eventually lose weight from useless, unsightly fat.

While this obvious benefit is taking place, you have another, quieter victory in progress. As you exert yourself, you breathe deeper and more rapidly and your heart beats faster. Your blood is circulated through the lungs, where it picks up extra oxygen and carries this off to both muscles and your brain. The brain 'eats' over 7 pints/4 litres of oxygen each day. If it has insufficient oxygen it feels 'tired'. If it gets 'enough', the chances are that you will feel better, which, in turn, gets you moving faster, and that burns more calories . . . from fat!

All this, however, depends upon your decision to apply the Minimax principles to your life and not only to *eat less* but to *move more* on a committed basis, come rain or shine.

Now . . . on to the move it and lose it recipes . . . Have fun and a good digestion!

Graham Kerr
Kirkland, Washington

VEGETABLE CHART

VEGETABLE	CALORIES	PROTEIN	COOKING METHODS/ TIME IN MINUTES
SPRING			
Asparagus	26	2.74	Steam, 10; Pressure Cook, 2
Mangetout Peas	40	3.14	Steam, 5; Pressure Cook, 2
Spinach	22	2.42	Steam, 8; Salads
Spring Cabbage	24	1.20	Steam, 9; Pressure Cook, 1
Spring Greens	16	1.27	Steam, 5; Pressure Cook, 1
Spring Onions	25	1.74	Steam, 5; Salads
SUMMER			
Beetroots	30	1.02	Bake, 45; Pressure Cook, 14
Broad Beans	227	18.81	Steam, 25; Pressure Cook, 2
Cabbage	20	0.92	Steam, 20; Pressure Cook, 2; Salads
Celery	14	0.46	Steam, 20; Pressure Cook, 3; Braise, 60
Chinese Cabbage	12	1.53	Steam, 3; Pressure Cook, 1
Courgettes	14	1.15	Steam, 15; Pressure Cook, 1; Bake, 30
Cucumber	13	0.54	Salads
Globe Artichokes	41	2.16	Steam, 30; Pressure Cook, 10
Green Beans	25	1.29	Steam, 15; Pressure Cook, 3
Leeks	11	0.80	Steam, 15; Pressure Cook, 5; Braise, 45
Marrow	14	1.15	Steam, 15; Pressure Cook, 1; Bake, 30
Peas	40	3.14	Steam, 12; Pressure Cook, 1
Radishes	17	0.60	Salads
Sweetcorn	82	3.05	Steam, 8; Pressure Cook, 1
AUTUMN/WINTER			
Broccoli	28	3.10	Steam, 10; Pressure Cook, 2
Brussels Sprouts	45	3.86	Steam, 10; Pressure Cook, 3
Cauliflower	18	1.56	Steam, 30; Pressure Cook, 5
Chard	16	1.54	Steam, 20
Endive	17	1.25	Salads
Jerusalem Artichokes	91	1.81	Steam, 25; Bake, 45
Kale	15	1.21	Steam, 25; Pressure Cook, 3
Kohlrabi	29	1.80	Steam, 20; Pressure Cook, 6
Okra	41	2.29	Steam, 15
Onions	24	0.76	Steam, 25; Pressure Cook, 3; Bake, 60
Parsnips	83	1.35	Steam, 35; Bake, 60
Spinach Beet	16	0.89	Steam, 20
Swedes	32	1.02	Steam, 20; Pressure Cook, 1; Bake, 60
Sweet Potato	80	1.34	Pressure Cook, 10; Bake, 60
Turnips	17	0.67	Steam, 20; Pressure Cook, 5
Winter Cabbage (Savoy)	24	1.20	Steam, 9; Pressure Cook, 1
ALL YEAR			
Aubergines	26	0.78	Braise, 45

VEGETABLE	CALORIES	PROTEIN	COOKING METHODS/ TIME IN MINUTES
Bean Sprouts	10	1.19	Steam, 3; Salads
Carrots	41	1.00	Steam, 20; Pressure Cook *(whole)*, 6, *(sliced)*, 3
Garlic	149	6.36	Seasoning
Lettuce	16	1.62	Salads
Mushrooms	19	0.50	Raw in Salads
Potatoes	104	2.18	Steam, 10; Pressure Cook, 25; Bake, 90
Sweet Peppers	17	0.60	Steam, 5; Braise, 30; Salads
Watercress	9	1.84	Salads

NOTE: I have included a few recipes using liquid egg substitute, which has not yet caught on in the UK. If you are on a low-cholesterol diet, lobby your local shopkeepers about this product – it will certainly extend your range of pudding choices. You can, of course, make the recipes with whole egg – use 1 large egg for each 2 fl oz/57 ml liquid egg substitute – but you will need to alter the nutrition figures as follows:

PER EGG OR EQUIVALENT	WHOLE EGG	LIQUID EGG SUBSTITUTE
Calories	75	46
Fat (g)	5	2
Calories from fat	60%	38%
Cholesterol (mg)	213	0
Sodium (mg)	63	80

Alternatively you can make your own egg substitute by using egg white with a touch of yellow colouring in it. You should make up exactly the same volume as required in the recipe on the basis that 2 egg whites are equal to 1 whole egg.

BAGUETTE OF MUSHROOMS

'𝒩othing could be finer than to be in Carolina . . . '?
Well . . . we've found it! Fresh wild mushrooms (chanterelles) in a very special sauce. We also tried this with button mushrooms and it came out equal with Carolina . . . our daughter, Tessa, happens to live there, so we know!

The pieces of French bread stick (baguette) are made to look like hollow tree trunks, filled to overflowing with wild mushrooms. I cut them diagonally for a main course and straight across for a starter. The main course needs a beautiful fresh salad of green leaves, herbs and edible flowers (see Helpful Hints).

Nutritional Profile

PER SERVING	CLASSIC	MINIMAX
Calories	497	324
Fat (g)	36	8
Calories from fat	66%	21%
Cholesterol (mg)	112	14
Sodium (mg)	1103	752
Fibre (g)	3	4

■ *Classic compared:* Chanterelles and Smoked Ham in Cream

Time Estimate

Hands On Unsupervised									
Minutes	10	20	30	40	50	60	70	80	90

Cost Estimate

Low	Medium	Medium High	Celebration

INGREDIENTS

4 teaspoons/20 ml extra light olive oil with a dash of sesame oil

3 shallots, peeled and finely chopped

2 tablespoons/30 ml loosely packed fresh thyme leaves

¼ teaspoon/1.25 ml nutmeg, freshly grated

⅛ teaspoon/0.6 ml black pepper, freshly ground

4 fl oz/113 ml de-alcoholized white wine

2 tablespoons/30 ml cornflour mixed with 2 table-spoons/30 ml de-alcoholized white wine

4 fl oz/113 ml evaporated skimmed milk (see page 197)

½ pint/284 ml chicken stock (recipe page 210)

4 fl oz/113 ml strained yogurt (recipe page 210)

2 oz/57 g back bacon, sliced thinly (see page 21)

1 lb/450 g chanterelle mushrooms (if not in season, use button mushrooms)

2 oz/57 g smoked turkey breast, cut in small strips

⅛ teaspoon/0.6 ml cayenne pepper

1 tablespoon/15 ml fresh parsley, chopped

A 12-inch/30-cm French baguette loaf

4 sprigs fresh thyme

NOW COOK

■ In a small saucepan, heat 1 teaspoon/5 ml of the olive oil. Add the shallots, 1 tablespoon/15 ml of the thyme, the nutmeg and the black pepper. Cook until the shallots are translucent.

■ Pour in the de-alcoholized wine and boil until reduced by half. Add the cornflour paste, bring to the boil and stir until thickened. Add the evaporated milk and 2 fl oz/57 ml of the chicken stock.

■ Put the pan into a bowl of iced water in order to cool it quickly, or just stand there and wait for it! When the sauce has cooled, add the yogurt and stir in the rest of the thyme. Strained yogurt can break up into little flecks if it is added to hot liquids. For this reason, do please cool the sauce so that the whitening effect can take place and the sauce will look smooth and glossy.

■ Heat the remaining oil in a low-sided stewpot. Add the bacon, mixing it lightly with the oil.

■ Separate the mushroom caps from the stems and slice the stems. Drop the stems into the stewpot and sauté for 5 minutes. Now add the caps and stir gently.

■ Add a little of the remaining chicken stock to kick up some steam, then add the rest, stirring lightly. Cover and simmer for 5 minutes. Remove from the heat.

■ Pour the cooking liquid from the stewpot through a fine mesh strainer into the yogurt sauce. Mix them thoroughly to blend. Pour the yogurt sauce back into the mushrooms and stir well. Add the turkey, cayenne pepper and parsley.

■ *To Serve:* Cut the baguette into 1-inch/2.5-cm slices and remove most of the soft centre, leaving only a thin layer of dough on the bottom, forming a shallow bread 'cup'. Put three bread slices per person on ovenproof plates and toast them in the oven until golden brown. Pour 4 fl oz/113 ml of the chanterelle cream over each serving and garnish with a sprig of thyme.

Helpful Hints and Observations

'GARDEN' SALAD – One of the truly great advances in modern food is the re-discovery of the herb salad. Start with crisp lettuce, radiccio, curly endive, a little watercress if you like it; then add sorrel, nasturtium leaves (hot!) and flowers, lemon balm, applemint, marigold petals, chive blossoms, sweet violets ... the list is almost endless and the result is literally fantastic! You may even experiment with the fruited vinegars, such as raspberry, mixed with a little oil and fresh lemon juice and sprinkled in at the last moment.

About the Ingredients

CHANTERELLE MUSHROOMS – These are one of the best-known and best-liked wild species of the almost 40,000 different varieties of mushroom in the world. Nestled in the nooks and crannies of forests around the globe, their caps look like frilly orange Oriental parasols. But unless you have a trained mushroom hunter with you, I wouldn't recommend gathering wild mushrooms on your own – many species are poisonous. Either hunt the delicious chanterelle down in your local greengrocer's or supermarket, or simply rush ahead and make the recipe with button mushrooms. Chanterelles are in season from July to December. They cannot be artificially cultivated, but may be available dried or tinned.

BAGUETTES – Long, thin, delicious loaves of white bread. Follow your nose to a bakery to enjoy the classic baguette. In France, you will often see them strapped to the back of bicycles as people pedal home with the evening groceries. This mode of transport is not strictly necessary, but, on the other hand, it's great aerobic exercise!

HUMMUS

$\mathcal{D}$*ips can be great fun: they help people to overcome initial shyness at social gatherings by giving them something to do with their hands. I've adapted the famous Middle Eastern Hummus for you so that it falls within our Minimax boundaries.*

Look out for classic Middle Eastern bowls and plates. They are very colourful and make great conversation pieces. Arrange the vegetable pieces and pitta bread slices on dishes surrounding the dip. It's a good idea to split the dip into two bowls for parties of six or more.

Nutritional Profile

PER SERVING	CLASSIC	MINIMAX
Calories	391	206
Fat (g)	33	3
Calories from fat	76%	14%
Cholesterol (mg)	21	0
Sodium (mg)	596	191
Fibre (g)	2	7

■ *Clasic compared:* Avocado Dip

Time Estimate

Hands On Unsupervised									
Minutes	10	20	30	40	50	60	70	80	90

Cost Estimate

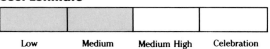

Low	Medium	Medium High	Celebration

INGREDIENTS

Two 15-oz/425-g tins chickpeas
6 tablespoons/90 ml sesame tahini
6 fl oz/177 ml water
4 garlic cloves, peeled and chopped
2 tablespoons/30 ml fresh parsley, chopped
5 tablespoons/75 ml lemon juice, freshly squeezed
¼ teaspoon/1.25 ml cayenne pepper
1 teaspoon/5 ml finely chopped fresh coriander leaves, or to taste
About 2 lb/900 g crunchy raw vegetables such as celery, carrots, sweet peppers, courgettes, button mushrooms, cauliflower florets, etc.
Wholewheat pitta bread

NOW ASSEMBLE

■ Drain the chickpeas and purée them in a food processor.

■ Thoroughly stir the tahini while it's still in the tin or jar in order to obtain a consistent mixture of solids and cream. Scoop the tahini into the processor with the chickpeas. Pour in the water.

■ Add the garlic, parsley, lemon juice and cayenne.

■ Continue processing until you have a creamy, smooth texture.

■ Add the coriander leaves and more cayenne to taste.

■ Wash the vegetables and cut them into large strips or chunks. Cut the pitta bread into triangular wedges.

■ Serve the Hummus with the vegetables and pitta bread triangles for dipping.

Helpful Hints and Observations

TAHINI – Be sure to shake the tin vigorously and then stir the contents well because the solids tend to settle. If you don't use the whole tin, store the leftovers in an airtight glass jar under refrigeration.

CHICKPEAS – The tinned variety are quite good for this dip but are usually much too soft for use either in a salad or as garnishes for chicken dishes. Please try the following method of cooking chickpeas from scratch.

DRIED LEGUMES FROM SCRATCH – Wash the chickpeas, then soak them overnight in 3 to 4 times as much water as chickpeas. Remove any that float – these may be mouldy. Pour off the water and rinse well. Re-cover with fresh water and bring the chickpeas to a slow boil. Chickpeas are quite hard. You may need to simmer them for as long as 3 hours until they're tender.

If you forget to soak your chickpeas overnight, there is a short cut. Put the chickpeas in a large pot and cover them with cold water. Bring to the boil and simmer for 2 minutes, then remove from the heat. Let them stand, tightly covered, for 1 hour. Now cook as suggested.

About the Ingredients

TAHINI – This 'sesame butter' is made from hulled and finely ground sesame seeds mixed with sesame oil. Sesame seeds have been used for centuries as a protein source in many countries, particularly in the Middle East and Africa. Tahini's uses won't stop with this recipe. Try it as a spread, or an ingredient in salad dressings, sauces and casseroles.

CHICKPEAS – These are also known as garbanzo beans, ceci (Italy) and chole (India). They came originally from the Middle East, where they are still a staple food. They are large, with an irregular circular shape like a hazelnut (or as their Latin name *arietinum* implies, 'like a ram'). These versatile legumes are a good source of calcium, phosphorus and potassium. Try them hot in beanpot recipes or cold in salads.

PITTA BREAD – This looks like a bread roll which has been put through an old-fashioned mangle! It is made from yeast dough which has been rolled to ¼ inch/1.25 cm thick and cooked at a very high temperature. The result is two hard 'crusts' with a soft centre, so that the breads can be cut in half and each half opened up to form a 'glove' which can be filled. Pitta bread is available from Greek bakers' and large supermarkets.

SHRIMP ROLLS 690

*Jhis is an excellent example of 'East meets West':
the blending of previously distinct cultures to come
up with unique ideas. One of the masters of this
craft is Jeremiah Tower, the chef/owner of several
popular San Francisco restaurants, including 690 on
Van Ness Avenue, where this is served. It needed very
little change to make it a great Minimax dish!*

*The idea is to serve these filled rice paper packages
as either a first course or a hot weather main dish. They
are literally bursting with aromas, colours and textures.*

Nutritional Profile

PER SERVING	CLASSIC	MINIMAX
Calories	473	152
Fat (g)	34	6
Calories from fat	65%	37%
Cholesterol (mg)	75	63
Sodium (mg)	757	341
Fibre (g)	8	2

■ *Classic compared:* Shrimp Rolls

Time Estimate

Hands On									
Unsupervised									

| *Minutes* | 10 | 20 | 30 | 40 | 50 | 60 | 70 | 80 | 90 |

Cost Estimate

Low	Medium	Medium High	Celebration

Serves 4

INGREDIENTS

8 fl oz/227 ml shelled and cooked shrimps or prawns, coarsely chopped

3 fl oz/85 ml strained yogurt (recipe page 210)

½ teaspoon/2.5 ml chilli powder

Salt and freshly ground pepper to taste

1 small sweet red pepper, halved lengthwise, cored and de-seeded

1 small sweet green pepper, halved lengthwise, cored and de-seeded

1 red chilli pepper, halved lengthwise, cored and de-seeded

8 fl oz/227 ml fish stock (recipe page 210)

1 teaspoon/5 ml ginger root, freshly grated

2 tablespoons/30 ml of 4-inch/10-cm lemon grass strands

4 tablespoons/60 ml fresh lime juice

1 tablespoon/15 ml low-salt soy sauce

3 tablespoons/45 ml extra light olive oil with a dash of sesame oil

¼ teaspoon/1.25 ml sesame oil

8 fl oz/227 ml water

1 teaspoon/5 ml turmeric

4 dried rice papers, 8–9 inches/20–23 cm diameter

1 small cucumber, peeled, de-seeded and cut into matchsticks

2 cabbage leaves, cut into fine strips

12 mint leaves, cut into fine strips

1 tablespoon/15 ml fresh coriander leaves

NOW COOK

■ Mix the shrimps with the strained yogurt and the chilli powder and season to taste with the salt and pepper.

■ Pre-heat the grill. Lay the peppers, skin side up, on a grill pan, and place the pan 3–4 inches/8–10 cm below the heat source. Grill until the skins are charred and black. Slip them directly into a heavyweight plastic storage bag and let them cool. Rub off the charred skins and cut the flesh into fine dice.

■ Boil the fish stock, grated ginger and lemon grass in a small saucepan until reduced by half. Strain the stock into a measuring cup. Whisk in 3 tablespoons/45 ml of the lime juice, the soy sauce and oils.

■ In a bowl, combine the warm water and the remaining lime juice. If you prefer a colourful set of rice papers, add turmeric to the water! Submerge the rice papers one at a time, until they start to soften – about 15 seconds. Remove to a damp napkin and cover

■ Fill each paper with shrimp mixture, cucumber, cabbage and mint. Roll them up loosely and place on individual plates.

■ Just before serving, stir the roasted peppers and coriander leaves into the sauce.

■ Pour a spoonful of sauce over each roll and serve.

About the Ingredients

RICE PAPER – Please don't let the presence of rice paper deter you from cooking this dish. It's simply a very thin South-East Asian pastry wrapper, that you may have eaten before as 'spring rolls'. Indeed, rice paper is as ordinary in Thai cooking as a sesame seed hamburger 'bun' in American cuisine. You should find it in Oriental foodstores. You'll see that rice paper is sold dried, in 1 lb/450 g packages, so you'll have enough sheets to experiment with many different fillings – you're only as limited as your imagination!

LEMON GRASS – See page 67.

TURMERIC – A bright yellow spice that is native to southern Asia. It is in the ginger family, technically a rhizome. A rhizome is actually an underground stem that gives rise to new roots and above-ground shoots. Turmeric is found dried and in powdered form and is used in curries, curry powder and natural dyes.

BLACK BEAN SOUP

This is one of Brazil's favourite foods. It is often served with side dishes of many kinds of boiled meats. Perhaps they use the leftover bones to make meat stocks to use in place of the often recommended water.

My recipe is simply a soup (no side dishes). But it does help to serve it from a tureen, preferably rustic in appearance . . . the tureen increases the mystique! Then add the dollop of the yogurt-coriander mixture at the table.

Nutritional Profile

PER SERVING	CLASSIC	MINIMAX
Calories	591	480
Fat (g)	29	15
Calories from fat	44%	29%
Cholesterol (mg)	19	36
Sodium (mg)	708	63
Fibre (g)	19	16

■ *Classic compared:* Black Bean Soup

Time Estimate

Hands On									
Unsupervised									
Minutes	10	20	30	40	50	60	70	80	90

Cost Estimate

Low	Medium	Medium High	Celebration

Serves 6

INGREDIENTS

1 lb/450 g black kidney beans
2 large ham hocks, stripped of all visible fat
4 teaspoons/20 ml extra light olive oil with a dash of sesame oil
2 large Spanish onions, peeled and diced
4 garlic cloves, peeled and chopped
5 pints/3 l water *or* good beef stock (recipe page 210)
½ teaspoon/2.5 ml black pepper, freshly ground
Pinch of cayenne pepper
4 teaspoons/20 ml ground cumin seed
4 sprigs fresh oregano
3 bay leaves
1 medium sweet red pepper, de-seeded and diced
3 tablespoons/45 ml fresh parsley, chopped
1 tablespoon/15 ml brown sugar
1 tablespoon/15 ml freshly squeezed lemon juice
2 teaspoons/10 ml grated orange rind
8 fl oz/227 ml strained yogurt (recipe page 210) mixed with 1 teaspoon/5 ml fresh coriander leaves, chopped

FIRST PREPARE

■ The night before making this splendid soup, place the black beans in a bowl of water and let them soak overnight.

■ Blanch the ham hocks by putting them in a medium saucepan with enough cold water to cover and bringing to the boil. Pour off the water and rinse out the pan.

NOW COOK

■ In a 10-inch/25-cm diameter stockpot, heat 1 tablespoon/15 ml of the olive oil and sauté the onions and garlic.

■ Rinse and drain the black beans thoroughly. Pour them into the pot and place the ham hocks in the centre. This allows the bean flavour to be evenly 'en-hocked'!

■ Cover with the water or stock, add the black pepper and stir in the cayenne, 1 tablespoon/5 ml of the cumin seed, the oregano and bay leaves. Bring to the boil and simmer for 1½ hours. Now remove the ham hocks and bay leaves, setting the ham hocks aside in a medium-sized bowl and discarding the bay leaves.

■ Remove 12 fl oz/340 ml of beans from the soup, along with 12 fl oz/340 ml of the cooking liquid, and purée these in a food processor. Pour this mixture through a sieve, into a large bowl. With a wooden spoon, push the beans through the sieve. Pour the purée back into the pot and discard the residue in the sieve.

■ Chop approximately 12 fl oz/340 ml of the lean ham hock meat into very small chunks and toss them back into the soup.

■ In a heated small saucepan, stir the remaining olive oil with the red pepper, parsley, the remaining cumin seed and the brown sugar. Mix in the lemon juice and orange rind and stir it all into the hot soup. What a fabulous aroma!

■ Take the soup to the table with the yogurt-coriander mixture on the side.

Helpful Hints and Observations

STOCK vs WATER – You can use fresh water or stock. There is enough flavour to succeed with water but given the choice, I'll always go for the depth of flavour that comes from a good beef stock.

HAM HOCKS – Do please watch out for their size. These are very heavily fatted in some cases and you need to strip away every vestige of visible fat before the long cooking process.

About the Ingredients

BLACK KIDNEY BEANS – A variety of the common bean *Phaseolus vulgaris*, these add a rich, almost purple colour to many dishes. And their taste is as deep and hearty as their colour. Black beans contain substantial amounts of potassium and phosphorus. They are a good source of calcium, and contain iron as well.

CUMIN – These zesty seeds come from a very dainty plant with small rose-coloured or white flowers. Their earthy spiciness is an essential part of curry-spice mixtures. Please don't leave their taste out of this recipe!

BAY LEAVES – Small, shiny, leathery leaves culled from an evergreen shrub, *Laurus nobilis*, sometimes called the Bay Laurel or Sweet Bay. Laurel leaves were used in ancient times to crown poets and heroes. The Romans used the name of the tree, *Laurus*, to mean a triumph or victory, and today the British still 'crown' a Poet Laureate. I use bay leaves in many dishes. Simmered in stocks, casseroles and soups, they add a quality which is difficult to describe but manages to be pungent, sweet and bitter at the same time.

BROAD BEAN SOUP PROCACCINI

This is the recipe that took away the dreaded 'Broken Spoon Award'! Back in 1970, Weight Watchers gave me this 'badge of dishonour' because of my liberal use of . . . well . . . everything! I created this dish for Nina Procaccini, who is head of recipe research for Weight Watchers, to demonstrate my new style of cooking. Broad beans are one of her favourite ingredients, and now, I hope, they will become one of yours!

This is the kind of soup that should be served from a tureen at the table. You could probably get a beautiful one at a great price in an antique shop. It's a good investment because you'll want to serve soup often as part of your Minimax lifestyle.

Nutritional Profile

PER SERVING	CLASSIC	MINIMAX
Calories	381	153
Fat (g)	22	2
Calories from fat	52%	10%
Cholesterol (mg)	48	0.01
Sodium (mg)	421	81
Fibre (g)	8	8

■ *Classic compared:* Soupe au Pistou

Time Estimate

Hands On									
Unsupervised									
Minutes	10	20	30	40	50	60	70	80	90

Cost Estimate

Low	Medium	Medium High	Celebration

INGREDIENTS

1 teaspoon/5 ml extra light olive oil with a dash of sesame oil

8 oz/225 g sweet onions, peeled and cut in ½-inch/1.5-cm cubes

2 large garlic cloves, peeled and thinly sliced

4 fl oz/113 ml Florence fennel, thinly sliced

A 6-oz/170-g tin no-salt tomato paste

1½ pints/850 ml water

A 19-oz/540-g tin broad beans

4 fl oz/113 ml rocket or leaf spinach

4 fl oz/113 ml spring greens

1 lb/450 g Italian plum tomatoes, peeled and sieved (see *Helpful Hints*)

Black pepper to taste

BOUQUET GARNI

6 whole cloves

12 black peppercorns

2 bay leaves, crushed

1 sprig rosemary, crushed

NOW COOK

■ Heat the olive oil in a large soup pot over medium heat. Fry the onions and garlic until soft. Add half the fennel, the tomato paste and the water. Stir and bring to the boil.

■ Drop in the bouquet garni and broad beans. Cook for 30 minutes.

■ Drop the rocket and spring greens in boiling water and blanch for 30 seconds. Plunge immediately into cold water to refresh. Set aside.

■ Slice the rocket and spring greens and add them to the soup. At the last minute, add the remaining fennel and the sieved tomatoes. Season with pepper to taste.

■ Remember to remove the bouquet garni before serving the soup ... things could get nasty if a wide-mouthed, talkative guest swallowed it!

Helpful Hints and Observations

TO PEEL TOMATOES – Drop them into a pot of boiling water for a minute or two. The skin will split and start to peel back. Remove them from the water. The skin will come off easily.

SWEATING THE VEGETABLES – In practically all my soups, sauces, stocks and casseroles, I use a standard technique that I think will do you a great deal of good. It's called 'sweating': a process where the vegetables cook in a small amount of olive oil, never more than 1 tablespoon/15 ml. Sweating raises the temperature of the vegetables enough to release their aromatic and flavourful volatile oils.

TO MAKE A BOUQUET GARNI – The method will depend on the ingredients: some can simply be held together with kitchen string, others need to be wrapped in butter muslin and tied with string. I used a wire mesh tea-ball for this one.

OIL – I use several different oils, mostly light in flavour because I look to other foods and seasonings to provide aromatic combinations. I do, however, add a touch of toasted sesame seed oil to my oil. This provides just enough nutty finish to release my fond memories of clarified butter! By the way, a 'touch' is about one-sixteenth by volume.

About the Ingredients

BROAD BEANS – Big beans with big, meaty taste and texture. You may also know them as fava beans. They are available fresh in their pods, tinned or dried. If you use dried beans, you have to soak them overnight, bring them to the boil, and then simmer for an hour or until tender. To save time, I've called for the pre-cooked, tinned beans in this recipe.

ROCKET – The name seems dependent on your nationality: rocket in Britain; arugula, pronounced, a-ROO-ga-la, in the United States and Italy; roquette in France. Rocket is a dark salad green with an unexpectedly nutty, peppery taste. If you can't find it in the shops, it is easily grown from seed. Although I've used it in soup for this recipe, don't miss using rocket as an addition to your fresh salads.

FLORENCE FENNEL – There are two types of fennel, both of which can be utilized in your kitchen. The dried seeds of common or wild fennel (an annual herb) are an aromatic addition to baked breads and the leaves are wonderful stuffed inside a grilled fish. In this recipe the root of Florence or sweet fennel is used, chopped like an onion.

SEATTLE CLAM CHOWDER

$\mathcal{N}$ew England clam chowders are velvet experiences – very dense, very white, very creamy. This was the classic we set out to match! I hope you like this creative alternative. It is very crisp, fawn-coloured, and almost Asian in its sweet and sour style.

Seattle is, after all, a Pacific rim gateway city; how better to celebrate its relationships?

I like very colourful chunky soup bowls, set on larger plates, with crisp oven-warmed French bread. Serve a salad on the side and this is a meal in itself.

Nutritional Profile

PER SERVING	CLASSIC	MINIMAX
Calories	430	281
Fat (g)	20	4
Calories from fat	43%	12%
Cholesterol (mg)	60	34
Sodium (mg)	784	354
Fibre (g)	6	5

■ *Classic compared:* Clam Chowder

Time Estimate:

Hands On									
Unsupervised									
Minutes	10	20	30	40	50	60	70	80	90

Cost Estimate:

Low	Medium	Medium High	Celebration

INGREDIENTS

1 teaspoon/5 ml extra light olive oil with a dash of sesame oil

8 fl oz/227 ml onion, peeled and diced

3 tablespoons/45 ml fresh thyme

3 bay leaves

8 fl oz/227 ml de-alcoholized white wine

1¼ pints/700 ml fish stock (recipe page 210)

6 lb/2.7 kg clams (yielding 10 oz/285 g clam meat when shelled)

1¼ pints/700 ml raw potatoes, peeled and diced

12 fl oz/340 ml raw leeks, chopped

16 fl oz/450 ml fresh sweetcorn kernels (3 fresh ears)

3 tablespoons/45 ml cornflour combined with 6 tablespoons/90 ml water to form a paste

8 fl oz/227 ml strained yogurt (recipe page 210)

4 oz/113 g back bacon, trimmed of fat and diced

¼ teaspoon/1.25 ml black pepper, freshly ground

2 tablespoons/30 ml fresh parsley, chopped

NOW COOK

■ Heat the olive oil in a high-sided stockpot and sauté the onion, thyme and bay leaves until the onion is translucent.

■ Stir in the de-alcoholized white wine and one-third of the fish stock. This becomes your steaming base. Keep it very hot, at a rolling boil.

■ Drop in the clams, making sure the steaming base is kept on the boil. Cover and steam for 3 minutes.

■ Using oven gloves, lift the stockpot, holding the lid tightly in place. Give it a vertical shake, which will distribute the steaming base evenly throughout the clams.

■ Place the stockpot back on the burner and steam for another 3 minutes. Uncover it, and the clams should be wide open. Discard any that remain firmly closed.

■ Pour the clams and steaming base into a strainer or colander set over a large bowl. The steaming base and clam juice should drain through the strainer into the bowl.

■ Wash out the stockpot, and return it to the hot burner. Add the remaining fish stock. Pour the clam juice and the steaming base through a strainer lined with muslin (this removes any sand particles from the juice), and add them to the stock. Now boil for 10 minutes to concentrate. (You should have about 2 pints/1.2 l total after boiling.) Strain once more, unless you are very confident!

■ Shell the clams, and chop them in half if extra large. Place them in a bowl and set aside.

■ Add the diced potatoes to the clam concentrate. Simmer for 5 minutes. Stir in the leeks and simmer for 5 more. Add three-quarters of the corn and cook for another 5 minutes.

■ Remove 8 fl oz/227 ml of the broth from the chowder and place it in a small bowl. Stir in the cornflour paste. Add the yogurt to the warm thickened broth and stir thoroughly (see *Helpful Hints*). Pour it back into the pot, bring to the boil and stir until thickened.

■ Add the bacon, clams and the remaining corn, and cook it all together for 5 minutes. Season with pepper and parsley.

Helpful Hints and Observations

ADDING NON-FAT YOGURT – Please note the way I have had to add the non-fat yogurt. I remove the hot stock from the heat and thicken it before adding the *cold* yogurt in order to stop it breaking into little tiny lumps. Another easy way is to add the cornflour to the yogurt and then add the stock, returning the thin cream to the heat to thicken. Your choice!

About the Ingredients

CLAMS – These marine molluscs are obtainable in three forms, depending where you live: in the shell, shelled and tinned. For this recipe, I buy them in the shell if possible. Make sure they are alive, with their valves tightly closed. Refrigerated at 40°F/4°C they should stay alive for several days. Shelled clams are the whole meat. They should be plump, free of broken shells, with a clear liquor. Clams are also available in tins, whole or minced, in brine or clam liquor. These are not much good for this recipe.

BACK BACON – Bacon on the Minimax menu? Well, not in any quantity and not just any bacon. Back bacon comes from a selection of boneless pork loin encircled in a very thin layer of fat, which is easily trimmed away. It's a borderline choice, and I use the least possible – just enough to let its flavour be known.

LEEKS – These are one of those foods that add wonderful taste without burdensome calories, fats, or sodium. They're a splendid addition to the greengrocer's display: like giant green onions with snow-white bulbs and flat green leaves. Buy leeks that appear crisp and unblemished. The only caveat: give them a good rinsing with cool water. Leeks can hide soil that literally goes along for the ride.

THAI SOUP *(Tom Yum Gai)*

*T*his is a good example of the classic Asian Hot and Sour Soup: a thin, broth-style liquid, chock full of aromatic seasonings that jostle each other for equal billing. It winds up not too spicy, not too sour, not too rich, but just right! When it's right, it's a great test of the cook's general ability to prepare good Asian food.

I often serve this as a 'revival' first course. Let's face it, I can't imagine a taste bud that couldn't be made to sit up and beg for more. Include all the bits and pieces, with the caution that you should not try to chew the galangal, lemon grass, or Kaffir lime leaves. They are strictly there to let you know that it's full of the most authentic flavours.

Nutritional Profile

PER SERVING	CLASSIC	MINIMAX
Calories	288	135
Fat (g)	17	5
Calories from fat	54%	35%
Cholesterol (mg)	40	34
Sodium (mg)	1569	154
Fibre (g)	0.1	1

■ *Classic compared:* Cream of Chicken Soup

Time Estimate:

Hands On									
Unsupervised									
Minutes	10	20	30	40	50	60	70	80	90

Cost Estimate

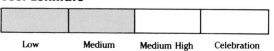

Low	Medium	Medium High	Celebration

INGREDIENTS

CHICKEN STOCK

1 tablespoon/15 ml extra light olive oil with a dash of sesame oil

1 medium onion, peeled and coarsely chopped

1 stalk celery, coarsely chopped

2 large carrots, peeled and coarsely chopped

1 small bunch fresh thyme

3 whole cloves

5 whole black peppercorns

2 bay leaves

1 whole chicken, about 3½ lb/1.6 kg

3 pints/1.7 l water

SOUP

1½ pints/850 ml prepared chicken stock

1 lemon grass stalk, crushed and cut in 1-inch/2.5-cm sections

3 Kaffir lime leaves*

2 slices galangal*

1 teaspoon/5 ml roasted chilli paste* (hot, hot, hot!)

2 tablespoons/30 ml fish sauce*

1½ tablespoons/23 ml fresh lemon juice

1 spring onion, sliced on the diagonal

8 fl oz/227 ml fresh mushrooms, quartered

1 tablespoon/15 ml fresh coriander leaves

16 fl oz/454 ml diced thigh and leg meat from the stock chicken

Available from Asian foodstores.

FIRST PREPARE THE STOCK

■ This is a phenomenal chicken stock, quite different from any you've ever eaten. In a large stockpot, over high heat, pour in the olive oil, add the onion, celery, carrots, thyme, cloves, peppercorns and bay leaves, and cook for 2 minutes to release the flavours. Drop the chicken in on top. Pour ½ pint/284 ml of the water over it all and cover. Let the chicken steam, with its sinews cracking and exploding with flavour, for 15 to 20 minutes. Add the remaining 2½ pints/1.3 l of water, cover and simmer gently for 30 minutes. Strain the chicken stock. Skin and de-bone the cooked chicken.

NOW COOK THE SOUP

■ Pour the strained chicken stock into a large saucepan. Do not pour in any of the sediments that have settled at the bottom. Add the lemon grass, Kaffir lime leaves and galangal. Bring to the boil, put the lid on and boil for 5 minutes.

■ Stir in the 1 teaspoon/5 ml of chilli paste – no more, this is hot stuff. Continue stirring in the fish sauce, lemon juice, spring onion, mushrooms, coriander leaves and cooked chicken meat. That's it . . . inhale deeply and savour the aromas!

Helpful Hints and Observations

'STEAM BURSTING' – The method described for preparing the stock is one of the most important I will ever give you. It takes even tough old birds and helps to make them tender, and it creates the most wonderful basic chicken stock.

FREEZING STOCK – It helps to overproduce good stocks so that you can freeze them either in ice-cube form for use in making small sauces or in sealable plastic bags for 1–2 pint/½–1 l quantities, for soups, stews, and so on. I always label mine clearly, date them, and use them within six months of freezing.

BASHING THE AROMATICS – When using small, whole pieces of food like lemon grass, crushing helps to break up the fibre and extract more of the flavour.

STOCKPOT – It really pays to invest in a good-sized stockpot. Over the years I have found that thin-walled (and thin-bottomed) pans just don't last. Better by far is the heavy-based aluminium pan that is completely sealed by some permanent non-stick glaze. It should be easy to clean inside and out and for the average home cook needn't hold more than 10 pints/5.5 l.

About the Ingredients

LEMON GRASS – See page 67.

KAFFIR LIME LEAVES – Leaves of the Kaffir lime and rinds of its pear-shaped fruits are used in South-East Asia for cooking. Highly aromatic, with a strong floral fragrance, they add peaks to Thai cuisine.

GALANGAL – Galangal resembles ginger root in appearance and is botanically in the same family. It is a rhizome, or underground stem, pale yellow in colour, with zebra-like stripes.

FISH SAUCE – Fish sauce is added to nearly every dish in South-East Asian cooking. It is made by packing fish, usually anchovies, mackerel, or both, in wooden barrels or ceramic crocks. The fish is then covered with brine and allowed to ferment in the tropical sun for months. The resulting brown liquid is drained off and used for dipping and seasoning.

RED SNAPPER YUCATAN

$\mathcal{T}$he famous anthropologist-explorer William Bartram visited the Seminole Indians in 1791 and was served red snapper steamed with fresh oranges. I picked up on this classic regional idea, developed by the Mexican people in the Yucatan peninsula, and consider it to be one of the great dishes of the world.

In the classic version the fish is usually served whole, but I have used the more readily available fillets. Steamed rice is an ideal accompaniment and if you like fresh spinach, then cook it quickly and serve it in the whole-leaf form, while it is still bright green – just squeeze it lightly to remove excess liquid before putting it on the plate.

Nutritional Profile

PER SERVING	CLASSIC	MINIMAX
Calories	513	273
Fat (g)	22	8
Calories from fat	38%	27%
Cholesterol (mg)	204	116
Sodium (mg)	1318	720
Fibre (g)	4	1

■ *Classic compared:* Baked Red Snapper

Time Estimate

Hands On									
Unsupervised									
Minutes	10	20	30	40	50	60	70	80	90

Cost Estimate

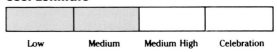

Low	Medium	Medium High	Celebration

Serves 4

INGREDIENTS

1 tablespoon/15 ml extra light olive oil with a dash of sesame oil

4 fl oz/113 ml onion, peeled and sliced

4 fl oz/113 ml sweet red pepper, sliced

4 fl oz/113 ml pimento-stuffed olives, sliced

2 teaspoons/10 ml + ½ tablespoon/8 ml fresh coriander leaves, chopped

4 tablespoons/60 ml orange juice, freshly squeezed

2 tablespoons/30 ml lemon juice, freshly squeezed

4 fillets of 6 oz/170 g each, red snapper *or* any firm-fleshed white fish

¼ teaspoon/1.25 ml salt, freshly ground

⅛ teaspoon/0.6 ml black pepper, freshly ground

1 teaspoon/5 ml arrowroot mixed with 2 fl oz/57 ml freshly squeezed orange juice

NOW COOK

■ Pre-heat the oven to 400°F/205°C/Gas Mark 6.

■ In a large ovenproof skillet, heat the oil and fry the onion until soft. Add the red pepper, olives, 2 teaspoons/10 ml of the coriander leaves, 3 tablespoons/45 ml of the orange juice and all the lemon juice and cook for 2 to 3 minutes.

■ Brush the fish fillets with the remaining orange juice, season with the salt and pepper and add them to the skillet. Bake on a rack in the top third of the oven for 12 minutes.

■ Transfer the cooked fish to a serving dish, reserving the juice and vegetables in the skillet. Remove the skillet from the oven, stir in the arrowroot paste, return to the stove top on low heat and stir until thickened.

■ Sprinkle the sauce with the remaining coriander leaves, pour it over the fish and serve.

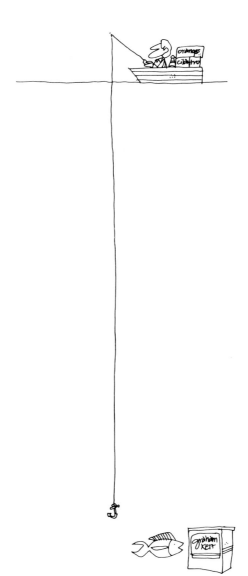

SALMON CHINA MOON

*B*arbara Tropp, one of my favourite cookbook writers and owner/chef of the China Moon restaurant in San Francisco, suggested this simple yet elegant salmon dish for our collaboration. It took only very minor changes to meet the Minimax nutrition profile.

This dish is very elegant, especially if it's served on one of those glossy black plates. The sauce is brushed on the fish but can also be strained into small pots for dipping.

Nutritional Profile

PER SERVING	CLASSIC	MINIMAX
Calories	386	403
Fat (g)	18	10
Calories from fat	43%	22%
Cholesterol (mg)	86	55
Sodium (mg)	209	143
Fibre (g)	1	2

■ *Classic compared:* Spicy Salmon

Time Estimate

Hands On									
Unsupervised									
Minutes	10	20	30	40	50	60	70	80	90

Cost Estimate

Low	Medium	Medium High	Celebration

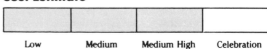

Serves 4

INGREDIENTS

4 fresh salmon steaks, 5–6 oz/140–170 g each,
cut ¾ inch/2 cm thick
16 fl oz/454 ml water
8 fl oz/227 ml long grain rice
¼ sweet red pepper, thinly sliced 1½ inches/4
cm long
4 spring onions, green parts only, finely sliced
1 teaspoon/5 ml extra light olive oil with a dash
of sesame oil
2 garlic cloves, peeled and finely minced
2 tablespoons/30 ml threads of fresh ginger root,
finely sliced
1 tablespoon/15 ml black fermented Chinese beans
1 teaspoon/5 ml dried red chilli flakes
1 tablespoon/15 ml rice wine vinegar
4 fl oz/113 ml de-alcoholized white wine

FIRST PREPARE

■ Remove the salmon's free bones (see *Helpful Hints*).

NOW COOK

■ Put the water in a medium saucepan, bring to the boil, add the rice and simmer for 15 minutes. The rice should have a firm texture, without sticking together. Add the peppers and half the sliced spring onions.

■ In a large sauté pan, heat the olive oil and sauté the minced garlic, half the ginger, the beans and red chilli flakes, stirring to blend, for 5 minutes. Add the rice vinegar and half the de-alcoholized white wine.

■ On an ovenproof plate or pie dish, at least 1 inch/2.5 cm smaller in diameter than your steamer, lay out the fish steaks next to one another, arranged back-to-belly for a pretty fit. Sprinkle with the remaining spring onions and ginger. Lightly press the onions with the broad side of a knife to release their juices before distributing them evenly over the fish. Use only a bare sprinkling of ginger if it is the stronger, thick-skinned variety. You can be more liberal with the subtle, young type. Now pour the bean mixture evenly over the top of everything.

■ Pour water into your steamer pot to a depth of 4 inches/10 cm and bring it to a full boil. Put the plate of prepared salmon in the steamer, cover tightly, and steam over medium-high heat for 8 minutes. While steaming, do not lift the lid to peek at the fish, or you will dissipate the heat. When properly steamed, the fish will still look moist and red, but will not be fleshy or raw.

■ Remove the plate from the steamer. Pour the steaming liquid through a strainer into a small saucepan. Stir in the remaining de-alcoholized white wine.

■ Serve the hot fish immediately. You can also serve this dish at room temperature: just remove the salmon from the steamer when it is about 1 minute underdone and let it cook to completion from its own inner heat.

■ Just before serving, remove the ribs and backbones and pull off the skin in a neat ribbon with the aid of a small knife. Discard most of the spring onion, leaving a few nuggets on top for colour, or garnish the salmon with one of the prettier whole spring onion stalks. Serve the fish in the steamer basket, or transfer it carefully to heated serving plates with a spatula.

■ Spoon the rice into small, individual moulds and flip on to each serving plate. Glaze the salmon and rice with the salmon's steaming liquid. Leftovers keep 1 to 2 days in the refrigerator and are very good cold. The salmon juices gel into a delicious aspic.

Helpful Hints and Observations

TO BONE SALMON STEAKS – Before you steam the salmon, remove the 'free' bones. They fan out on either side of the backbones in a 'V' shape. Press down either side of the bone ends as this will make them protrude. Using a pair of fine needle-nosed pliers, pull out the bones and discard. After the fish is cooked, strip off the outer skin and carefully remove the ribs and backbones.

About the Ingredients

FERMENTED BLACK BEANS – According to some historians, fermented salted black soybeans are the oldest recorded soyfood in history! A very popular Chinese seasoning in the modern age, you'll find them packaged in heavy plastic bags. They may be labelled Chinese black beans, salted beans, fermented black beans, or even ginger black beans. They're made by cooking small black soybeans until soft, mixing them with a mould, and then covering them with a brining solution for 6 months. A few shreds of ginger or maybe orange peel can be added in the final soaking stage. Stored in an airtight container at room temperature, away from light, heat and moisture, they will keep indefinitely. If you are concerned about sodium, rinse the beans under cold running water before using them to remove the salt.

SALMON PISEGNA

$\mathcal{T}$his dish was created for one of my 'nutritional heroes'. Chef David Pisegna was a very highly regarded executive chef at a luxury hotel when he decided to make a remarkable career change to become executive chef at a hospital! Now Chef Pisegna creates nutritious and delicious food for hospital patients. Don't we all wish we could check into his hospital when we are in need of treatment and recuperation? I created this dish for him, using his favourite ingredients: the famous Copper River sockeye salmon and asparagus.

I suggest serving this poached salmon cold, adorned with the creamy asparagus sauce. Steamed carrots and courgettes would add a splash of bright colour contrast.

Nutritional Profile

PER SERVING	CLASSIC	MINIMAX
Calories	608	435
Fat (g)	35	18
Calories from fat	52%	37%
Cholesterol (mg)	225	99
Sodium (mg)	110	505
Fibre (g)	0.03	2

■ *Classic compared:* Salmon with Mayonnaise Sauce

Time Estimate

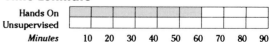

Hands On
Unsupervised

Minutes 10 20 30 40 50 60 70 80 90

Cost Estimate

Low   Medium   Medium High   Celebration

Serves 6

INGREDIENTS

1 tablespoon/15 ml extra light olive oil with a dash of sesame oil
1 large onion, peeled and coarsely chopped
4 fl oz/113 ml celery leaves, chopped
4 sprigs fresh thyme
12 whole cloves
2 bay leaves
3 sprigs fresh tarragon
3 sprigs fresh dill
3 pints/1.8 l water
1 teaspoon/5 ml salt, freshly ground
1 whole salmon (4 lb/1.8 kg), head and tail removed
2 fl oz/57 ml balsamic vinegar

ASPARAGUS SAUCE
1½ lb/680 g asparagus
4 fl oz/113 ml strained yogurt (recipe page 210)
1 tablespoon/15 ml fresh tarragon, finely chopped
White pepper, freshly ground

NOW COOK

■ Heat the oil in a fish poacher. Add the onion, celery, thyme, cloves, bay leaves, tarragon and dill and cook for about 2 minutes to release the volatile oils. Add the water, bring to the boil, cover and simmer for 15 minutes.

■ Sprinkle the salmon with the salt, put it in the fish poacher, add the vinegar and cover. The fish should poach for 4 minutes per pound. This 4-lb/1.8-kg salmon should poach for 16 minutes.

■ After the salmon is cooked, let it cool in the poaching liquid. When completely cool, remove the skin and bones using a relatively simple technique (see *Helpful Hints*).

■ *The Sauce:* Cut off the tough stem ends of the asparagus and discard. Cut off the very tips and keep them separate. In two separate pans, steam the asparagus tips and stems until just tender. The reason to keep them separate is that the tips need just about 4 minutes and the stems about 10 minutes.

■ Put the cooked stems in a food processor or blender and purée. You should have about 4 tablespoons/60 ml of asparagus purée.

■ In a small bowl, mix the purée with the yogurt, tarragon and pepper to taste. Fold in the asparagus tips. The sauce is now ready to adorn your salmon.

Helpful Hints and Observations

BONELESS AND BEAUTIFUL – To de-bone your salmon and keep one side whole for a lovely presentation, use the following simple technique.

Carefully remove the salmon to a cutting board just large enough to hold it. First remove the skin on the top side. Cut down to the bone along the natural flank line. Slice the fish down one side of the backbone from head to tail. Gently pry the entire back fillet away from the bones. It should come off in one piece. Repeat with the belly cut. This is harder to keep intact. Now the spine and rib-bones are exposed. Starting at the tail, carefully, gently, pull out the spine and rib-bones. Take your salmon pieces and re-form them over the de-boned fish. Needless to say, this is now your slightly untidy side!

Ready for the incredibly clever part? Put a long oval serving plate over the fish, hold the board to the plate, and, in one graceful movement, flip the whole thing over! There on your serving plate is the other side of the salmon. Carefully strip off the skin and you've got a whole, completely boned salmon to delight your guests! Yes, you may pat yourself on the back for this one. You may also see why television is so helpful when explaining these tricky techniques!

About the Ingredients

BALSAMIC VINEGAR – Here's a Minimax ingredient that adds great flavour: a vinegar from Northern Italy that, by law, must be aged for 10 years, going through stages in oak, chestnut, mulberry and juniper barrels. It will also be a tasty addition to your salad dressings, marinades and fruit desserts.

ASPARAGUS – This vegetable is best when it's purchased in season – late spring and early summer – from local sources. Controversy rages in culinary circles over the relative tenderness of thick-stemmed or thinner-stemmed spears. I think this is an issue you'll have to decide for yourself, since I'm an enthusiast for both!

SHARK STIR-FRY ARIEL

This is a dish created for one of my heroes: a person pushing back boundaries, making news, providing creative alternatives for society. The hero is Barry Gnekow, who's developed wonderfully fragrant and elegant de-alcoholized wines. This dish is made with Barry's favourite ingredients. It may become one of your favourites – if you can get used to the idea of eating shark or its relatives. One way to do this is to ponder Barry's low key response on tasting his dish on camera for the first time . . . 'I guess you could say we won!'

The very nature of stir-fry is that all is included, and when it is done . . . it is done, and must be consumed immediately. I always provide chopsticks for the pure fun of it – and it helps both digestion and conversation.

Nutritional Profile

PER SERVING	CLASSIC	MINIMAX
Calories	662	379
Fat (g)	51	8
Calories from fat	70%	20%
Cholesterol (mg)	115	39
Sodium (mg)	1328	150
Fibre (g)	1	8

■ *Classic compared:* Chinese Stir-Fried Beef and Mushrooms

Time Estimate

Hands On
Unsupervised

| Minutes | 10 | 20 | 30 | 40 | 50 | 60 | 70 | 80 | 90 |

Cost Estimate

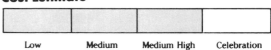

Low   Medium   Medium High   Celebration

Serves 6

INGREDIENTS

RICE

8 fl oz/227 ml wild rice
8 fl oz/227 ml water
1 tablespoon/15 ml fish sauce
3 tablespoons/45 ml pine nuts

STIR-FRY

1 tablespoon/15 ml extra light olive oil with a dash
of sesame oil
7 spring onions, chopped (both the white and green
parts)
1 tablespoon/15 ml fresh ginger root, grated
1 lb/450 g shark meat, cut in 1-inch/2.5-cm cubes
(if necessary, substitute dogfish, monkfish, or huss)
4 oz/113 g fresh water chestnuts, peeled and thinly
sliced
4 oz/113 g mangetout peas, strings removed
24 fresh coriander leaves
4 oz/113 g fresh white seedless grapes (taste one
before buying, if possible, to make sure they're sweet)
8 fl oz/227 ml de-alcoholized white wine
1 tablespoon/15 ml arrowroot, mixed with 1 table-
spoon/15 ml de-alcoholized white wine
¼ teaspoon/1.25 ml ground cayenne pepper

FIRST PREPARE

■ Remember, all stir-fries are based upon one
principle: everything is cut up and measured *before*
you start cooking!

NOW COOK

■ Use a pressure cooker to reduce the cooking
time of wild rice from 40 to 15 minutes. Place the
wild rice and water in the pressure cooker and stir
in the fish sauce. Check to make sure that the lid hole
is clear, fasten and put on high heat. Cook the rice for
15 minutes from when the cooker starts 'hissing'. Stir
in the pine nuts and set aside.

■ Heat the olive oil in a wok on high heat. When a
drop of water hits the wok and disappears immediately, the wok is ready! Drop in the spring onions, ginger
and shark meat. Keep stirring.

■ As the shark meat whitens, drop in the water
chestnuts and mangetouts. Keep stirring. Add the
coriander leaves and grapes. At the last moment
pour in the wine.

■ Stir the arrowroot paste into the wok. In moments
you have a glistening, gorgeous wine sauce.

■ Sprinkle the sparkling red cayenne pepper over
the top to add taste-bud heat. Serve with the wild
rice and pine nuts.

About the Ingredients

SHARK – Its rich white meat can be wonderfully
delicious and should be only lightly cooked, as in my
stir-fry method. But don't despise its poorer relations
if your fishmonger can't oblige.

DE-ALCOHOLIZED WINE – Ariel is a California winery
producing superior de-alcoholized products. They're
so good that they're winning awards over alcoholic
wines in blind taste tests. The alcohol-free wines
available in Britain vary in quality and you may need
to experiment a bit before you find one to your taste.
The sweeter ones are best avoided, as they can turn
sugary. Look out for German labels – some of these
work well.

WATER CHESTNUTS – At one time these were only
available in tins, but you may find them now in Asian
foodstores. Choose those that are very hard and have
a gloss to them. If fresh water chestnuts are not
available, use tinned ones, but drain them in advance
of cooking and pat dry with kitchen paper.

SOLE WITH SAFFRON SAUCE

I was inspired to create this dish from a Sole with Café de Paris Sauce original. This classic featured moist, thick Dover sole, stuffed with highly seasoned butter and nestling in a bath of butter sauce. Today, I have used no butter at all! I can almost hear your sharp gasp, saying, 'No, it isn't possible!' But it may be that you won't even miss the butter. Let your taste buds be the judge!

Great accompaniments to this dish are tiny steamed new potatoes, and green beans, sprinkled with a touch of nutmeg, parsley and mint.

Nutritional Profile

PER SERVING	CLASSIC	MINIMAX
Calories	780	88
Fat (g)	66	1
Calories from fat	77%	13%
Cholesterol (mg)	258	40
Sodium (mg)	2073	147
Fibre (g)	1	0.2

■ *Classic compared:* Sole with Café de Paris Sauce

Time Estimate

Hands On Unsupervised									
Minutes	10	20	30	40	50	60	70	80	90

Cost Estimate

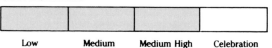

Low   Medium   Medium High   Celebration

Serves 6

INGREDIENTS

FISH

6 sole fillets, 6 oz/170 g each

FUMET

1 teaspoon/5 ml extra light olive oil with a dash of sesame oil

1 large onion, peeled and sliced

2 sprigs fresh parsley

2 bay leaves

2 sprigs fresh thyme

2 whole cloves

1 lb/450 g fish bones

2½ pints/1.4 l water

SAFFRON SAUCE

8 fl oz/227 ml prepared fish fumet

¼ teaspoon/1.25 ml fresh tarragon, chopped

½ teaspoon/2.5 ml fresh dill, chopped

1 tablespoon/15 ml fresh parsley, chopped

2 tablespoons/30 ml spring onions, chopped

2 anchovy fillets, mashed to a paste

1 tablespoon/15 ml capers

1 clove garlic, peeled and chopped

2 teaspoons/10 ml English mustard

1 tablespoon/15 ml lemon juice

Pinch of saffron threads

1 tablespoon/15 ml arrowroot

2 fl oz/57 ml de-alcoholized white wine

FIRST PREPARE

■ When you get the sole fillets home from the fishmonger's, put them in ice-cold salted water. This Scottish crofter's technique, called 'crimping', will remove the 'woofy' smell.

NOW COOK

■ *The Fumet:* This reduced fish stock is the most important element of this dish's flavourful sauce.

■ Heat the olive oil in a medium saucepan over medium heat. Add the onion, parsley, bay leaves, thyme, cloves and fish bones.

■ Pour in the water and bring to the boil. Reduce the heat and simmer for 30 minutes – no longer, or the fumet will become bitter.

■ Strain out the liquid.

■ Discard the solids and transfer the liquid to another saucepan, bring to the boil and reduce by 50%. You should have about 8 fl oz/227 ml after reduction – the fumet.

■ *The Fish:* Just anoint your grill pan with a touch of olive oil. Place the sole fillets in the pan.

■ Position the pan 4 inches/10 cm from the grill heat source for about 6 minutes.

■ Remove the fish while it's tender and snowy white. Don't wait until it browns or becomes crisp.

■ *The Sauce:* In a small saucepan, over medium heat, mix the reduced fumet with the tarragon, dill, parsley, spring onions, anchovies, capers, garlic, mustard and lemon juice.

■ Now for a burst of colour: stir in the saffron threads. Note that the yellow hue is very similar to that of butter!

■ In a small bowl, dissolve the arrowroot in the white wine. Take the saucepan from the heat and stir in the arrowroot mixture. Return to the heat and stir until thickened.

■ *To Serve:* Remove the fish to a warmed serving plate and spoon some saffron sauce over each portion.

Helpful Hints and Observations

CRIMPING – A few more words about this very important idea. I've seen many people wrinkle their noses when they talk about fish. 'I don't like the way it smells.' 'It's sticky to the touch.' Well, it is true that even perfectly fresh fish can become surface tacky in a warm car, but it can be refreshed using this ancient Scottish crofters' method called 'Crrrrrimping'! The trick is to get cold tap-water tasting like seawater by adding sea salt – a mean 1 tablespoon/15 ml for 3 pints/1.7 l. Now add a bunch of ice-cubes to drop the temperature to North Sea levels and then slip your fish directly from the wrapper into the iced 'seawater' and leave it there for about 15 minutes. When you dry it off, give it a sniff – it should have a sea-fresh aroma. If it doesn't, it may not have been the 'right stuff' when you bought it.

About the Ingredients

ANCHOVY FILLETS – See page 59.
SAFFRON THREADS – See page 61.

BANGKOK STEAMED TROUT

*W*hole fish cooked in this Thai marinade is absolutely delicious. You might also like to try it with a chicken breast or your favourite fillet of fresh fish.

Since this fish is so well garnished with its vegetables it needs only some well-steamed rice served on the side.

Nutritional Profile

PER SERVING	CLASSIC	MINIMAX
Calories	516	200
Fat (g)	30	5
Calories from fat	52%	23%
Cholesterol (mg)	246	76
Sodium (mg)	434	274
Fibre (g)	1	2

■ *Classic compared:* Trout Woolpack

Time Estimate

Hands On Unsupervised									
Minutes	10	20	30	40	50	60	70	80	90

Cost Estimate

Low	Medium	Medium High	Celebration

INGREDIENTS

1 whole trout (2 lb/900 g)
8 fl oz/227 ml celery, sliced thinly on the diagonal
1 sweet red pepper, de-seeded and cut into matchstick strips
8 fl oz/227 ml green Chinese cabbage (pe-tsai) *or* roundhead cabbage, cut in 1-inch/2.5-cm squares
4 fl oz/113 ml straw mushrooms *or* small button mushrooms
Chopped coriander leaves for garnish

MARINADE
¾ pint/475 ml chicken stock
2 tablespoons/30 ml dried cranberries
2 chilli peppers, finely chopped
1 tablespoon/15 ml fresh ginger, grated
4 cloves pickled garlic, mashed
2 tablespoons/30 ml fresh lime juice
2 tablespoons/30 ml soy sauce

FIRST PREPARE

■ For this recipe you will need either a long fish steamer with a perforated rack or a large baking pan with a grill that fits inside another covered pan.

■ Clean and wash the fish. Cut a long piece of foil, 3 inches/8 cm larger than the fish. Place the fish in the centre of the foil and fold up the edges to make a 'pool' around the fish. This 'pool' will hold the marinade.

■ Add water to the steamer pan, being sure that the perforated base or wire grill is raised above the water line.

■ Place all the marinade ingredients in a saucepan. Boil for 5 minutes.

NOW COOK

■ Bring the water in the steamer to the boil and then slip the fish in its 'aluminium foil pool' on to the rack. Pour the marinade over the fish so that it now sits in a broth of seasonings. Cover and steam for 15 minutes, until the fish is just tender.

■ Place the sliced celery in another pan and steam for 4 minutes. Add the red pepper, cabbage and mushrooms and steam for 30 seconds.

■ Carefully lift the fish from the steamer to a serving plate and garnish with the steamed vegetables and chopped coriander leaves.

Helpful Hints and Observations

REMOVING THE FISH FROM THE FOIL – My description of this manoeuvre is really simplistic, so I'll use this space to try and illustrate the entire technique.

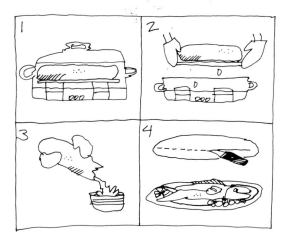

1 This shows the construction of the steamer.
2 Lift out the grid with the fish in its boat.
3 Pour out all the marinade and cooking liquids.
4 Lay the foil boat on its side and cut a slot along its full length. Lift the fish out through the slot and on to the serving plate.

About the Ingredients

STRAW MUSHROOMS – These long-stemmed white mushrooms with small caps are indigenous to Japan, but are available at supermarkets worldwide. They are usually sold wrapped in plastic to preserve freshness because they oxidize very quickly, turning light brown. Select mushrooms that are firm and white. Avoid slimy stems and loose packaging. Substitute button mushrooms if necessary.

DRIED CRANBERRIES – You might think these look a lot like raisins, only they are bright red and have a wonderfully tangy flavour. If you can't find them at your supermarket, try the local health food shop. Sometimes marketed as craisins, they should be dry but moist internally like a raisin.

PICKLED GARLIC – Very common in Asia and a favourite of the Koreans. If you have an Asian foodstore nearby, you will find it with other pickled condiments. Otherwise substitute the same amount of crushed fresh garlic and a dessertspoon/10 ml red wine vinegar in the marinade.

GOLDEN TUNA

*O*ur very special 'celebrity on the street' for whom we created this dish was Jeff Gold, a retired IBM representative who has had serious health problems related to his diet. Jeff flew in from New York to taste this dish which comprised all his favourite foods – and he loved it!

Nutritional Profile

PER SERVING	CLASSIC	MINIMAX
Calories	956	871
Fat (g)	84	8
Calories from fat	79%	9%
Cholesterol (mg)	303	66
Sodium (mg)	890	265
Fibre (g)	2	12

■ *Classic compared:* Tuna with Pasta

Time Estimate

Hands On									
Unsupervised									
Minutes	10	20	30	40	50	60	70	80	90

Cost Estimate

Low	Medium	Medium High	Celebration

Serves 2

INGREDIENTS

1 teaspoon/5 ml extra light olive oil with a dash of sesame oil

⅜ teaspoon/1.9 ml salt

¼ teaspoon/1.25 ml black pepper, freshly ground

2 pieces of fresh tuna steak, 4 oz/113 g each

3 large nectarines

2 tablespoons/30 ml fresh lime juice

¼ teaspoon/1.25 ml cayenne pepper

16 fl oz/450 ml dried pasta (ziti or elbow macaroni)

3 pints/1.8 l boiling water

4 fl oz/113 ml de-alcoholized white wine

1 tablespoon/15 ml fresh basil, chopped

1 tablespoon/15 ml fresh parsley, chopped

1 tablespoon/15 ml mild Cheddar or Parmesan cheese, freshly grated

FIRST PREPARE

■ Pour the olive oil on to a plate. Add one-third of the salt and two-thirds of the pepper and gently mop it up with the tuna, making sure each piece is lightly oiled on both sides.

■ Remove the stones from the nectarines and cut them in quarters. Purée them in a food processor or blender, then push through a sieve into a large bowl. Stir in the lime juice and cayenne pepper.

NOW COOK

■ Drop the pasta into the boiling water with the remaining salt and cook for 11 minutes or until *al dente* (slightly resistant to the teeth). Drain in a colander, then return the pasta to the warm pot and set aside.

■ While the pasta is cooking, place the tuna in a hot skillet, cover and cook for 6 minutes on medium heat. Turn the tuna, add the de-alcoholized white wine and increase the heat to high. Cover and cook for another 3 minutes.

■ Pour the puréed nectarine sauce over the tuna and allow it to heat through. Sprinkle with basil and the remaining black pepper.

■ Turn the tuna out on to hot serving plates. Pour half the heated sauce over the tuna pieces and the rest over the pasta. Sprinkle with the parsley and cheese.

Helpful Hints and Observations

TUNA SUBSTITUTES – I am often asked if you could do this dish with chicken breast. The answer is, yes. In fact, whenever you encounter a potentially difficult main food item, you can think to yourself, how would it taste with something else? In this case, imagine the tart-sweet taste of a nectarine and the smooth taste of chicken – what do you think of that? If it works for you, then have a go at it! In this way you learn how to 'springboard' off other people's recipes and literally do your own thing.

I want you to go in for the tuna.

About the Ingredients

TUNA – Yummy! And don't think you've experienced the taste with the tinned variety. Fresh tuna is a unique taste in its own right. I recommend the yellow fin for this dish but don't be afraid to substitute whatever's fresh and best at your local fishmonger.

NECTARINES – Golden, juicy, sweet and tangy! Select nectarines that are fairly firm, but give slightly under pressure. Store the fresh, ripe fruit in the refrigerator for 3 to 5 days until ready to eat.

CATFISH POORBOY

This is one of the great 'foods of the people' dishes in America and deserves to be world famous. At its simplest, it is really a long bread roll ('Poorboy') filled with fried fish, perhaps some mayonnaise and often with a pickle. In this case, I have done an 'upgrade' to increase the aroma, colour and texture.

I suppose that you could attack this 'filled roll' with a knife and fork, but frankly, you'd miss out on all the fun! This is a super creative choice for a barbecue or picnic. A big, crisp, tossed salad with Treena's Vinaigrette (see Helpful Hints) would go really well.

Nutritional Profile

PER SERVING	CLASSIC	MINIMAX
Calories	657	446
Fat (g)	25	9
Calories from fat	34%	19%
Cholesterol (mg)	136	50
Sodium (mg)	2914	611
Fibre (g)	4	3

■ *Classic compared:* Catfish Poorboy

Time Estimate

Hands On									
Unsupervised									
Minutes	10	20	30	40	50	60	70	80	90

Cost Estimate

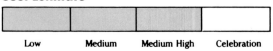

Low	Medium	Medium High	Celebration

INGREDIENTS

4 white bread rolls, about 7–8 inches/18–20 cm
long, 3–4 inches/8–10 cm in diameter. I find the
best roll carries the name 'Continental Breakfast Roll'.
See *About the Ingredients*.

1 tablespoon/15 ml extra light olive oil with a dash
of sesame oil

4 fl oz/113 ml onion, peeled and chopped

2 sweet red peppers, de-seeded and and chopped
in ¼-inch/0.75 cm cubes

1 red chilli pepper, de-seeded and finely diced

1 garlic clove, crushed

2 tablespoons/30 ml tomato paste

2 tablespoons/30 ml fresh basil, chopped

1 tablespoon/15 ml fresh lime juice

4 fl oz/113 ml water

4 fillets of salmon trout or catfish, 7 oz/200 g each

FIRST PREPARE

■ Split the rolls in half lengthwise, leaving one side
joined. Scoop out the doughy centre. Set aside.

NOW COOK

■ Heat the oil in a large frying pan. Over high heat
cook the onion, peppers and garlic until the onion is
translucent. Add the tomato paste, half the chopped
basil leaves and the lime juice. Then pour in the water,
reduce the heat to low and cook for 2 minutes.

■ Arrange the four fish fillets on the sauce in the
frying pan. Brush with the surrounding sauce. Put
under the grill for about 8 minutes. (It helps to have
a frying pan with a handle that withstands a very high
temperature, otherwise crowd the fillets to one side
and keep the handle out in the cool.)

■ Slip the well-sauced fish fillets into the rolls. Spoon
sauce on top and sprinkle each roll with the remaining
basil.

■ Serve immediately. Totally delicious!

Helpful Hints and Observations

PAN GRILLING – This is another relatively new
technique that you may wish to consider for some
future creation of your own. The idea is simple: you
create a colourful, aromatic sauce of vegetables and
herbs, then lay fish fillets (or veal fillets, chicken
breasts, etc.) on this 'bed'. Brush the fish with the pan
juices, slip the pan under a hot grill, about 4 inches/10
cm from the heat source, and let it cook for about 8
minutes. The fish will be perfect, and if you have used
sweet peppers and onions they will have roasted on
the exposed surfaces to give a smoky taste.

SCOOPING OUT THE BREAD – Be careful here! It's
easy to dig too far and make a hole. Then all the
great juice will end up on your shirt!

TREENA'S VINAIGRETTE – A lovely dressing for a
side salad to this dish. Just blend together 1 part olive
oil, 2 parts white wine vinegar and 1 garlic clove. Add
dry mustard powder, cayenne pepper and soft brown
sugar to taste. Use sparingly over crisp salad greens
and freshly sliced celery, tomatoes and purple onions.
A few sunflower seeds add texture.

About the Ingredients

CATFISH – An American
freshwater fish which likes
calm water and is mainly found
in the Mississippi basin, the
catfish has delicious
practically boneless, slightly
oily flesh. A much larger
relative, *Silurus glanis*, or Wels
catfish, has been introduced to
Britain, but it has rather fatty
flesh, a little like eel, and is not
widely available. So I have

substituted salmon trout – but you could use any
good quality oily fish such as mackerel or herring.
Ask you fishmonger to fillet the fish for you, and be
wary of remaining small bones!

CONTINENTAL BREAKFAST ROLLS – These rolls are
chosen for their crisp crust, which will hold in all the
wonderful juice. If you are lucky enough to live within
reach of a sourdough baker's, look for the 'Italian
Spaghetti Roll' which will add an extra dimension of
flavour.

KEDGEREE

$\mathcal{K}$evin Graham, *Chef de Cuisine of the famed Windsor Court Hotel in New Orleans, makes a very rich Kedgeree. He obliged me by setting a much higher fat standard than usual. Mine is a 'flip side' alternative. Don't risk buying poor quality fish. Get the best, the moister the better.*

Kedgeree is really either a breakfast or supper dish and is complete in itself.

Nutritional Profile

PER SERVING	CLASSIC	MINIMAX
Calories	693	456
Fat (g)	56	11
Calories from fat	73%	22%
Cholesterol (mg)	296	189
Sodium (mg)	1187	1224
Fibre (g)	1	2

■ *Classic compared:* Kedgeree

Time Estimate

Hands On		
Unsupervised	2 Hours	
Minutes	10 20 30 40 50 60 70 80 90	

Cost Estimate

Low	Medium	Medium High	Celebration

INGREDIENTS

1 lb/450 g smoked haddock, *or* similar smoked white fish

Cold milk – enough to cover the fish in a small bowl

3 hard-boiled eggs (boiled 5 minutes)

1 teaspoon/5 ml extra light olive oil with a dash of sesame oil

1 large onion, peeled and finely diced

2 teaspoons/10 ml garam masala

½ teaspoon/2.5 ml turmeric

¼ teaspoon/1.25 ml ground cardamom

8 fl oz/227 ml uncooked basmati or any good long grain rice, rinsed

1½ pints/800 ml homemade fish stock (recipe page 210)

1 bay leaf

2 tablespoons/30 ml fresh parsley, chopped

¼ teaspoon/1.25 ml freshly ground sea salt if needed, no more

TURMERIC SAUCE

8 fl oz/227 ml homemade fish stock (recipe page 210)

1 tablespoon/15 ml arrowroot

½ teaspoon/2.5 ml turmeric

FIRST PREPARE

■ Remove and discard the skin from the smoked fish. Soak it for 1 to 2 hours in sufficient cold milk to cover. This helps leach out the salt.

■ Separate the hard-cooked egg whites from the yolks. Slice the egg whites into thin strips and set aside. Discard the egg yolks. (Pet dogs appreciate these egg discards.)

NOW COOK

■ Heat the olive oil in a large saucepan and cook the onion, garam masala, turmeric and cardamom together until the onion is soft, about 5 minutes.

■ Add the rice to the onion, stir and leave to cook for 2 minutes. Add 1 pint/568 ml of fish stock and the bay leaf. Cook on medium heat, uncovered, for 18 to 20 minutes, until all the stock has been absorbed into the rice.

■ Remove the fish from the milk. Into a small saucepan on very low heat, flake the fish into 1-inch/2.5-cm pieces. Feel carefully for small bones. Add the remaining fish stock, bring to a simmer, cover and cook gently for 5 minutes. Add the sliced egg whites, and cover.

■ Instead of a high-fat butter sauce, make the turmeric sauce by pouring the fish stock into a hot saucepan. Stir in the turmeric and arrowroot. Almost instantaneously the sauce will become glossy and smooth. This sauce is used to add the 'mouth feel' and colour of butter without which a Scotsman would declare the dish 'stingy'.

■ Stir the thickened sauce into the rice. Gently stir in the fish and eggs.

■ Taste for salt. I feel a dish with this much rice needs some salt. But be careful not to add more than ¼ teaspoon/1.25 ml. This is all the sodium an average adult needs each day!

■ Transfer the Kedgeree to a serving dish and garnish with chopped parsley.

Helpful Hints and Observations

REPLACING FAT – In this recipe I faced a good deal of classical and cultural difficulty. As I've already implied, a Scot's idea of ultimate 'stinginess' (and they have the reputation to start with) is someone who doesn't add sufficient butter to kedgeree. My father was pure Scot and my family goes back for many generations. We come from the lowlands just south of Edinburgh. Hence, if I'm stingy with the butter, I'm in trouble! I actually took this recipe to Scotland to test it. It was accepted without condemnation. In fact, those who tried it preferred the lighter taste. Some of the reasons for this breakthrough were the reduced fish stock (fumet) that provides richness and flavour from the bones; the turmeric that gives it a yellow butter colour; and the arrowroot that adds a glossy sheen.

About the Ingredients

SMOKED HADDOCK – This fish is easily found on the eastern seaboard of the United States and off the coasts of England and France. At one time, haddock was the most plentiful of all the white fish, accounting for almost half the catch in the North Atlantic. Smoked haddock has been split in half lengthwise as soon as it is caught, rubbed lightly with salt, and left to smoke for 24 hours. It should have a dull, pale yellow surface. Very bright yellow colouring is artificial. Substitute smoked cod if haddock is not available.

GARAM MASALA – See page 111.

BASMATI RICE – See page 47.

TACOS DE PESCADO

$\mathcal{A}t$ *lunchtime in the heart of Phoenix, Arizona's business district, lines of people are waiting to eat at Fina Cocina. Owner and head chef Norman Fierros dazzles his patrons by presenting the great flavours of Mexican cuisine with a masterful light touch. This recipe is an adaptation of one of his most popular dishes and makes wonderful sense for lunch.*

Mexican salads rely mainly on colour and freshness, which, come to think of it, isn't a bad combination! This taco is served with a finely sliced onion, cabbage and tomato salad: the finer the cut, the better!

Nutritional Profile

PER SERVING	CLASSIC	MINIMAX
Calories	613	298
Fat (g)	36	6
Calories from fat	53%	18%
Cholesterol (mg)	108	39
Sodium (mg)	2589	402
Fibre (g)	5	10

■ *Classic compared:* Tacos

Time Estimate

Hands On									
Unsupervised									

Minutes 10 20 30 40 50 60 70 80 90

Cost Estimate

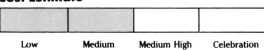

Low   Medium   Medium High   Celebration

INGREDIENTS

CORIANDER PESTO

1¼ pints/700 ml coriander leaves

4 fl oz/113 ml extra light olive oil with a dash of sesame oil

5 garlic cloves, peeled

2 red chilli peppers, cored and de-seeded

8 fl oz/227 ml walnuts

8 fl oz/227 ml very mild feta cheese

Juice of 1 lemon

2 fl oz/57 ml iced water

TACOS

4 fillets of sole, 6 oz/170 g each

2 tablespoons/30 ml sea salt

1½ pints/900 ml iced water

½ teaspoon/2.5 ml white pepper, freshly ground

6 Italian plum tomatoes, de-seeded and finely sliced

6 spring onions, chopped

½ head of purple cabbage, thinly sliced

1 teaspoon/5 ml extra light olive oil with a dash of sesame oil

8 wholewheat tortillas

Juice of 1 lime

4 lime wedges

FIRST PREPARE THE PESTO

NOTE: The quantities given are for 1¼ pints/700 ml. We only use 5 tablespoons/75 ml for the four servings in this recipe. Note that each tablespoon contains 23 calories and 2 grams of fat.

■ Place all the ingredients in a food processor and purée into a thick paste. Refrigerate until needed.

NOW COOK THE TACOS

■ Dissolve the sea salt into the iced water. Slip the fish fillets into the salty water and let them refresh for 10 minutes. Remove the fillets, and pat them dry with paper towels. Sprinkle them with white pepper and set aside.

■ Mix together the tomatoes, spring onions, cabbage and 1 tablespoon/15 ml of the pesto.

■ Lightly grease a skillet with the oil and put it on medium heat. Dip the tortillas in water and then quickly steam-sauté them on both sides. Remove them from the pan and keep them warm until needed. (I use a plate set over a small saucepan of boiling water, covering the cooked tortillas with a clean cloth.)

■ Place the fish fillets on a lightly oiled rack in a grill pan and grill for 4 minutes. Sprinkle with the lime juice.

■ To assemble, spread a warm tortilla with 1 table-spoon/15 ml of coriander pesto, place a fish fillet on it and cover it with the salad mixture. Roll up like a taco or simply leave it open-faced for your guests to do the rolling – it looks more attractive this way. Serve with lime wedges on the side.

Helpful Hints and Observations

PROCESSOR HEAT – The food processor is a wonderful piece of equipment and really essential when making a good pesto. However, because of its speed it does work up a certain amount of friction heat which can discolour the green tint of the pesto. This is the reason for the iced water: it saves the mixture from heat discoloration.

HEATING TORTILLAS – Be careful not to let your steam-heated tortillas stay too long under the towel – 10 minutes should be maximum. My personal preference is to use wholewheat tortillas. I like the taste and nutrition better and, as an added bonus, they're much easier to handle.

About the Ingredients

FETA CHEESE – Made of sheep's milk, feta is curdled, heated and then cured or pickled in a mixture of brine and its own whey. Look for feta that is white, moist and crumbly in texture.

CORIANDER – This bright green leaf herb adds a fresh, distinctive flavour to your cooking. Another name for coriander is Chinese parsley, and to make matters even more confusing, its dried seeds are also marketed as coriander! Look for coriander in your supermarket, or any greengrocer's with a good selection of herbs. Like many herbs, coriander is quite easy to grow in the garden, or on a sunny windowsill. It is an annual, so save some seed for the following year.

CREPES FRUITS DE MER

This dish comes from my past! My parents opened Gravetye Manor near East Grinstead back in 1958. Under Peter Herbert's direction, it is now one of the very best small hotels in Europe. We originally invented this dish for the head of the seafood company, Young's. He was delighted! Now it is re-invented for you.

I love to serve this on a large plate with six to eight portions all lined up! However, unless you have a presentable fish slice or a long palette knife, it's probably best to slosh it up in the kitchen. Freshly steamed green beans and small boiled potatoes make up a great supper.

Nutritional Profile

PER SERVING	CLASSIC	MINIMAX
Calories	1433	525
Fat (g)	63	8
Calories from fat	39%	13%
Cholesterol (mg)	588	223
Sodium (mg)	2509	507
Fibre (g)	7	10

■ *Classic compared:* Crêpes Fruits de Mer

Time Estimate

Hands On									
Unsupervised									
Minutes	10	20	30	40	50	60	70	80	90

Cost Estimate

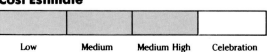

Low	Medium	Medium High	Celebration

INGREDIENTS

CREPE BATTER (*makes 8 crêpes*)
4 fl oz/113 ml plain flour
1 whole egg
1 egg yolk
8 fl oz/227 ml skimmed milk
1 teaspoon/5 ml extra light olive oil with a dash
of sesame oil
8 fresh dill sprigs

FILLING
A 15-oz/425-g tin of butter beans, drained and rinsed
4 fl oz/113 ml de-alcoholized white wine
1¼ pints/710 ml skimmed milk
12 oz/340 g lemon or Dover sole, cut in finger-sized
strips
6 oz/170 g scallops
6 fl oz/170 ml button mushrooms, quartered unless
very small
2 tablespoons/30 ml arrowroot mixed with 4
tablespoons/60 ml de-alcoholized white wine
1 teaspoon/5 ml fresh dill, finely chopped
⅛ teaspoon/0.6 ml cayenne pepper
6 Italian plum tomatoes, peeled, de-seeded and
chopped
1 tablespoon/15 ml fresh parsley, chopped
6 oz/170 g small cooked prawns
2 tablespoons/30 ml Parmesan cheese, freshly grated

GARNISH
1 lemon, cut into wedges
Fresh parsley, chopped

FIRST PREPARE THE CREPES

■ In a medium bowl combine the flour, whole egg, egg yolk and milk and leave them to stand for 30 minutes. Heat a crêpe pan, swish the oil around in it to prepare the surface, then pour the oil into the batter. Mix in well. This will make each crêpe self-releasing.

■ Pour a small ladle of batter into the hot crêpe pan. When it begins to bubble and look waxy, gently loosen the edges. Place a fresh dill sprig on the uncooked surface and flip the crêpe over. Continue to cook the remaining crêpes in the same manner. Cover them with a damp cloth to await filling.

THEN COOK THE FILLING

■ Purée the butter beans in a food processor, adding 2 fl oz/57 ml of the wine to make a paste. Set aside.

■ Heat the milk in a large skillet. Place the sole strips, scallops and mushrooms in the milk. Poach for 4 to 5 minutes but do not boil. When tender, remove from the milk and keep warm.

■ Take out 8 fl oz/227 ml of the poaching milk and place it in a small saucepan. Remove from the heat and add half the dissolved arrowroot solution. Return to heat and stir until thickened.

■ Add the rest of the wine to the milk in the large skillet. Stir in the remaining arrowroot mixture to thicken, and add 4 fl oz/113 ml of the butter bean purée. Return the poached fish mixture to the sauce.

■ Add the dill and cayenne pepper to the sauced fish. Add the tomatoes and chopped parsley for colour, and the prawns. Stir very gently to avoid breaking the sole.

NOW ASSEMBLE

■ Lay the reserved crêpes in an ovenproof pan, dill-side down. Fill each one with the fish mixture and fold. Turn seam-side down. Pour the sauce over the herbed tops – they should just show through.

■ Sprinkle with Parmesan cheese. Place under a hot grill until the cheese melts and browns – about 2 minutes.

■ Serve with lemon wedges on the side and a good scattering of chopped parsley. A little paprika will add colour to compensate for the light touch with the cheese.

Helpful Hints and Observations

■ BUTTER BEAN SAUCE – In this recipe I have tried to use the very lightly flavoured butter bean to add some 'body' to the sauce. It works for me – please see if it's a technique you can adapt to other recipes. You will get a certain amount of grainy texture that is different from the velvet softness achieved by a flour-and-butter roux based sauce but you will notice from the nutritional comparison that we had a substantial amount of work to do!

■ PRE-PREPARATION – You can prepare this dish up to 6 hours in advance, as far as filling the crêpes and laying them in the pan. Cover the filled crêpes with plastic wrap and keep cool until needed. Reserve the sauce separately. Reheat the crêpes in a 250°F/120°C/Gas Mark ½ oven. Reheat the sauce, pour it over the heated crêpes, sprinkle with cheese, grill and serve. This works well at a dinner party when you want more time with your guests.

SCALLOPS AND PRAWNS VINCENT

*C*hef *de cuisine Vincent Guerithault of the restaurant Vincent's at Camelback in Phoenix, Arizona, gave me permission to adapt his popular scallops and shrimp appetizer to provide a quick and elegant main dish. As you'll see, the recipe utilizes an unusual method: one in which the seafood juices go to make up a lovely fresh orange sauce in only a matter of minutes.*

Chef Vincent serves this dish as an appetizer in miniature bamboo steamers. I have increased the size of each portion and added basmati rice to make it a main course.

Nutritional Profile

PER SERVING	CLASSIC	MINIMAX
Calories	643	324
Fat (g)	18	2
Calories from fat	25%	6%
Cholesterol (mg)	78	45
Sodium (mg)	1636	163
Fibre (g)	8	3

■ *Classic compared:* Scallops and Shrimp Vincent

Time Estimate

Hands On
Unsupervised
Minutes   10   20   30   40   50   60   70   80   90

Cost Estimate

Low   Medium   Medium High   Celebration

INGREDIENTS

16 fl oz/454 ml water

4 fl oz/113 ml uncooked Basmati rice, rinsed

½ teaspoon/2.5 ml extra light olive oil with a dash of sesame oil

1 shallot, peeled and finely sliced

1 teaspoon/5 ml ginger root, freshly grated

Zest of half an orange

1 tablespoon/15 ml fresh basil, finely sliced

8 fl oz/227 ml de-alcoholized white wine

6 uncooked prawns, peeled, de-veined and the shells reserved

6 scallops

1 orange, segmented, pitted and the pith removed

1 tablespoon/15 ml arrowroot mixed with 2 table-spoons/30 ml de-alcoholized white wine

GARNISH

Fresh basil, finely sliced, to taste

White pepper, freshly ground, to taste

NOW COOK

■ Put the water in a medium saucepan, bring to the boil, add the Basmati rice and cook for 10 minutes. Drain in a metal sieve or colander. Fill the saucepan about a quarter full with hot water. Put the sieve or colander filled with rice over the saucepan and cover. Not only will this keep the rice warm, it also helps the grains be separate and fluffy (see *Helpful Hints*).

■ Heat the oil in a pot large enough to hold a steamer platform to cook the seafood. Add the shallot, ginger root, orange zest and basil. Heat and stir.

■ Add the de-alcoholized white wine and the reserved prawn shells. Put the steamer platform in place, cover and bring to the boil. Place the prawns and scallops on the steamer tray and steam for 5 minutes (try not to overcook seafood – 5 minutes should be enough). Remove the prawns and scallops and keep warm.

■ Take the poaching liquid off the heat and strain it into a smaller saucepan. Add the arrowroot paste, return to the heat and stir until thickened.

■ Return the prawns and scallops to the thickened poaching liquid and add the orange segments. Sprinkle with additional fresh basil and white pepper to taste.

■ Serve the glistening, fragrant seafood in a nest of the steamed rice.

Helpful Hints and Observations

PERFECT RICE – A major goal in most nations' rice cookery is to achieve separate, fluffy grains. Clogged, starchy rice masses are not, as a rule, enjoyable, except when using chopsticks!

Clogging happens through overcooking in too great a volume of water and from surface starch created by movement of the rice grains against themselves in packing and shipping.

The obvious first step must be to rid the rice of its surface starch by rinsing it under cold water until the water runs clear. Caution: don't rinse the rice marked as 'enriched' or having 'added nutrients'. These are put in the package in powder form and will rinse away. My recommendation would be to avoid these 'nutrient added' products unless you consume a great deal of rice as your sole grain source.

Put the rinsed rice into a saucepan with 4 fl oz/113 ml of boiling water for each fl oz/28 ml of rice. Boil for 10 minutes and strain through a metal sieve or colander. Put the sieve or colander full of rice back over the saucepan a quarter filled with boiling water. Cover and steam for 15 minutes. Each grain will be separate and fluffy.

This will always work if you follow the directions exactly.

About the Ingredients

BASMATI RICE – A fragrant long grain rice from India and Pakistan, Basmati rice can usually be found in the special foods section of your local supermarket. If necessary, you can substitute any good-quality long grain rice.

SCALLOPS – Succulent, sweet and oh, so good to eat, scallops are molluscs (shellfish with hinged shells) with white flesh and an orange roe enclosed in pinkish-brown shells. They are usually sold opened – ask your fishmonger if you want the shells too. Look for firm white flesh and bright-coloured roe and make sure the liquid surrounding them is thick with a sweet fragrance. Scallops are in season from September to March, but should be obtainable frozen at other times.

PRAWNS – Small soft-shelled grey or brownish crustaceans, the shells of which turn bright red and the flesh pink when boiled. It is worth tracking down uncooked prawns if you can – if pre-cooked they will have lost some of their flavour in the cooking water. Select prawns which are firm and fragrant, not fishy.

PRAWN GUMBO

This Minimax version of a Creole classic is based upon the marvellous rendition served by Chef Leah Chase at her fabulous restaurant in New Orleans, Dooky Chase. One food critic called Leah's Gumbo 'the kind of dish that makes you want to throw down your spoon, rush into the kitchen and kiss the cook'! I hope this Minimax version inspires similar emotions – it could be the beginning of world peace!

Nutritional Profile

PER SERVING	CLASSIC	MINIMAX
Calories	415	510
Fat (g)	17	3
Calories from fat	36%	5%
Cholesterol (mg)	197	107
Sodium (mg)	1974	204
Fibre (g)	14	11

■ *Classic compared:* Gumbo

Time Estimate

Hands On									
Unsupervised									
Minutes	10	20	30	40	50	60	70	80	90

Cost Estimate

Low	Medium	Medium High	Celebration

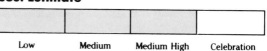

Serves 4

INGREDIENTS

1 lb/450 g uncooked prawns in their shells
2½ pints/1.4 l water
8 fl oz/227 ml uncooked long grain rice, rinsed
4 flat tablespoons/60 ml plain flour
Two 14-oz/400-g tins cut okra, drained
2 tablespoons/30 ml extra light olive oil with a
dash of sesame oil
A 6-oz/170-g tin no-salt tomato paste
1 large onion, peeled and chopped
3 stalks celery, chopped
2 sweet green peppers, de-seeded and chopped
2 garlic cloves, peeled and chopped
6 thyme sprigs
2 bay leaves
½ teaspoon/2.5 ml cayenne pepper
Spring onions and fresh parsley, chopped, for garnish

FIRST PREPARE

■ Peel and de-vein the prawns, saving the shells.
Cut each prawn into three pieces and set aside.

■ Put the prawn shells into a medium saucepan and
cover with ¾ pint/425 ml of the water. Bring to the
boil and simmer for just a couple of minutes. Strain out
the shells, reserving the liquid. This flavour-infused
water will be used to cook your rice.

NOW COOK

■ Cook the rice in the reserved prawn shell water
until all the liquid is absorbed and the rice is cooked
through.

■ Put the flour in a saucepan over medium heat. Stir
constantly until it turns light brown. Remove from the
heat and cool. This step is crucial in developing a nice
toasty flavour and brown colour for your gumbo.

■ Put the drained okra in a large plastic bag. Pour
in the cooled flour. Seal off the top and shake until
the okra is completely coated with flour.

■ Heat 1 tablespoon/15 ml of the oil in a large pot.
Add the flour-coated okra and the flour, one half at
a time. You want the okra to fry and become really
brown. Push the okra to one side of the pot.

■ On the other side of the pot, add the tomato
paste and cook, stirring often. Continue cooking
until the tomato paste turns a dark brown. This is
a caramelizing called the Maillard reaction. Now stir
the tomato paste into the okra pieces. Turn the cooked
okra out on to a plate, scraping up all the tasty brown
pan residue.

■ Add the remaining oil to the same pot. Add
the onion, celery, green pepper and garlic. Let the
vegetables swelter and fry over high heat. Stir in the
cooked okra and continue frying over high heat.

■ Pour in the other 1¾ pints/975 ml of water,
thyme, bay leaves and the Creole Torpedo – the
cayenne pepper. Simmer for 30 minutes.

■ Just before you're ready to serve, stir in the prawns.
Cook for about 4 minutes only. The prawns should not
be overdone.

■ To serve, spoon the rice, fragrant from the prawn
shells, into a bowl. Sprinkle the chopped spring onions
over the rice. Top with the Prawn Gumbo. Sprinkle
with emerald flecks of chopped fresh parsley.

Helpful Hints and Observations

WHAT TO DO WITH THE ROUX? – A really tough issue:
can it be Creole without roux, the incredible invention
that provides both depth of taste and silky thickening
to so many wonderful dishes? Roux is almost equal
amounts of flour and butter, stirred together over mild
heat to cook. This combination can actually thicken
up to six times its own weight in liquid! It is also rich
in saturated fat and calories. I started out by toasting
the plain flour in a dry saucepan over medium heat –
stirring continuously until it was a deep brown colour.
I then tossed the okra in a bag. This gave each piece
an even coating that soaked up spare surface juices
and allowed the pieces to colour in the very hot oil.
In order to put depth in the dish, I added tomato paste
and fried it to change its colour. With the right amount
of cayenne pepper we eventually made it!

OKRA – Fresh okra wasn't available when we made
this dish on the television programme, so we tried
the canned variety, which turned out to be just fine
and much less complicated (or slippery). The fresh
okra doesn't have a good, high nutrient value, so the
normal canning loss wasn't too much of a threat.

About the Ingredients

OKRA – A pod vegetable related to the cotton plant,
whose origin is traced back to Africa. Brought to the
Americas during the slave trade, okra is popular in
the southern United States. Used as a thickener, okra
replaced filet-powder, a thickener made of ground
sassafras leaves. If using fresh okra, select pods that
are a light to medium green. Fresh okra will keep only
3 to 5 days. It can be blanched and frozen.

PRAWNS – See page 47.

JAMBALAYA

C*ajun – a term derived from Arcadian – is a mixed*
style of cooking often confused with Creole and Soul.
This is not too surprising when you note that the same
geographical area of Louisiana was first peopled by
Choctaw Indians, followed by the Spanish, Africans,
Arcadians from Nova Scotia and then the French.
Jambalaya – so like Paella – is almost certainly of
Spanish origin.

This famous dish is always served as it cooks
(eventually!) from pot to plate. For my taste, I
really enjoy a crisp salad with Treena's Vinaigrette
(see Helpful Hints, *page 39) and lots of fresh salad*
herbs.

Nutritional Profile

PER SERVING	CLASSIC	MINIMAX
Calories	704	456
Fat (g)	41	16
Calories from fat	52%	31%
Cholesterol (mg)	241	178
Sodium (mg)	2312	981
Fibre (g)	2	3

■ *Classic compared:* Austin's Jambalaya

Time Estimate

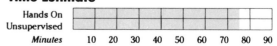

Hands On
Unsupervised

Minutes   10 20 30 40 50 60 70 80 90

Cost Estimate

Low   Medium   Medium High   Celebration

Serves 6

INGREDIENTS

1 lb/450 g smoked ham hocks
1½ pints/850 ml water (for second stage)
4 bay leaves
1¾ lb/800 g uncooked prawns in their shells
¾ pint/425 ml boiling water
1 teaspoon/5 ml extra light olive oil with a dash
of sesame oil
1 onion, peeled and chopped
2 garlic cloves, peeled and chopped
4 fl oz/113 g celery, chopped
1 tablespoon/15 ml no-salt tomato paste
8 oz/225 g lean ham steak
1 teaspoon/5 ml fresh thyme
⅛ teaspoon/0.6 ml whole cloves
½ teaspoon/2.5 ml fresh cayenne pepper (more if
your tongue is asbestos)
12 fl oz/340 ml uncooked long grain rice, rinsed
A 28-oz/800 g tin Italian plum tomatoes, drained and
roughly chopped
2 fl oz/57 ml fresh parsley, chopped

NOW COOK

■ Cover the ham hocks with cold water. Bring to
the boil and cook for 5 minutes. Remove the hocks
and discard the water.

■ Place the blanched ham hocks in the 1½
pints/850 ml of fresh water, add the bay leaves
and simmer for 1 hour, or pressure cook for 20
minutes.

■ Remove the ham hocks. Strain and reserve the
liquid. Cut the lean meat in shreds and discard all the
fat and bone. Return the reserved liquid to a saucepan
and reduce to ¾ pint/425 ml to make a ham hock
stock. Skim off any surplus fat.

■ Cook the prawns in the ¾ pint/425 ml boiling
water for 3 minutes. Remove the prawns and pour
the liquid into the ham hock stock.

■ Put the cooked prawns straight into iced water;
peel, de-vein and slice in half lengthwise. Put the
shells into the ham hock stock and continue cooking
until it has reduced to 1¼ pints/710 ml.

■ In a large sauté pan, heat the oil and fry the
onion, garlic and celery. After 2 minutes, add the
tomato paste and cook for 1 minute. Heat caramelizes
the tomato paste into a deep brown colour. Called the
Maillard reaction, this adds both colour and the depth
of taste so essential when a lot of fat is removed from
a recipe.

■ Cut the ham steak into bite-sized cubes and add to
the vegetables with the shredded meat from the ham
hocks.

■ Place the thyme, cloves and cayenne pepper in
a coffee bean grinder or a small food mill. Grind the
spices to create a wonderfully fragrant powder. Put
half the mixture in the ham hock stock and half in
the vegetables.

■ Remove the prawn shells from the stock.

■ Cook the rice in the ham hock stock for about
20 minutes, or until all the liquid has been absorbed.
Never stir the rice while cooking – that can break its
texture into a mush.

■ Combine the cooked rice with the vegetables and
ham. Add the tomatoes and the prawns.

■ Stir in the parsley and a scattering of chopped
fresh thyme. Now taste it. Add more cayenne pepper
if everyone likes it hot and spicy. Serve it hot!

Helpful Hints and Observations

RICE COOKED SEPARATELY – I have separated the
rice from the other ingredients in order to avoid the
common problem of having the rice 'catch' if you don't
use a heavy enough pan. Removing so much of the
fat makes the sticking problem even worse. However,
please note that I have used a good stock to cook the
rice ... so nothing is lost ... only fat and frustration.

About the Ingredients

LONG GRAIN RICE – The rice plant, *Oryza sativa*,
probably originated in southern India and spread to
China, where it was known and cultivated over 3,000
years ago. Of the 2,500 or so varieties, there are two
main types: the subspecies *japonica*, which is short
and sticky, and *indica*, which is long and fluffy. The
short or round grain varieties are mainly used in
puddings, as they have thickening properties and
hold together. Long grains, preferred for savoury
dishes, remain separate – unless overcooked, when
they turn to an unappetizing mush.

CAYENNE PEPPER – I like to call this spice the
'Creole Torpedo'. It comes from the fruit of a South
American hot pepper plant. Cayenne chillies have an
oval shape, growing 2–6 inches/5–15 cm long. They
start out green and turn red or orange as they ripen.
Their dried, ground seeds form the product we are
most familiar with. The flavour is strong, and rather
sharp. Use with caution!

RIVER CAFE SUCCOTASH

$\mathcal{D}$avid Burke has a problem with his restaurant . . . it's the view! The River Café is located just east of the Brooklyn Bridge in New York City and sits right on the river bank with nothing to obscure the Manhattan skyline. But David wants people to look at his food, so he has to fight for attention.

As a result, David's cuisine is remarkable for its display. In a way he is a modern Antonin Careme (a chef with remarkable presentation skills in the 1800s) with a sense of humour. This dish is somewhat altered, but owes its concept to David's genius for presentation.

I set the Succotash off against freshly cooked spinach fettuccini – great colours and no other vegetable needed.

Nutritional Profile

PER SERVING	CLASSIC	MINIMAX
Calories	484	202
Fat (g)	17	4
Calories from fat	32%	16%
Cholesterol (mg)	253	45
Sodium (mg)	2673	110
Fibre (g)	10	6

■ *Classic compared:* Sauteed Shrimp and Ravioli with Pumpkin Succotash

Time Estimate

Hands On
Unsupervised

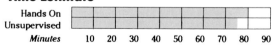

Minutes   10   20   30   40   50   60   70   80   90

Cost Estimate

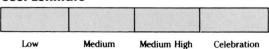

Low   Medium   Medium High   Celebration

Serves 4

INGREDIENTS

4 mini pumpkins *or* 1 medium-sized pumpkin
1 tablespoon/15 ml extra light olive oil with a dash of sesame oil
16 fl oz/450 ml prawn stock (recipe page 210)
12 large uncooked prawns, shells removed
8 fl oz/227 ml sweet red pepper, diced
8 fl oz/227 ml sweet yellow pepper, diced
4 fl oz/113 ml de-alcoholized white wine
8 fl oz/227 ml cooked corn kernels
8 fl oz/227 ml cooked butter beans
1 tablespoon/15 ml fresh sage, chopped
¼ teaspoon/1.25 ml salt, freshly ground
4 fl oz/113 ml fresh chives, chopped
1½ pints/900 ml cooked spinach fettuccine

FIRST PREPARE

■ Cut the stem and top off each pumpkin. Remove the seeds and stringy material. (The seeds can be toasted and reserved to use on my breakfast cereal, Kerrmush, page 162.) Scoop the pumpkin flesh out with a melon baller, leaving the shell ¼ inch/0.75 cm thick. Place the balls in a saucepan with the prawn stock. Bring to the boil, then reduce the heat and simmer until the pumpkin balls are tender – about 20 minutes. Purée in a food processor until smooth.

NOW COOK

■ Pre-heat the oven to 350°F/180°C/Gas Mark 4. Place the hollowed-out pumpkins on a rack in a roasting tin with a small amount of water in the bottom. Cover with foil and bake for 35 minutes.

■ Heat the oil in a large skillet and sauté the prawns and peppers until the prawns are lightly brown. Place them in a small bowl and set aside. Pour the wine into the skillet, add the corn, butter beans and sage and cook for 30 more seconds. Add the pumpkin purée and simmer for another 1 to 2 minutes. Season with the freshly ground salt.

■ *To Serve:* Place the medium pumpkin shell on a large plate or place the mini pumpkins on four individual plates. Place two prawns in the bottom of each pumpkin and pour in the Succotash. Top with one more prawn and a sprinkle of the chives. Serve with spinach fettuccini fresh from the pot.

About the Ingredients

PUMPKINS – Such a festive and beautiful vegetable for presenting your Succotash! Look for pumpkins without brown blemishes and no soft spots. But don't think of pumpkins just for decoration. Not only do they yield tasty flesh, they are also wonderful sources of what are believed to be anti-cancer nutrients: vitamin C, fibre and carotene.

SAGE – When you think of the aroma of turkey stuffing, you're probably thinking about sage. And it's probably the common garden sage, although there are over 500 varieties of this herb. This is a strong herb for strong uses. It even holds up well when you throw it on barbecue coals to impart fragrance to grilling. But really, dried sage doesn't taste anything like fresh, so try to find or grow the real thing.

APRICOT-CORIANDER CHICKEN

*O*nce in a while, Treena and I visit a restaurant that we really like. Triples, on the west side of Lake Union in Seattle, Washington, is one of the best. One of their simple yet wonderful dishes is a plump chicken breast with a chutney-like sauce, using apricots, coriander leaves and a special spice mix. With their permission, I've trimmed the fat down a little, resulting in some excellent nutritional numbers (that's because it was so good to start with!).

I serve this dish with saffron-tinted rice and steamed kale. This is a recipe you must try – it is full of aroma, colour and texture, almost the perfect Minimax dish!

Nutritional Profile

PER SERVING	CLASSIC	MINIMAX
Calories	659	443
Fat (g)	22	6
Calories from fat	30%	12%
Cholesterol (mg)	97	86
Sodium (mg)	2177	151
Fibre (g)	6	7

■ *Classic compared:* Chicken with Apricot-Coriander Sauce

Time Estimate

Hands On Unsupervised									
				3 Hours					
Minutes	10	20	30	40	50	60	70	80	90

Cost Estimate

Low	Medium	Medium High	Celebration

Serves 6

INGREDIENTS

6 chicken breasts with skin, 6 oz/170 g each, trimmed of fat and de-boned

MARINADE

2 tablespoons/30 ml lemon juice, freshly squeezed
1 tablespoon/15 ml Dijon mustard
⅛ teaspoon/0.6 ml cayenne pepper
⅛ teaspoon/0.6 ml black pepper, freshly ground
2 tablespoons/30 ml de-alcoholized white wine
1 tablespoon/15 ml fresh thyme, chopped

SAUCE

12 fl oz/340 ml hot water
8 fl oz/227 ml dried unsulphured apricots
2 whole cloves
1-inch/2.5-cm piece of cinnamon stick
¼ teaspoon/1.25 ml coriander seeds
¼ teaspoon/1.25 ml black pepper, freshly ground
12 Italian plum tomatoes, de-seeded and diced
1 teaspoon/5 ml extra light olive oil with a dash of sesame oil
1 medium onion, peeled and diced
1 tablespoon/15 ml fresh ginger root, cut in fine strips
2 tablespoons/30 ml apricot preserve
2 tablespoons/30 ml fresh coriander leaves, chopped

RICE

1½ pints/850 ml water
10 fl oz/284 ml long grain rice
Pinch of saffron (enough to colour the rice pale yellow)

BOUQUET GARNI

4 whole cloves
6 black peppercorns
6 coriander seeds
2-inch/5-cm piece of cinnamon stick
1-inch/2.5-cm square piece of fresh ginger root
2 sprigs fresh coriander

GARNISH

2½ pints/1.4 l kale leaves
Fresh coriander sprigs

FIRST PREPARE

■ Mix all the marinade ingredients in a medium-sized bowl. Put the chicken breasts in the marinade and refrigerate for 3 hours.

■ Pour the hot water over the dried apricots and soak them for 1 hour. Strain, reserving the water. Finely dice four of the apricots and set aside to use later in the rice. Chop the remaining apricots.

■ In a small food processor, or using a pestle and mortar, grind the cloves, cinnamon, coriander seeds and black peppercorns for the sauce. Push the spice powder through a sieve, trapping any large particles.

NOW COOK

■ *The Rice:* Pour the water into a medium-sized saucepan, add the bouquet garni and bring to the boil. Add the rice and saffron, cover and boil for 10 minutes. Strain through a metal sieve, or a colander with very small holes! Place the sieve with the rice over the saucepan which has been a quarter filled with boiling water. Stir in the four chopped apricots. Cover and steam for 15 minutes.

■ Remove the chicken breasts from the marinade and place them in a hot skillet skin-side down. Brown for 1 minute, then reduce the heat and continue cooking for 5 minutes on each side. Remove and set aside. Pour 8 fl oz/227 ml of the reserved apricot soaking water into the skillet to de-glaze the pan residues.

■ *The Sauce:* Heat the oil in a medium saucepan and cook the onion and ginger for 2 minutes. Stir in the tomatoes and apricots. Strain the apricot and pan juices into the saucepan and bring to a rapid boil. Stir in the spice powder and apricot preserve to add a lovely gloss.

■ Strip the skin off the chicken breasts and return them to their original skillet. Coat with the sauce and sprinkle with the chopped coriander leaves. Keep warm over medium heat.

■ Just before serving, steam the kale leaves for 3 to 4 minutes.

■ *To Serve:* Divide the kale leaves between six dinner plates. Spoon 4 fl oz/113 ml of rice in the centre in the shape of a nest. Pour a spoonful of sauce on the rice and lay a sauce-coated chicken breast on top. Garnish with a large sprig of fresh coriander and serve hot!

Helpful Hints and Observations

CHICKEN SKIN – See page 59.

CHICKEN ENGLISH MEHSON

This dish was created for a viewer whom we met in the streets of New York. Gary Mehson just happened to be English, but that didn't stop him from raving on about chicken in a rich sauce with mushrooms . . . on pasta . . . with LOTS of sauce. So I created Chicken English Mehson just for him. In the end, he flew from London to Seattle to put it to the ultimate personal test. He liked it, so it carries his name.

A crisp salad to follow wouldn't hurt!

Nutritional Profile

PER SERVING	CLASSIC	MINIMAX
Calories	1231	699
Fat (g)	53	18
Calories from fat	39%	23%
Cholesterol (mg)	248	100
Sodium (mg)	2296	628
Fibre (g)	7	9

■ *Classic compared:* Poulet Sauté Maison

Time Estimate

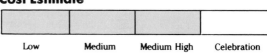

Hands On
Unsupervised
Minutes   10   20   30   40   50   60   70   80   90

Cost Estimate

Low   Medium   Medium High   Celebration

INGREDIENTS

3 teaspoons/15 ml extra light olive oil with a dash of sesame oil
1 medium onion, peeled and thinly sliced
2 teaspoons/10 ml shallots, peeled and thinly sliced
1 oz/28 g back bacon, fat removed and cut into matchsticks
1 teaspoon/5 ml fresh thyme
1 tablespoon/15 ml fresh parsley, chopped
2 chicken breasts, 6 oz/170 g each, with skin
1 tablespoon/15 ml tomato paste
2 oz/57 g pimento cut into matchsticks
6 fl oz/170 ml de-alcoholized white wine
24 button mushrooms, quartered
14 pitted black olives, halved
5 teaspoons/25 ml capers
16 fl oz/450 ml beef stock (recipe page 210)
2 tablespoons/30 ml arrowroot
4 oz/113 g spaghetti
5 pints/2.75 l water
8 fl oz/227 ml leaf spinach
Chopped fresh parsley for garnish

NOW COOK

■ In a large skillet, heat 1 teaspoon/5 ml of the olive oil and sauté the onion and shallots until translucent.

■ Add the back bacon, thyme and parsley and cook for 2 to 3 minutes. Turn the contents of the pan out on to a plate and set aside.

■ Heat 1 more teaspoon/5 ml of the olive oil and brown the chicken breasts on medium heat for 4 minutes on each side. Add the tomato paste and pimento. Cook until lightly browned. Remove the chicken and place it on a dish. Deglaze the pan with 4 fl oz/113 ml of the de-alcoholized white wine. Remove the skin from the chicken.

■ Return the cooked onion mixture and chicken breasts to the skillet. Add the mushrooms, the olives and 4 teaspoons/20 ml of the capers. Pour in the beef stock.

■ Make a paste of the arrowroot and the remaining wine. Remove the pan from the heat and stir in the arrowroot paste to thicken.

■ Cook the spaghetti in the 5 pints/2.75 l of water for 10 minutes. Pour the spaghetti into a strainer set over a serving bowl. Tip the hot water out and place the spaghetti in the heated bowl. Toss with the spinach and the remaining capers.

■ *To Serve:* Make a bed of pasta and place the chicken breasts in the centre. Spoon the sauce over the chicken and garnish with chopped parsley.

Helpful Hints and Observations

SAUCE COLOUR – Beef stock is usually dark in colour but we wanted it a deep reddish-brown. The pimento and tomato paste combined with the olive oil did the trick. I cooked it at medium high heat and it quickly began to darken. When you try this, keep stirring and don't fuss if the pan gets almost black – but don't let it burn! You'll get the hang of it quite easily. The trick is to aim for real darkness by stirring as the sugar content caramelizes. Then add the stock all at once and stir to loosen the glaze on the bottom. When you thicken it with the tablespoon/15 ml of arrowroot it simply needs to be strained to remove any overcooked solids and you are ready! This method works well to create a quick, savoury and great-coloured low fat sauce for all kinds of dishes.

About the Ingredients

OLIVES – Green, black, small, large, smooth, wrinkled, there are so many different kinds of olive you really must try a few and see which ones suit your taste. Green olives are the unripe fruit of the olive tree picked in September; black olives are the same fruit left to ripen on the tree and picked in November; oil olives are the same fruit left on the tree until January. Olive trees normally live anything from 300 to 600 years!
PIMENTO – See page 139.

CHICKEN POLESE

This dish began many years ago in Sydney, Australia, at a truly wonderful Italian restaurant called Beppies, owned by Guiseppe Polese. The recipe has remained a favourite over the years and has gone through most of my changes. I hope you enjoy the '90s version!

That's Chicken Polese...
Not Chicken Police.

Nutritional Profile

PER SERVING	CLASSIC	MINIMAX
Calories	907	293
Fat (g)	56	11
Calories from fat	55%	33%
Cholesterol (mg)	308	85
Sodium (mg)	1748	515
Fibre (g)	2	3

■ *Classic compared:* Chicken Polese

Time Estimate

Hands On									
Unsupervised									
Minutes	10	20	30	40	50	60	70	80	90

Cost Estimate

Low	Medium	Medium High	Celebration

INGREDIENTS

1 teaspoon/5 ml extra light olive oil with a dash of sesame oil
1 garlic clove, peeled and diced
2 boneless chicken breasts, 6 oz/170 g each, with skin
½ sweet red pepper, de-seeded and finely diced
2 Italian plum tomatoes, peeled, de-seeded and finely diced
1 tablespoon/15 ml fresh oregano, finely chopped
Black pepper, freshly ground
1 tablespoon/15 ml fresh parsley, chopped
2 slices low-fat Mozzarella cheese
4 anchovy fillets
2 tablespoons/30 ml capers
½ teaspoon/2.5 ml arrowroot
2 tablespoons/30 ml de-alcoholized white wine

NOW COOK

■ In a large skillet, heat the olive oil and fry the garlic until brown. Remove the garlic and discard.

■ In the same skillet, fry the chicken breasts for about 3 minutes on each side. Remove the skin and discard it. Set the chicken aside.

■ In the same skillet, fry the red pepper for 2 minutes. Add the tomatoes, oregano, black pepper to taste and 1 teaspoon/5 ml of the parsley.

■ Return the chicken to the pan, cover and reheat for about 2 minutes.

■ Cover each breast with a slice of cheese, two crisscrossed anchovy fillets and a sprinkle of capers. Cover and cook until the cheese melts – about 1 minute. Remove the chicken to a warm plate.

■ In a small bowl, mix the arrowroot and wine into a thin paste. Remove the pan from the heat and stir the arrowroot thickening into the pan juices. Return to low heat and stir until the sauce thickens.

■ Serve the chicken breasts in a juicy pool of sauce dusted with the remaining parsley.

Helpful Hints and Observations

REMOVAL OF SKIN – A matter of timing! By now you will know that I always remove the fatty skin from poultry, except for poussins which are too fiddly and too small to matter.

I do not, however, take the skin off before I cook the chicken when it is to be boiled, grilled, shallow-fried, or roasted. The exception is when a bird has to be cut into sections for a casserole or stew.

The reason for retaining the skin for cooking is that it helps to keep the moisture in. The fat skin acts as a barrier to the escaping steam as the temperature rises.

It is sometimes messy and almost always a sacrifice to remove it when it's golden and crispy, but if you can remember these numbers, it may help: chicken, 3 lb/1.4 kg, roasted with skin on, skin removed before eating, 871 calories for the whole bird, 32% calories from fat; chicken, 3 lb/1.4 kg, skin eaten, 1,333 calories for the whole bird, 47% calories from fat. This adds up to 51 grams of fat, or a total of 462 calories, usually divided among four people, to equal over 115 calories a head for skin!

BONING WHOLE CHICKENS – Whole chickens make good budget sense. Bone the chickens, then use the bones for the stock and freeze leftover portions for later use.

About the Ingredients

ANCHOVY FILLETS – You may respond with a gasp of 'Oh, no!' Please let me encourage you to experience a wonderful taste sensation. Anchovies from a tin can be superb, but at the same time some brands can be just awful. When purchasing anchovies, buy a good quality brand packed in olive oil. If your store has several brands, the best idea is to taste the most expensive. If they are not evenly sized and coloured or if they are frayed at the edges, take them back for a refund!

CAPERS – These are actually the unopened flower buds of a desert shrub, often found in the Sahara, but farmed commercially in southern France, close to the Mediterranean. The buds are pickled and lend a terrific flavour to foods they accompany. Buy capers of good quality. The most valued are capers that are the least developed. They may be more expensive, but they're worth it. Look for capers near the pickles in your local supermarket. When opened, they keep well in the refrigerator provided the brine solution covers the buds.

CHICKEN YANKOVA

Treena and I first ate this dish in Moscow back in 1970 BG (Before Glasnost). The original is a modified Chicken Kiev in which a chicken is smothered in butter, packed into a puff pastry envelope and slow-baked. Delicious, but just look at the nutritional analysis of the classic: 70 grams of fat per serving!

The crisp bread loaf is best served whole and cut slice-by-slice on a wooden board. A great dish to serve with a colourful salad.

Nutritional Profile

PER SERVING	CLASSIC	MINIMAX
Calories	1232	491
Fat (g)	70	10
Calories from fat	51%	18%
Cholesterol (mg)	336	48
Sodium (mg)	791	798
Fibre (g)	4	5

■ *Classic compared:* Chicken Yankova

Time Estimate

Hands On									
Unsupervised									
Minutes	10	20	30	40	50	60	70	80	90

Cost Estimate

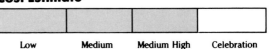

Low	Medium	Medium High	Celebration

INGREDIENTS

12 oz/340 g mushrooms, sliced
2 teaspoons/10 ml extra light olive oil with a dash of sesame oil
1 tablespoon/15 ml fresh lemon juice
¼ teaspoon/1.25 ml cayenne pepper
½ teaspoon/2.5 ml dried dill weed
1 French bread loaf (approximately 4 × 3 inches/30 × 10 × 8 cm)
2 oz/57 g mild Cheddar cheese, grated
4 skinned chicken breasts
8 fl oz/227 ml chicken stock (recipe page 210)
2 sprigs fresh tarragon or 1 teaspoon/5 ml dried
Black pepper, freshly ground, to taste
⅛ teaspoon/0.6 ml saffron
1 tablespoon/15 ml arrowroot mixed with 2 fl oz/57 ml de-alcoholized white wine
Sprigs of fresh tarragon or parsley for garnish

FIRST PREPARE

■ Put the mushrooms into a large bowl. Sprinkle them with half the olive oil, the lemon juice, cayenne pepper and dill. Cover the bowl with a plate and shake it thoroughly. Now the mushrooms are evenly coated with the flavouring ingredients.

■ Cut lengthwise into the bottom of the French bread loaf at a 30° angle on both sides, taking a triangular section out of the loaf. Now cut the dough off the triangular section, leaving you with the crust, which you will use as a cap. Hollow out the rest of the loaf, leaving a practically dough-free loaf surrounded by crust. Sprinkle ½ oz/14 g of the grated cheese over the cap and the rest into the hollowed loaf.

■ Pre-heat the oven to 300°F/150°C/Gas Mark 2.

NOW COOK

■ Pour the remaining olive oil on to a plate and mop it up with the chicken breasts, coating both sides. Put the oiled breasts into a large pre-heated skillet and brown for 4 minutes on each side. Take the chicken breasts out of the pan and set them aside.

■ Drop the mushrooms into the same pan and sauté for 2 to 3 minutes. Remove them on to a plate. Take another plate of similar size and place it on top of the mushrooms. Now squeeze the plates together while holding them over a small saucepan. The juice should drizzle into the saucepan!

■ Pour the chicken stock into the skillet, scraping the residue off the bottom of the pan. Pour this deglazed sauce into the small saucepan with the mushroom juice and keep on low heat.

■ Put the chicken breasts inside the bread loaf. Lay one long sprig of tarragon over each chicken breast. If you can't get fresh tarragon, then sprinkle with the dried.

■ Season the mushrooms with pepper and pack them in over the chicken. Place the cap on the loaf, so that the filling is packed solid and enclosed. Cover with foil and bake in the pre-heated oven for 10 minutes, just to warm through. The crust should not become over-crisp.

■ *The Sauce:* Stir the saffron into the sauce in the small saucepan. Mix in the arrowroot paste off the heat, then bring it to the boil to thicken.

■ *To Serve:* Carve the loaf with a good serrated bread knife and place a couple of 1-inch/2.5-cm slices of Chicken Yankova on each plate. Drizzle with the sauce and garnish with the rest of the grated cheese and a sprig of fresh tarragon or parsley – enjoy!

Helpful Hints and Observations

DIG OUT THE DOUGH! – No, this isn't a hold-up! I mean scoop out all the soft inner bread, leaving only a thin coating in the crust. You can dry this doughy centre bread in the oven at 150°F/70°C/Gas Mark ¼ for about 20 minutes to make white breadcrumbs. Pop them in a blender or processor, then store in an airtight container in a cool place.

TOSSING THE MUSHROOMS IN SEASONINGS – This is a very special way to reduce the amount of oil you add to vegetables, especially mushrooms. Please try it . . . and you'll be amazed at the result!

About the Ingredients

SAFFRON – It takes the stigmas from a minimum of 70,000 blooms of the saffron crocus to produce 1 lb/450 g of saffron! That is one reason why it's one of the most expensive spices in the world. Fortunately, a very small amount goes a long way. Saffron can be bought in three different forms: threads, cakes, or powder. One man said that saffron 'refreshes the spirit and is good against fainting fits and palpitation of the heart'. Well, at least enjoy its rich yellow colour in your Minimax cooking.

POULET BASQUAISE

I've often used this recipe as an example of how fresh foods in season were simply assembled in a geographically isolated area between France and Italy to become a significant flavour combination that identified the region.

Couldn't this happen all over again where you live? Simply restrict yourself to foods grown within, say, 20 miles/32 km in a specific season and see what you get!

This is a 'food of the people' dish – nothing haute cuisine about it. Dishes like this one are best served in a shallow clay casserole that is roughly glazed with bold colours. Be very sure to check out the lead content before you purchase an imported piece of pottery. No need for other vegetables . . . it's complete as it is.

Nutritional Profile

PER SERVING	CLASSIC	MINIMAX
Calories	1001	604
Fat (g)	57	14
Calories from fat	51%	20%
Cholesterol (mg)	176	133
Sodium (mg)	1461	249
Fibre (g)	4	6

■ *Classic compared:* Poulet Basquaise

Time Estimate

Hands On
Unsupervised
Minutes 10 20 30 40 50 60 70 80 90

Cost Estimate

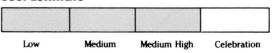

Low   Medium   Medium High   Celebration

INGREDIENTS

1 whole chicken (3½ lb/1.6 kg)
2 teaspoons/10 ml extra light olive oil with a dash of sesame oil
6 fl oz/170 ml mushrooms, finely diced
2 garlic cloves, peeled and chopped
A 6-oz/170-g tin no-salt tomato paste
2 sweet green peppers, cored, de-seeded and diced
1 sweet red pepper, cored, de-seeded and diced
6 fl oz/170 ml de-alcoholized dry white wine
4 large tomatoes, de-seeded and diced
Black pepper, freshly ground, to taste
1 tablespoon/15 ml fresh parsley, chopped
10 fl oz/285 ml uncooked long grain rice, rinsed
3¼ pints/1.8 l water
3 mushrooms, sliced
1 tablespoon/15 ml fresh basil leaves, sliced
2 tablespoons/30 ml fresh parsley, chopped
1 teaspoon/5 ml baking powder

NOW COOK

■ Cut chicken into three pieces: the whole breast and two legs with thighs. Remove all the skin.

■ In a large, low-sided casserole, heat half the oil and sauté the mushrooms and garlic for 2 minutes. Turn out on a side dish and reserve.

■ Pour the remaining oil into the casserole, turn the heat up high and brown the chicken pieces, turning often. Stir in the tomato paste, making sure the chicken gets coated. The tomato paste caramelizes and turns brown: the Maillard reaction. Add the diced peppers. Make sure you dredge up any brown residue off the bottom of the pot. This provides a smokiness that gives depth of taste without fat.

■ Pour in the wine, the reserved mushrooms and the tomatoes. Grind in fresh black pepper to taste. Add the parsley. Make sure the chicken breast is turned meat-side down to ensure thorough cooking. Cover and simmer at medium heat for 35 minutes.

■ While the Poulet Basquaise is simmering, cook the rice. In a medium saucepan, boil the water. Add the rice, bring to the boil again, cover and simmer for 10 minutes. Drain the rice through a metal strainer or colander. To keep the rice hot, add 2 inches/5 cm of hot water to the pan. Put the strainer full of cooked rice on top, cover with a small lid and keep on medium heat for up to 15 minutes. The rice will continue to cook in a gentle steam and will be perfectly fluffy without becoming overcooked.

■ After the chicken is done, remove it from the pot on to a cutting board and carve it into nice chunks. By cooking the chicken in large pieces you get a much more attractive and succulent piece of meat.

■ Drop the chicken pieces back into the sauce. Stir in the sliced mushrooms, chopped basil and parsley – a fresh, field-like touch to your finished dish! And now an ingredient that will make an astonishing taste difference: stir in the baking powder. This smooths out the flavour, cancelling any acidity and allowing the sweetness to come through.

■ Put the cooked rice into a large serving dish, make a well in the middle and fill with the chicken.

Helpful Hints and Observations

SMOKY DEPTH – This is a standard for me: to cook tomato paste along with the peppers until it begins to brown. It develops an unusual, smoky, sweet yet acid taste that compensates to some degree for the loss of fat.

About the Ingredients

TOMATOES – When selecting tomatoes for this recipe, look for unpackaged ones so you can examine them. Watch out for bruises, cracks, mouldy spots and other blemishes. Choose tomatoes that are ripe, firm and plump. Two varieties that would be good for this recipe are the round or beefsteak tomatoes or the Italian plum tomatoes (the pear-shaped ones) that are fleshy, have few seeds and are a little sweeter than American varieties.

BASIL – This herb is often proclaimed as the perfect accompaniment to anything that includes tomato. A pungent herb, basil has been used in the kitchen since at least 400 BC. Its name, from the Greek *basilikon*, means 'kingly'. Indeed, in many places custom demanded that the king himself cut the first basil of the season with a golden sickle! But please don't wait for a king to cut basil for your use in the kitchen. Its fragrant leaves complement many vegetables and meats.

SMOKED CHICKEN BREASTS

$\mathcal{M}$y very good friend Chef de Cuisine Ludger Szmania has mastered the art of aroma, colour and texture for alternative cuisine. This smoked chicken idea got mixed up with a Chinese pot steamer technique and came out very well. It really is a new style of cooking for you to try. You might like to try cooking fish or even a whole chicken or duck in the same manner.

Nutritional Profile

PER SERVING	CLASSIC	MINIMAX
Calories	846	119
Fat (g)	50	2
Calories from fat	53%	14%
Cholesterol (mg)	150	0
Sodium (mg)	1721	622
Fibre (g)	2	2

■ *Classic compared:* Chicken with Cream Gravy

Time Estimate

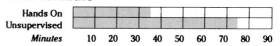

Hands On									
Unsupervised									
Minutes	10	20	30	40	50	60	70	80	90

Cost Estimate

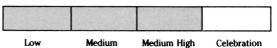

Low	Medium	Medium High	Celebration

Serves 4

INGREDIENTS

4 chicken supremes – skinless and boneless chicken breasts, 7–8 oz/200–225 g each. You can cut these from whole birds! If you do, leave on the first section of the wing so that the breast is not entirely boneless.

MARINADE

½ teaspoon/2.5 ml cinnamon
2 fl oz/57 ml red wine vinegar
3 whole cloves, crushed
½ teaspoon/2.5 ml fresh ginger root, grated
2 fl oz/57 ml low-salt soy sauce
3 sprigs fresh thyme
Nutmeg, freshly grated
Black pepper, freshly ground

SMOKE

Contents of 2 Earl Grey tea-bags
2 tablespoons/30 ml brown sugar
2 tablespoons/30 ml brown rice
1 cinnamon stick

CINNAMON SAUCE

1 medium sweet onion, peeled and finely sliced
1 tablespoon/15 ml brown sugar
1 teaspoon/5 ml extra light olive oil with a dash of sesame oil
8 fl oz/227 ml chicken broth
1 cinnamon stick
2 sprigs fresh thyme

FIRST PREPARE

■ Put the chicken breasts in a bowl. Mix the marinade ingredients, pour on top and marinate for at least 30 minutes.

■ Fold a large piece of aluminium foil in several crumpled layers to make a small wrinkled cushion with a depression in the centre. This cushion should fit in the bottom of a large, heavy-based stockpot, in which you will eventually smoke the chicken. Place the ingredients for the smoke on the depression in the centre of the foil cushion, then put the whole thing in the pot.

NOW COOK

■ Place the onion slices in a saucepan along with the brown sugar and oil. Cook on medium heat until caramelized. Add the chicken broth, cinnamon stick and thyme sprigs. Bring to the boil and reduce the volume by about one-third.

■ Purée the reduced sauce in a food processor. Strain through a fine sieve into a saucepan and keep warm.

■ Remove the chicken from the marinade and set aside.

■ Add the marinade to the sauce and cook for 2 minutes on medium heat.

■ Start smoking the chicken. Put the lid on the stockpot 'smoker' and place it over high heat. In about 6 minutes it should begin to smoke. Set a steamer basket over the smoke. Set the chicken on it and smoke for 10 minutes. It will be a lovely dark brown! Remove the stockpot from the heat and let it sit for 5 minutes.

NOTE: When you take the chicken out, it's a good plan to wrap the aluminium foil and smoke ingredients and take them out to the dustbin immediately. This rids your home of any potential for residual smoke smell!

■ Serve the smoked chicken breasts with a lovely rice. Saffron rice adds great yellow colour! Pour the cinnamon sauce on top, garnish with a sprig of fresh thyme, and serve fresh vegetables on the side.

Helpful Hints and Observations

■ THE STOCKPOT – I use a heavy-based aluminium pan with a permanent non-stick glaze and a capacity of 11 pints/6 l. It works very well, and afterwards I simply rinse it out with warm, soapy water and it is as good as new. It has a glass lid which goes through the dishwasher!

■ THE SMOKE – There is a great deal to be said about various 'smoke' woods, and each one does add its own flavour. But to my taste this unique blend of Earl Grey tea, brown rice, cinnamon and brown sugar is a delight – well worth a try!

About the Ingredients

EARL GREY TEA – A scented black China tea, originally created for the 2nd Earl Grey, under whose premiership slavery was abolished throughout the British Empire. The scent is oil of bergamot, a Mediterranean citrus fruit. Try to find individually wrapped tea-bags, or buy loose tea and make sure the tin you store it in is airtight, or it will rapidly lose its aroma.

■ CINNAMON – A native spice of South-East Asia, it is the dried inner bark of two related evergreen trees. Of these trees one produces true cinnamon, the other a spice properly named cassia. Mostly what is sold as cinnamon is truly cassia. The way to tell them apart is by colour. Cinnamon is a tan-brown colour, cassia is reddish-brown. The spice we know as cinnamon is one of the world's oldest commodities.

EVIL JUNGLE PRINCESS

$\mathscr{I}$ would be delighted to learn where this classic Thai dish got its somewhat odd title. If you know, please write. We tried to find out from the charming Thai chef, and co-collaborator on this dish, Malee Chu, but it was the only thing she didn't know!

Malee runs a restaurant in Scottsdale, Arizona, called Malee's at the Borgata.

Serve this attractive dish with a small bowl of short grain white rice on the side. You can sprinkle the rice with some rice wine vinegar and cayenne pepper for extra flavour.

Our numbers are for strained coconut milk, not shop-bought coconut cream. Using the cream would increase the calories from fat to 43%.

Nutritional Profile

PER SERVING	CLASSIC	MINIMAX
Calories	525	202
Fat (g)	41	6
Calories from fat	71%	27%
Cholesterol (mg)	225	58
Sodium (mg)	803	114
Fibre (g)	1	4

■ *Classic compared:* Chicken à la King

Time Estimate

Hands On									
Unsupervised									
Minutes	10	20	30	40	50	60	70	80	90

Cost Estimate

Low	Medium	Medium High	Celebration

Serves 2

INGREDIENTS

1 teaspoon/5 ml peanut oil

2 garlic cloves, peeled and crushed

2 tablespoons/30 ml lemon grass, finely chopped

2 Kaffir lime leaves, softened in a little warm water and finely chopped

1 chicken breast, 8 oz/227 g, skin removed, and sliced into 2 × ¼ inch/5 × 0.75 cm strips

2 fl oz/57 ml unsweetened coconut milk (can be purchased in tins)

2 fl oz/57 ml good quality chicken stock (recipe page 210)

½ teaspoon/2.5 ml chilli powder

1 teaspoon/5 ml sugar

7 fresh peppermint leaves, finely chopped

2 tablespoons/30 ml fish sauce

½ teaspoon/2.5 ml cayenne pepper, or to taste

2 tablespoons/30 ml fresh squeezed lemon juice, or to taste

8 fl oz/227 ml Chinese cabbage (pak-choi) or spinach, finely sliced

8 fl oz/227 ml red cabbage, finely sliced

14 fl oz/400 ml straw mushrooms or small button mushrooms

NOW COOK

■ Heat the peanut oil in a large skillet and add the garlic. Cook until the oil has been infused with the garlic flavour, about 1 minute, then remove and discard the garlic.

■ Add the lemon grass, lime leaves and chicken, and stir-fry until the chicken just loses its raw look.

■ Add the coconut milk, chicken stock and chilli powder and stir-fry until the chicken turns completely white and the sauce has cooked down into a coating, not floating, cream.

■ Stir in the sugar, mint leaves and fish sauce. You also need to add the cayenne pepper at this time, but remember: the amount of cayenne you add will determine a one- to five-star heat factor. I can't go past ** but my wife, Treena, can manage at least a ***** or 1 full teaspoonful/5 ml!

■ Stir in the lemon juice to suit your taste.

■ Turn the sliced cabbages and the mushrooms into a hot skillet with a little chicken stock or water (just enough to create some steam), heat them through (about 2 minutes), then turn out on to a serving plate.

■ Serve the vegetables with the sauced chicken on top.

Helpful Hints and Observations

COCONUT MILK – See page 203.

About the Ingredients

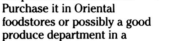

LEMON GRASS – Here's the reason why a Thai or Vietnamese dish will have a compelling flavour you can't quite put your finger on. Lemon grass doesn't give a strong lemon flavour, just a subtle lemon perfume, due to the presence of citric oils. Purchase it in Oriental foodstores or possibly a good produce department in a large supermarket. A powdered form is sold as 'Sereh Powder'.

KAFFIR LIME LEAVES – See page 23.

PEPPERMINT – One of the three most common varieties of mint, the others being applemint (or Bowles mint) and spearmint. Peppermint has the highest menthol content of the three, hence its characteristic cooling flavour.

FISH SAUCE – See page 23.

STRAW MUSHROOMS – See page 35.

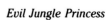

SLOPPY JOE

*E*veryone raised in North America seems to have a Sloppy Joe in their gastronomic experience and every recipe has its own secret ingredient. I've got several in this recipe, and they all add up to Minimax flavour with much less fat and refined carbohydrate. It's also a lot of fun and easy to make.

Serve on a hot plate with a crisp, colourful salad on the side.

Nutritional Profile

PER SERVING	CLASSIC	MINIMAX
Calories	470	338
Fat (g)	29	7
Calories from fat	54%	20%
Cholesterol (mg)	77	51
Sodium (mg)	1165	592
Fibre (g)	3	6

■ *Classic compared:* Not So Sloppy Joe

Time Estimate

Hands On									
Unsupervised									
Minutes	10	20	30	40	50	60	70	80	90

Cost Estimate

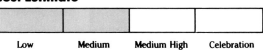

Low	Medium	Medium High	Celebration

Serves 4

INGREDIENTS

1 tablespoon/15 ml extra light olive oil with a dash of sesame oil

8 fl oz/227 ml onion, peeled and diced

2 fl oz/57 ml carrot, peeled and diced

2 fl oz/57 ml celery, diced

2 garlic cloves, peeled and chopped

½ sweet green pepper, cored, de-seeded and finely chopped

12 oz/340 g ground turkey or turkey breast (see *About the Ingredients*)

2 fl oz/57 ml bulgur wheat

3 tablespoons/45 ml tomato paste

1 tablespoon/15 ml dark brown sugar

1 tablespoon/15 ml fresh oregano

⅛ teaspoon/0.6 ml salt, freshly ground

¼ teaspoon/1.25 ml black pepper, freshly ground

12 fl oz/340 ml de-alcoholized red wine

8 fl oz/227 ml low-salt tomato sauce

1 tsp/5 ml creamed horseradish

4 wholewheat hamburger rolls

NOW COOK

■ Heat the oil in a large wok and stir-fry the onion, carrot, celery, garlic and green pepper until just tender. Tip the vegetables into a bowl and set aside.

■ In the same wok or a large frying pan, brown the ground turkey. Stir in the bulgur, tomato paste and brown sugar and cook until the tomato paste's colour darkens.

■ Sprinkle in the oregano and return the cooked vegetables to the pan. Season with the salt and pepper to taste.

■ Pour in 8 fl oz/227 ml of the wine and half of the tomato sauce. Cover and cook for 15 minutes.

■ Meanwhile, put the hamburger rolls into a low oven to toast.

■ Just before serving, stir in the remaining wine and tomato sauce and the horseradish. Place the bottom side of a toasted roll on a plate and spoon the Sloppy Joe mixture over it. Set the top of the roll just slightly over to one side to expose the filling.

Helpful Hints and Observations

ADDING LIQUIDS IN TWO PLACES – In this recipe you'll note that I add the de-alcoholized wine and tomato sauce in equal amounts at either end of the cooking process. The reason for this is fresh taste and aroma. I get the flavours of both the wine and the tomato into the meat and vegetables in the simmering process but then I pick up tremendous freshness of aroma, taste and colour by the last minute addition.

Please give it a try. Taste it before you make the final addition and then again when it's added. Now you can try this idea with other dishes that call for tomato juice and/or wine.

DE-ALCOHOLIZED WINE HELPS – De-alcoholized wine allows for last moment addition without concern for the alcohol steam-off which can take some time.

About the Ingredients

GROUND TURKEY – Leaner (especially in the saturated fat department) and less expensive than ground beef, turkey is a good substitute in many dishes. Don't wait until next Christmas. If you can't find it ready-ground in your supermarket, buy turkey as breast or thigh, according to the recipe, and grind it yourself. If your butcher stocks it he will grind it for you.

WHOLEWHEAT ROLLS – Every bit of fibre helps! When you look for wholegrain buns, don't just grab the first brown-coloured bread you see. Brown colour might just indicate that there's a lot of molasses in the recipe. Let me suggest that you read the label. You'll get the most nutrients if one of the first ingredients listed is 100% wholewheat flour that is stoneground. The next best thing is wholewheat or other wholegrain flour (not stoneground).

■

SUPER BURRITOS

I'm not as practised with Mexican food as I would like to be, but I've travelled in Mexico and eaten in some truly wonderful restaurants. I had missed out on burritos and therefore was delighted to 'have a go'. What a happy combination this recipe turned out to be. We love it . . . hope you do, too!

Nutritional Profile

PER SERVING	CLASSIC	MINIMAX
Calories	1357	783
Fat (g)	68	13
Calories from fat	45%	15%
Cholesterol (mg)	185	62
Sodium (mg)	1657	1211
Fibre (g)	10	17

■ *Classic compared:* Super Burritos

Time Estimate

Hands On Unsupervised									
Minutes	10	20	30	40	50	60	70	80	90

Cost Estimate

| Low | Medium | Medium High | Celebration |

Serves 4

INGREDIENTS

8 flour tortillas, 8 inches/20 cm diameter

8 fl oz/227 ml dried pinto beans

2 pints/1.15 l chicken stock (recipe page 210)

8 fl oz/227 ml uncooked brown rice

2 red chilli peppers, diced

1 tablespoon/15 ml extra light olive oil with a dash of sesame oil

8 fl oz/227 ml onion, peeled and chopped

4 fl oz/113 ml sweet green pepper, chopped

1 garlic clove, peeled and diced

12 oz/340 g ground chicken (from a 1¼-lb/570-g chicken breast with bone)

1 tablespoon/15 ml chilli powder

¼ teaspoon/1.25 ml ground cumin

8 fl oz/227 ml strained yogurt (recipe page 210)

5 large Italian plum tomatoes, de-seeded and diced

2 fl oz/57 ml fresh coriander leaves, chopped

2 fl oz/57 ml spring onion, chopped

8 fl oz/227 ml lettuce, shredded

2 oz/57 g mild Cheddar cheese, grated

FIRST PREPARE

■ Stack the tortillas and wrap them tightly in foil. Heat them in a 350°F/180°C/Gas Mark 4 oven for 10 minutes to soften.

NOW COOK

■ Put the pinto beans and ¾ pint/425 ml of the chicken stock into a pressure cooker and cook for 10 minutes. Add the brown rice, the remaining chicken stock and half the red chilli peppers and cook for 15 minutes more.

■ In a medium-sized casserole, heat the olive oil, add the onion, green pepper and garlic, and cook until the onion is soft and slightly translucent.

■ Add the ground chicken to the mixture, tossing and breaking up the chicken until the mixture is an even texture throughout.

■ Add the chilli powder and cumin. Stir in half of the remaining red chilli peppers.

■ Mix 12 fl oz/340 ml of the rice and beans into the chicken filling.

■ Spoon a scant 2 fl oz/57 ml of filling on to the lower half of each warmed tortilla. Fold the opposite sides in until they meet. Fold the bottom and top edges just over the filling and turn over on a baking sheet so that all the folds are underneath. Bake in a 350°F/180°C/Gas Mark 4 oven for 10 to 12 minutes.

■ Make the sauce by combining the strained yogurt, tomatoes and the remaining red chilli peppers in a medium-sized bowl. Stir in the coriander leaves and spring onion.

■ Slit the cooked burritos down the middle and spoon the sauce into the top. Serve them on a bed of shredded lettuce, with a sprinkling of mild Cheddar cheese and the remaining beans and rice on the side.

Helpful Hints and Observations

THE BREAD TRICK – After placing meat in the grinder, finish it off with a piece of bread. When you see the bread coming through, you'll know you've ground all the meat!

MUCHO GRANDE CALORIES – It's a big meal at 783 calories. So if you are watching the numbers you could settle for one burrito at 392. The fat numbers are actually very good.

About the Ingredients

TORTILLAS – If you want to start a fight in Mexico, probably a good way to do it would be to declare one tortilla better than another. In one province alone you can buy 30 different types! So in the interests of maintaining peace, keep this information under your hat: I recommend a trip to the grocery store to look for wholewheat tortillas. Now, I know corn tortillas are the classic. But in this case I'm being an advocate for whole grains in your Minimax experiments.

PINTO BEANS – Have you run into these yet? When you buy them raw they're quite festive: beige with white speckles. When cooked, they lose their speckles. Pintos are the traditional bean used to make *frijoles refritos* or Mexican re-fried beans. Like all beans, they're quite nutritious, but need to be complemented with grains, nuts, or seeds in order for your body to complete their incomplete protein. Guess what? Eating pinto beans with tortillas is a simple way to do this!

CREPES ANTONIN CAREME

Antonin Careme was a famous chef whose complex display provided the great Escoffier (1784–1833) with an opportunity to propose a simple method of 'modern' cookery, and so the urge to simplify goes on and on . . . Today's approach is one in which to simplify also means to reduce risk, while at the same time enhancing aroma, colour and texture.

I have found this to be an enormously popular recipe. It does take time but it is definitely inexpensive and it looks and tastes wonderful. If you serve it from a large dish, or straight from the grill, you will need a long-bladed palette knife.

Nutritional Profile

PER SERVING	CLASSIC	MINIMAX
Calories	537	285
Fat (g)	31	8
Calories from fat	53%	25%
Cholesterol (mg)	178	155
Sodium (mg)	651	154
Fibre (g)	2	1

■ *Classic compared:* Crêpes Antonin Careme

Time Estimate

Hands On									
Unsupervised									
Minutes	10	20	30	40	50	60	70	80	90

Cost Estimate

Low	Medium	Medium High	Celebration

Serves 4

INGREDIENTS

FILLING
2 celery stalks, finely chopped
12 oz/340 g cooked chicken meat, diced

CREPE BATTER
1 whole egg
1 egg yolk
9 fl oz/255 ml skimmed milk
2 oz/57 g plain flour
White pepper, freshly ground
1 teaspoon/5 ml extra light olive oil with a dash of sesame oil
1 teaspoon/5 ml fresh tarragon, chopped

SAUCE
6 fl oz/170 ml skimmed milk
¾ pint/425 ml chicken stock (recipe page 210)
3 tablespoons/45 ml arrowroot mixed with 4 fl oz/113 ml de-alcoholized white wine
⅛ teaspoon/0.6 ml nutmeg, freshly grated
⅛ teaspoon/0.6 ml white pepper, freshly ground
4 fl oz/113 ml double cream, stiffly whipped – *optional*

GARNISH
½ teaspoon/2.5 ml Parmesan cheese, freshly grated
Fresh parsley, chopped

FIRST PREPARE AND COOK

■ *The Crêpes:* In a large bowl, beat together the whole egg, egg yolk and milk. Beat in the flour and pepper until fully incorporated. Set aside to rest for half an hour before cooking the crêpes.

■ Pour the oil into a crêpe pan, swish it around to cover all surfaces, then pour the excess into the crêpe batter. This helps to make the crêpes self-releasing and precludes having to re-oil the pan.

■ Over medium to high heat, pour a small ladle of batter into the prepared pan. Tilt the pan so the batter spreads evenly over the entire bottom surface. When the crêpe begins to bubble and looks waxy – about 2 to 3 minutes – use a spatula to gently loosen the edges. Sprinkle it with one-eighth of the tarragon, then flip it over. Cook until golden-brown on the second side – about 1 minute. Make eight crêpes in this manner.

■ *The Filling:* Poach the chopped celery in boiling water until just tender – about 10 minutes. Drain and set aside. When cool, combine with the diced chicken.

■ *The Sauce:* In a small saucepan, over medium heat, mix the milk and stock. Remove the saucepan from the heat and stir in the arrowroot mixture. Return to the heat and stir until thickened. Season with nutmeg and pepper. At this point you can add the whipped cream for its extra whitening effect and depth of taste, but don't forget to count the cost first: it adds 103 calories per serving and 11 grams of fat, which will make the percentage of calories from fat 44%!

■ Combine half the thickened sauce with the chicken filling. Reserve the other half to pour over the crêpes.

NOW ASSEMBLE

■ Place a crêpe on a large, ovenproof serving dish, herbed-side down. Spoon one-eighth of the filling in a line down the centre. Fold the edges over the filling and then turn the crêpe over so it is seam-side down. Fill all the crêpes in this way.

■ Pour the remaining sauce over the crêpes, sprinkle with Parmesan cheese and pop them under the grill until the cheese melts – about 1 minute. Scatter a little parsley on top and *'Voilà!'* (as they say in most kitchens . . . whether French is spoken or not!).

Helpful Hints and Observations

FLIPPING CREPES! – This recipe is literally chock full of techniques, but sometimes it is really hard to describe something as simple as turning a very fine crêpe – almost too fragile to flip! Here, then, is a simple illustration that may help you to avoid the frustration of seeing your limp masterpiece draped over the edge and slowly slipping on to the stove!

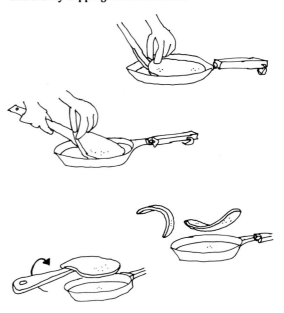

About the Ingredients

BAY LEAVES – See page 17.

ENCHILADAS FINA COCINA

Norman Fierros is a man with a mission: to upgrade the tastes and appeal of classic Mexican food. His Fina Cocina restaurant in downtown Phoenix is proof that this new 'pudding' is worth eating – in fact, it's wonderful and highly inventive. I've 'springboarded' off one of Norman's ideas with one of my own. Now why don't you do the same with mine?

A man with a mission

Nutritional Profile

PER SERVING	CLASSIC	MINIMAX
Calories	826	385
Fat (g)	50	12
Calories from fat	55%	27%
Cholesterol (mg)	182	30
Sodium (mg)	1858	447
Fibre (g)	10	8

■ *Classic compared:* Enchilada

Time Estimate

Hands On Unsupervised									
Minutes	10	20	30	40	50	60	70	80	90

Cost Estimate

Low	Medium	Medium High	Celebration

Serves 4

INGREDIENTS

TOMATILLO SAUCE

1 teaspoon/5 ml extra light olive oil with a dash of sesame oil
1 medium onion, peeled and sliced
2 cloves garlic, peeled and chopped
1 lb/450 g tomatillos or tomatoes, peeled and diced into ½-inch/1.25-cm cubes
1 red chilli pepper, de-seeded and finely chopped
8 fl oz/227 ml water
8 fl oz/227 ml chicken stock
3 tablespoons/45 ml arrowroot mixed with 3 tablespoons/45 ml water

FILLING

1 tablespoon/5 ml extra light olive oil with a dash of sesame oil
1 red onion, peeled and sliced very thinly
1 sweet red pepper, de-seeded and sliced
2 fl oz/57 ml chicken stock
1 teaspoon/5 ml cumin seed
1 teaspoon/5 ml cayenne pepper
8 oz/227 g cooked chicken meat, preferably thigh and leg, without skin, fat, or bone
1 tablespoon/15 ml fresh coriander leaves, chopped
1 tablespoon/15 ml fresh parsley, chopped
Reserved arrowroot mixture

TO SERVE

8 flour tortillas, 10 inches/25 cm diameter
Chopped coriander leaves for garnish

FIRST MAKE THE SAUCE

■ Heat the olive oil in a medium saucepan. Add the onion, garlic, tomatillos or tomatoes, and the chilli pepper. Stir together, letting the volatile oils fill the room. Ah! Ambrosia! Cook for 1 minute, then add the water and bring to the boil. Boil for 7 minutes.

■ Strain the sauce through a sieve to remove the skin and seeds. I use a machine that separates the juice from the skin and seeds for you (see page 145).

■ Put the strained sauce into a medium saucepan. Stir in the chicken stock and boil for 2 minutes.

■ Remove the tomatillo sauce from the heat and stir in 1 tablespoon/15 ml of the arrowroot paste to thicken it. Reserve the rest.

NOW COOK THE FILLING

■ In a large sauté pan, heat the olive oil over high heat. Drop in the red onion and red pepper and cook for 1 minute.

■ Add the chicken stock, cumin seed, cayenne pepper, chicken meat, coriander leaves and parsley.

■ Add the remaining arrowroot paste and stir to thicken the filling and gloss the vegetables.

TO ASSEMBLE

■ Warm the tortillas by placing them on a plate which is covering a pot of hot water. Cover with a clean cloth.

■ Place a warm flour tortilla on a warm serving plate. Spoon filling down the middle. Roll into a cylinder. Spoon tomatillo sauce over the top. Garnish with a dollop of the colourful filling on the side and a sprinkling of coriander leaves.

Helpful Hints and Observations

TART TASTES – You may have noticed that some Mexican recipes (and others) that use lots of tomatoes, green peppers and especially tomatillos will have a tart, even metallic taste: a little like touching your tongue to a small battery connection! If this taste is simply too sour for you, there is a solution. Add 1 level teaspoon/5 ml of baking powder to the sauce. It will froth when it's added, and in doing so, it's actually neutralizing some of the acids. Now take a second taste and see if you need a little more, adding and tasting until you've got it right. Please don't overdo it. You can get a terribly powdery taste by adding too much too soon.

About the Ingredients

TOMATILLOS – A Mexican tomato covered with a paper husk. You may find them marketed as *tomate verde* or, when they grow larger, as *tomate manzano*. You must remove the paper-like husk and rinse the tomatillo. You will find them to be sticky. This is natural and there is no need to wash it off. Choose tomatillos that are firm and green. If you substitute tomatoes, look for green ones in season.

CUMIN – An essential ingredient in many Mexican dishes, this spice is a native of West Asia where it is a component of Indian curry. Cumin gives a spicy edge and is used in chilli and numerous sauces. Often confused with caraway, cumin seeds are long and light brown, while caraway seeds are curved.

TORTILLAS – Available in corn, flour, or wholewheat, and the choice is yours to make. Corn tortillas are the most traditional but flour tortillas work better when making filled dishes that need to be folded. Tortillas freeze well and should be refrigerated to maintain their freshness.

PHEASANT WITH CHESTNUT SAUCE

$\mathcal{P}$heasant is now raised commercially on special farms. It is larger and less 'gamey' than its wild cousin. This dish is quite expensive but good results can also be achieved using a fresh 3-lb/1.4-kg chicken.

Couple this with steamed broccoli and some long, thin, steamed and glazed whole carrots and you have a fabulous special dinner dish.

Nutritional Profile

PER SERVING	CLASSIC	MINIMAX
Calories	1149	439
Fat (g)	51	10
Calories from fat	40%	20%
Cholesterol (mg)	12	64
Sodium (mg)	1	99
Fibre (g)	1	6

■ *Classic compared:* Roast Pheasant and Cumberland Sauce

Time Estimate

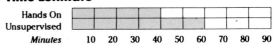

Hands On									
Unsupervised									
Minutes	10	20	30	40	50	60	70	80	90

Cost Estimate

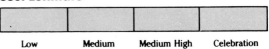

Low	Medium	Medium High	Celebration

Serves 2

INGREDIENTS

1 whole pheasant (2 lb/900 g)

HERB STUFFING

½ tablespoon/8 ml fresh parsley, chopped
1 teaspoon/5 ml fresh thyme, chopped
1 teaspoon/5 ml fresh sage, chopped
¼ teaspoon/1.25 ml fresh tarragon, chopped
¼ teaspoon/1.25 ml black peppercorns, cracked
⅛ teaspoon/0.6 ml salt
2 tablespoons/30 ml onion, peeled and chopped

CHESTNUT SAUCE

1 teaspoon/5 ml extra light olive oil with a dash
of sesame oil
1 onion, peeled and sliced
1 garlic clove, peeled and finely chopped
1 stalk celery, sliced
1 medium carrot, peeled and sliced
1½ pints/900 ml water
¾ pint/450 ml de-alcoholized red wine
2 tablespoons/30 ml arrowroot mixed with 2 table-
spoons/30 ml de-alcoholized red wine
4 oz/113 g peeled chestnuts
¼ teaspoon/1.25 ml fresh tarragon
¼ teaspoon/1.25 ml fresh thyme
½ teaspoon/2.5 ml fresh parsley

BOUQUET GARNI

2 bay leaves
6 stalks parsley
4 sprigs thyme

RICE PILAF

See recipe page 83. Use chicken stock (recipe page 210) instead of turkey stock and the reserved pheasant leg meat instead of prawns.

FIRST PREPARE

■ Make the herb stuffing. Combine all the ingredients in a small bowl and mix well.

■ Wash the pheasant and dry with absorbent paper. To remove the leg and thigh portion from the bird, cut down between the breast and thigh joint. Carefully bone the breast meat off the pheasant. Make sure to cut away any visible fat. Reserve the legs, thighs and bones.

■ Cut the breast in half. Coat the inner surface of the breast halves with the herb stuffing. Place one breast half on top of the other and squash them together so that all the stuffing is on the inside.

■ To make a bouquet garni, tie the herbs together and wrap them in butter muslin. Bruise the herbs with the back of a knife until the muslin is stained green.

NOW COOK

■ Pre-heat the oven to 375°F/190°C/Gas Mark 5. Place the stuffed pheasant breast on a rack in a roasting tin and roast for 35 minutes, or until the internal temperature reaches 165°F/75°C on a meat thermometer (see page 85).

■ *The Sauce:* Heat the olive oil in a large stockpot. Add the onion, garlic, celery, carrot, bouquet garni and the pheasant bones. Cook for 5 minutes.

■ Pour in the water and de-alcoholized wine and simmer gently until reduced to 1½ pints/900 ml. Add the reserved pheasant legs and thighs and cook for 35 minutes more. Remove and strip the meat from the bones, reserving the meat. Add to the rice pilaf before serving. Skim off all surface fat and strain the stock.

■ Transfer the strained stock into a small saucepan and boil rapidly until reduced to 12 fl oz/340 ml.

■ Remove the pan from the heat and mix in the arrowroot paste. Return to the heat and stir until thickened. Add the chestnuts, tarragon, thyme and parsley.

■ *To Serve:* Remove the pheasant breast from the oven and transfer to a carving dish. Slice off the skin and carve the meat vertically into thick slices. Serve the pheasant on a bed of rice pilaf, coated with the chestnut sauce.

Helpful Hints and Observations

LEGS AND THIGHS – These are cooked separately from the breast meat because they need to cook for 60 minutes, and the breast for only 40.

About the Ingredients

PHEASANT – Ask about pheasant at a licensed poulterer's or fishmonger's. Fresh wild pheasant is only available from October to January. Otherwise frozen oven-ready birds may be obtainable. Remember, pheasant meat is so lean that you must cook it very carefully to avoid drying it out.

CHESTNUTS – Chestnuts should feel soft when rubbed lightly with your fingers. Before you use them, throw them in boiling water for 10 minutes and then peel them. Peeled chestnuts in tins are usually available in large supermarkets.

POUSSINS AND PILAF KIRKLAND

$\mathcal{T}$he American original of this recipe uses Rock Cornish game hens. These are fed a diet of acorns and cranberries, which gives them a slightly 'wild' taste and a fuller flavour than chicken. They are a distinctive American invention, having been secretly bred from an English Cornish game cockerel and an American Plymouth Rock white hen. Ah, such romance, but then just look where it got them!

The rice pilaf provides enough carbohydrate so there's no need for potatoes or beans. I usually add a heap of steaming fresh-cooked spinach or Swiss chard with a pinch of freshly ground nutmeg. Be sure to squeeze out the excess water before you add it to the plate.

Nutritional Profile

PER SERVING	CLASSIC	MINIMAX
Calories	948	374
Fat (g)	62	12
Calories from fat	59%	29%
Cholesterol (mg)	251	103
Sodium (mg)	535	155
Fibre (g)	3	3

■ *Classic compared:* Game Hens Coq au Vin

Time Estimate

Hands On										
Unsupervised										
Minutes	10	20	30	40	50	60	70	80	90

Cost Estimate

Low	Medium	Medium High	Celebration

Serves 4

INGREDIENTS

2 poussins, about 1 lb/450 g each

RICE PILAF

1 tablespoon/15 ml extra light olive oil with a dash of sesame oil
1 large Spanish onion, peeled and finely diced
1 garlic clove, peeled and crushed
8 fl oz/227 ml mixed uncooked grains (I recommend a mixture of half mixed long grain rice, one-quarter pearl barley and one-quarter wild rice)
16 fl oz/455 ml chicken stock (recipe page 210)
2 bay leaves
1 sprig thyme
1 sprig parsley
6 fl oz/170 ml small green peas
14 fl oz/400 ml large mushrooms, sliced ½ inch/1.5 cm thick

SAUCE

2 fl oz/57 ml de-alcoholized white wine
1 tablespoon/15 ml arrowroot, mixed with 1 table-spoon/15 ml de-alcoholized white wine
½ tablespoon/8 ml fresh coriander leaves, chopped
1½ tablespoons/23 ml fresh parsley, chopped
1 sweet red pepper, de-seeded and finely diced

FIRST PREPARE THE POUSSINS

■ Cut each bird in half by making a cut on one side of the backbone. Make a second cut on the other side of the backbone. Take out the back and open up the bird. Cut through the breast-bone from the inside. Remove the fine rib-bones and cut the wing-tips off. Save the wing-tips and backbones for stock. Dry the poussins well with paper towels. Place on a rack in a roasting pan so that they do not touch the baking surface.

NOW COOK

■ *The Pilaf:* In a casserole pan, heat the oil and cook the onion and garlic until the onion is translucent. Add the rice and stir to coat. Cover with the stock and lay the herbs on top. Cook uncovered in a 375°F/190°C/Gas Mark 5 oven for 45 minutes. After 15 minutes, put the poussins into the oven as well.

■ When the pilaf is cooked, remove the herbs, stir in the peas and mushrooms, and return to the oven to heat through for 5 minutes. Meanwhile, take out the poussins.

■ *The Sauce:* Rinse the juice from the chicken roasting pan by adding de-alcoholized white wine. Pour into a fat strainer (this separates the fat from the juice), let sit for a few moments for the fat to rise to the surface, then pour the juice back into the pan through a fine sieve. You should end up with 4 fl oz/113 ml of juice.

■ Stir in the arrowroot paste until the sauce has thickened. Stir in the coriander leaves, parsley and diced red pepper.

■ *To Serve:* Place the poussins on a bed of pilaf and coat with the colourful sauce!

Helpful Hints and Observations

THICK-CUT MUSHROOMS – This is a new technique I'd like you to try out carefully. The mushrooms must be fresh, white, and cut in the full ½-inch/1.5-cm slices suggested. They are slipped raw into the very hot pilaf and cook (or rather warm) in about 5 minutes. The result is remarkable: each slice has an almost meat-like texture that adds significantly to the dish.

FAT STRAINER – Here is another one of those simple ideas that make you ask 'Why didn't someone think of that before?' In this recipe I make a sauce by keeping all the pan  drippings, adding the wine and pouring the liquid directly into this fat strainer. The fat rises to the surface and lets you pour the clear juices out from under the fat layer. Nifty? It works, and in my opinion is a must in a Minimax kitchen.

About the Ingredients

WILD RICE – Actually the seed of water grass that grows on lakes and is harvested in August and September. The wild rice you buy at the supermarket today is domesticated, or what is called 'paddy wild rice'. Wild rice keeps very well in a tightly covered container set in a cool, dry place.

BARLEY – Believed to be the first cultivated grain, mentioned in Far-Eastern writings and dating back 4,000 years. Today barley is mainly used in the making of beer, but as a food source it is a tasty addition to soups, stews, casseroles and pilaf dishes. Store barley as you would rice, in a covered container in a cool, dry place.

THANKSGIVING TURKEY AND STUFFING PIE

I hope that by cooking a turkey breast in a toaster oven you'll see how little space it can take to create a family feast. Have a great time with your loved ones. Tell each other some good news and in whatever way you feel comfortable, try saying 'Thank you' to God.

Here are two recipes for a slimmed-down version of the traditional Thanksgiving meal. In America it would be followed by Pumpkin Pie, and you'll find the recipe for a terrific pumpkin dessert on page 184.

In Britain turkey means Christmas, and the follow-up is the classic Plum Pudding. On page 186 there's a lean version which won't put you flat on your back. And since many people will admit to a preference for something lighter, they'll be delighted if you serve up a beautifully presented Trifle (page 208) instead.

Nutritional Profile

PER SERVING	CLASSIC	MINIMAX
Calories	1367	253
Fat (g)	58	6
Calories from fat	38%	21%
Cholesterol (mg)	470	88
Sodium (mg)	657	165
Fibre (g)	12	3

■ *Classic compared:* Roast Turkey with Chestnut Dressing

Time Estimate

Hands On Unsupervised	1 Hour, 40 Minutes
Minutes	10 20 30 40 50 60 70 80 90

Cost Estimate

Low	Medium	Medium High	Celebration

Turkey Breast in a Toaster Oven

Serves 12

INGREDIENTS

1 whole turkey breast (4 lb/1.8 kg)
4 fresh sage leaves
4 sprigs immature thyme
2 garlic cloves, peeled and chopped
¼ teaspoon/1.25 ml white pepper, freshly ground
⅛ teaspoon/0.6 ml salt, freshly ground
8 fl oz/227 ml good quality chicken stock (recipe page 210)
1 tablespoon/15 ml arrowroot mixed with 2 tablespoons/30 ml de-alcoholized white wine
1 tablespoon/15 ml fresh parsley, chopped

FIRST PREPARE

■ Remove the skin from the turkey and set it aside. Carefully remove the centre breastbone, keeping the two sides of the breast connected. Remove the tenderloin piece of turkey that forms an inner muscle of the breast. You can use this for other dishes. By removing it you make room for the herb dressing.

■ Spread the two boned breasts out flat on a chopping board. Place the sage leaves on top of one breast. Place the thyme sprigs and sprinkle the garlic, pepper and salt on the other.

■ Fold the breasts together with the seasonings inside. Place the breasts in a standard size meat loaf pan. Cut a piece of the reserved turkey skin to completely cover the top.

NOW COOK

■ Bake the turkey breasts in a large toaster oven at 325°F/165°C/Gas mark 3 for 35 minutes per lb/450 g. Check the turkey skin halfway through the cooking process. If the skin has shrunk, replace it with another piece of the reserved skin. Remove the cooked turkey to a serving dish, reserving the juices in the meat loaf pan.

■ To make a great gravy, pour the chicken stock into the meat loaf pan and dredge up any turkey residue. Now pour the stock into a saucepan and bring to the boil. Remove from the heat and pour the stock into a fat strainer. Let the fat rise to the surface – about 5 minutes. When separated, pour the clear, fat-free stock back into the saucepan.

■ Remove the gravy saucepan from the heat, stir in the arrowroot paste, then return to the heat and stir until thickened. Add the parsley.

■ Slice the turkey breast and serve with the gravy and Thanksgiving Stuffing Pie on the side.

Thanksgiving Stuffing Pie

Serves 8

INGREDIENTS

2 teaspoons/10 ml extra light olive oil with a dash of sesame oil
7 thin slices wholewheat bread
Leaves from 6 sprigs fresh thyme, chopped
8 fresh sage leaves, finely chopped
1 medium onion, coarsely chopped
10 oz/284 g parsnips, coarsely chopped
10 oz/284 g carrots, coarsely chopped
2 fl oz/57 ml turkey stock (recipe page 210)
½ teaspoon/2.5 ml nutmeg, freshly grated
2 tablespoons/30 ml whole berry cranberry sauce

FIRST PREPARE

■ Brush 1 teaspoon/5 ml of the olive oil on the bottom and sides of a standard size loaf pan. Set 2 pieces of bread aside. Cut the rest of the bread into 1-inch/2.5-cm wide strips and lay them side by side to cover the bottom and sides of the pan. These will guide you later in cutting serving slices.

■ Sprinkle 1 teaspoon/5 ml each of the thyme and sage over the bread lining.

NOW COOK

■ Pre-heat the oven to 350°F/180°C/Gas Mark 4.

■ Heat the remaining olive oil in a saucepan and fry the chopped onions for 2 minutes. Add the parsnips and carrots and cook for 5 minutes. Add the turkey stock and the remaining thyme and sage and simmer until the vegetables are tender – about 20 minutes. Then mash them roughly, but well, and stir in the nutmeg.

■ Spread half the mashed vegetables over the bottom layer of bread. Spread 1 tablespoon/15 ml of cranberry sauce on top. Repeat with another layer of vegetables and then more cranberry.

■ Finish with slices of bread cut to cover the top.

■ Bake the pie in the pre-heated oven for 30 minutes. Let it cool for 5 minutes, then turn it out of the pan on to a serving plate. Slice it and use a fish slice to serve.

About the Ingredients

THYME – A strong herb, essential in French cooking, it is a classic addition to the bouquet garni (with parsley and bay leaves). There are over a hundred species of thyme, but the superior flavour and aroma of garden or 'winter' thyme is usually preferred in cooking. For certain dishes the milder lemon thyme is a better choice. Bees love it!

TURKEY TREENESTAR

This recipe is named for my wife Treena. It came about on the day she came home having given birth to our first child, Tessa. I had a very small chicken, a tin of shrimps and some Swiss asparagus soup powder. From such humble and romantic beginnings comes this . . . turkey?

Serving a whole roasted turkey for a party is popular but messy. This idea works well and when the meat is built up on a mound of fragrant rice pilaf and coated with the sauce of prawns and asparagus tips it's great fun! Nutmeg-seasoned carrots and some more freshly steamed asparagus go very well.

Nutritional Profile

PER SERVING	CLASSIC	MINIMAX
Calories	688	648
Fat (g)	25	11
Calories from fat	33%	15%
Cholesterol (mg)	150	146
Sodium (mg)	396	395
Fibre (g)	3	2

■ *Classic compared:* Chicken Treenestar

Time Estimate

Hands On									
Unsupervised									
Minutes	10	20	30	40	50	60	70	80	90

Cost Estimate

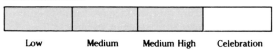

Low	Medium	Medium High	Celebration

Serves 6

INGREDIENTS

1 whole turkey breast with ribs and backbone (5 lb/2.25 kg), to yield 1 lb 10 oz/740 g cooked turkey meat
4 sprigs immature thyme
8 fresh sage leaves
¼ teaspoon/1.25 ml black pepper, freshly ground
⅛ teaspoon/0.6 ml salt, freshly ground
7 oz/200 g fresh asparagus (use frozen if out of season)
¾ pint/450 ml turkey stock (recipe page 210)
8 fl oz/227 ml evaporated skimmed milk
2 fl oz/57 ml cornflour mixed with 4 tablespoons/60 ml de-alcoholized white wine
Pinch of white pepper, freshly ground
4 oz/113 g cooked prawns
1 teaspoon/5 ml dried dill weed
1¾ pints/1 l cooked rice pilaf (recipe follows)

RICE PILAF

1 teaspoon/5 ml extra light olive oil with a dash of sesame oil
1 onion, peeled and thinly sliced
12 fl oz/340 ml long grain rice, well rinsed and drained
6 stalks parsley
1 sprig thyme
1 bay leaf
24 fl oz/680 ml turkey stock (recipe page 210)
4 oz/113 g shrimps or tiny prawns
½ teaspoon/2.5 ml dried dill weed
⅛ teaspoon/0.6 ml salt, freshly ground

GRANISH

Fresh parsley, chopped
Paprika

FIRST PREPARE

■ Using a sharp knife, cut the backbone and ribs out of the whole breast. Remove the inner fillet, known as the supreme. Set the bones aside for the stock. Cut the breast into two even sections. You should have approximately 2¼ lb/1 kg of uncooked meat.

■ Set the meat skin-side down on a board. Place the thyme sprigs and the sage leaves down the centre of one side. Sprinkle with the fresh pepper and salt. Now place the other breast section on the seasoned section so that the skin is on the outside and the thick muscles are at either end, to make a more even sized package.

■ Wrap the turkey in butcher's net as described on page 125.

■ Cut the asparagus tips from the spears and pass a knife through the tips a few times just to break them up without mashing them. The tips will be added to the sauce. Cut the rest of the asparagus into ½-inch/1.5-cm slices and steam them to serve as a side dish.

NOW COOK

■ Place the prepared turkey on a trivet or rack in a roasting tin. Roast at 375°F/190°C/Gas Mark 5 for 1 hour 15 minutes, or until the centre of the turkey has reached 185°F/85°C on a meat thermometer.

■ Approximately 25 minutes before the turkey is fully cooked, begin to prepare the sauce. In a large saucepan over medium heat, combine the heated stock and the evaporated skimmed milk. Bring it to the boil then stir in the cornflour paste. Turn the heat up a bit, stirring constantly to prevent the milk from sticking to the pan. This can happen because the milk proteins have no fat attached to them. Bring it up to the boil to thicken.

■ Lower the heat and add a pinch of white pepper, the prawns, reserved asparagus tips and the dill weed.

■ *The Pilaf:* Pre-heat the oven to 450°F/230°C/Gas Mark 8. Heat the oil in a small saucepan and fry the onion until softened, but not brown. Add the rice and cook for 1 to 2 minutes, stirring to coat the rice with oil. Add the herbs and turkey stock. Bake uncovered in the pre-heated oven for 20 minutes. (If you want to bake it at the same time as the Turkey Treenestar, cook it at 375°F/190°C/Gas Mark 5 for 30 minutes.) Remove the herbs and use a fork to fluff up the rice. Stir in the prawns (the heat of the rice will warm them). Season with the dill weed and salt and serve hot.

■ *To Serve:* Remove the turkey from the oven, cut off the net and slice the meat into twelve ⅓-inch/1-cm slices. Press the pilaf into a narrow loaf tin and turn out on to serving plate. Lay the turkey slices on the rice and coat them with the sauce. Dust with parsley and paprika.

About the Ingredients

IMMATURE THYME – Mature sprigs of thyme have thicker, woody stems while young sprigs are green and tender.
SAGE – See page 53.
ASPARAGUS – See page 29.

ROAST BEEF AND YORKSHIRE PANCAKES

$\mathcal{T}$his is truly a great-tasting change from Yorkshire Pudding when cooking responsibly for loved ones. The Yorkshire Pancake is much easier to make at home or for a party, and everyone will love it.

I'm sure none of us wants to see the end of the family meal where the large cut of meat is carved by Dad in Norman Rockwell style. However, in this case I've kept the amount of meat down to just enough for eight portions – and 2 lb/900 g isn't a large enough piece to carve at the table. Two lovely side vegetables are steamed carrots with a touch of nutmeg and freshly steamed broccoli (unless President Bush is coming to dinner).

Nutritional Profile

PER SERVING	CLASSIC	MINIMAX
Calories	1485	313
Fat (g)	113	13
Calories from fat	68%	38%
Cholesterol (mg)	419	113
Sodium (mg)	428	275
Fibre (g)	1	1

■ *Classic compared:* Roast Beef and Yorkshire Pudding

Time Estimate

Hands On / Unsupervised									
Minutes	10	20	30	40	50	60	70	80	90

Cost Estimate

Low	Medium	Medium High	Celebration

Serves 8

INGREDIENTS

PANCAKE BATTER
2 oz/57 g plain flour
1 whole egg
1 egg yolk
8 fl oz/227 ml skimmed milk
1 tablespoon/15 ml extra light olive oil with a dash
of sesame oil
1 tablespoon/15 ml fresh sage, chopped
1 tablespoon/15 ml fresh mint, chopped
Horseradish cream, about 1 teaspoon/5 ml for each
pancake

BEEF
2 lb/900 g silverside of beef, boned
Black pepper, freshly ground
1 large garlic clove, peeled, and sliced in 4 pieces
¾ pint/425 ml good quality beef stock (recipe page
210)
1 tablespoon/15 ml arrowroot

FIRST PREPARE

■ Sift the flour into a bowl and make a well in
the centre. Lightly beat the egg and egg yolk together
and pour into the well. Gradually pour in the milk,
beating the ingredients together until a smooth batter
is formed. Let it sit for 30 minutes.

■ Cut all but a thin layer of fat from the meat and
season the roast with freshly ground black pepper.

■ Cut small shallow pockets underneath the roast
and push the garlic slivers into the incisions.

NOW COOK

■ Place the roast on a trivet in a roasting pan, fat
side up, and roast in a 325°F/165°C/Gas Mark 3 oven
until an internal temperature of 120°F/48°C for rare
(about 50 minutes), 140°F/60°C for medium (about 60
minutes), 160°F/71°C for 'spoiled' (about 70 minutes)
is reached.

■ Meanwhile, make the pancakes. Lightly oil an
8-inch/20-cm diameter crêpe pan with the olive oil,
then tip the surplus into the batter and mix. This
will make each pancake self-releasing. When the pan
is hot, pour in sufficient batter to cover the bottom.
Sprinkle some of the sage and mint on top of each
pancake. Once bubbles appear on the surface of the
pancake and it goes dull and waxy, flip it over and
cook the underside 1 minute longer.

■ Transfer the pancake to a plate and spread the
plain side with 1 teaspoon/5 ml of the horseradish
cream. Fold it in half and in half again. Keep the
prepared pancakes warm while you finish cooking
the roast and its gravy.

■ When the roast is done, turn off the oven, open
the door and let stand for 20 minutes to set the juices
before carving. Remove the roast to a carving plate,
leaving the meat juices in the pan.

■ Add the beef stock to the meat juices and scrape
out all the residue into a fat strainer. Let the fat rise
to the top and then pour the juice through a fine mesh
sieve into a small saucepan.

■ In a small bowl, mix the arrowroot with 1 table-
spoon/15 ml water to make a paste and add it to the
meat juice in the saucepan. Stir over gentle heat until
it thickens into a clear gravy.

■ Carve the beef in thin slices, about ¼ inch/1 cm
thick. You should get two or even three slices for a
4–5 oz/113–142 g serving – it's delicious!

Helpful Hints and Observations

SITTING BATTER – Sounds a little like an unusual
tribal name! Always let flour mixes rest before use.
This allows starch cells to soften and take up more
of the moisture, which gives a finer texture.

SHALLOW GARLIC POCKETS – Keep garlic slivers
very close to the bottom surface. If dug in too deep
they appear in mid-slice, and for some this is just too
much!

THE TRIVET – This is simply a rack that holds the
meat away from the direct heat of the pan and stops
both excessive evaporation of the meat surface and
making a mess of your pan.

MEAT THERMOMETER – I really do urge you to buy
a good one: a very small and thin probe is best. Don't
keep it in during cooking. It is better to drive it into the
middle of the roast about 10 minutes before it is due
to be done, and then remove it – testing again later if
necessary.

THICKNESS OF CUT – I cut beef, and in fact all
meat cuts, in thin (¼-inch/0.75-cm) slices. This does
two things: it covers more of the plate than a single
thicker slice and prevents my choking my friends and
family. The typical thick cut prime rib is the culprit in
a surprisingly large number of rather public incidents.

About the Ingredients

SILVERSIDE OF BEEF – See page 97.

FILLET OF BEEF BENEDICT

*J*ust think of it: beef so tender it melts in your mouth, a hint of bacon peeking through egg and Mozzarella cheese, all on a muffin! Could a brunch dish so delicious be on a healthy Minimax menu? You bet!

Because the percentage of calories from fat is a little high, make Fillet of Beef Benedict something you serve only occasionally. It's a great dish for a special holiday brunch.

Nutritional Profile

PER SERVING	CLASSIC	MINIMAX
Calories	678	324
Fat (g)	47	12
Calories from fat	62%	32%
Cholesterol (mg)	537	67
Sodium (mg)	1513	659
Fibre (g)	0	1

■ *Classic compared:* Fillet of Beef Benedict

Time Estimate

Hands On								
Unsupervised								
Minutes	10 20	30	40	50	60	70	80	90

Cost Estimate

Low	Medium	Medium High	Celebration

INGREDIENTS

12 oz/340 g fillet of beef, fully trimmed
Black pepper, freshly ground
3 oz/85 g back bacon
2 oz/57 g skimmed Mozzarella cheese
1 tablespoon/15 ml extra light olive oil with a dash of sesame oil
8 fl oz/227 ml liquid egg substitute
2 teaspoons/10 ml horseradish sauce
2 muffins, cut in half and toasted
White pepper, freshly ground
4 fl oz/113 ml de-alcoholized white wine
1 teaspoon/5 ml arrowroot mixed with 1 tablespoon/15 ml water
Fresh parsley, chopped
Paprika

FIRST PREPARE

■ Slice the beef into 1-inch/2.5-cm thick medallions (or tournedos). Pound the meat with your fist or a mallet until it is 3½–4 inches/9–10.5 cm in diameter – slightly bigger than the muffins. Sprinkle with finely ground black pepper to taste.

■ Trim the skin and any fat off the bacon. Mince two slices (1 oz/28 g) very finely.

■ Cut four thin slices (approximately ⅛ inch/0.5 cm thick) of cheese. Trim them to make circles 4 inches/10 cm in diameter.

NOW COOK

■ Pour the olive oil into a dish and sop both sides of the beef circles. Drop the beef into a hot frying pan and brown for about 2 minutes on each side. Push the beef to one side of the pan, and brown the four whole bacon slices. Allow about 30 seconds for each side.

■ While the meat is browning, combine the liquid egg substitute with the minced bacon. Pour the egg mixture into non-stick egg poaching cups and set them in a skillet containing ½ inch/1 cm of steaming water. Poach the eggs until set.

■ Spread ½ teaspoon/2.5 ml horseradish sauce on each of the muffin halves, then layer with bacon, beef and eggs and top with a slice of cheese. Season with freshly ground white pepper.

■ Set the grill pan 4 inches/10 cm from the heat source. Pop the muffins under the grill. Check after 1 minute and remove them when the cheese is just beginning to brown.

■ *The Sauce:* Heat the wine in the meat sauté pan, scraping up any brown residue from the bottom of the pan. Remove the pan from the heat and slowly stir in the arrowroot mixture. Place it back on the heat and cook until the sauce has thickened.

■ *To Serve:* Pour the sauce over and around the grilled muffins and garnish with parsley and a sprinkling of paprika.

About the Ingredients

MOZZARELLA CHEESE – This is a favourite ingredient of many people, but do you know how it got its name? Mozzarella is made from a curd that is broken up and heated in water until it forms an elastic thread. This thread is wound into a ball, from which pieces are sliced off to form the cheese. This last stage is where the name comes from, because *mozzare* means 'to slice off'!

FILLET OF BEEF – Where does it come from? This lean, boneless piece of meat is from just below the ribs of the sirloin and is the most expensive cut available.

MUFFINS – British muffins are light-textured rolls, round and flat, made with yeast dough. Traditionally they are eaten in winter, served split, toasted and buttered for tea, sometimes with jam. Wholemeal muffins are now widely available, but you will have to look for them at your local supermarket or baker's – they are no longer sold in the street, as they were in Victorian times, by bell-ringing 'muffin men'.

FILLET OF BEEF MEURICE

$\mathcal{T}$*reena and I first ate this dish in France back in 1970, when we visited the famous Hotel Meurice in Paris. Those were the days when cream, butter, eggs, beef and pâté de foie gras were 'just part of my job'. Now things have changed – and so have we!*

This is a romantic dinner for two, or a special dinner for four (just double the quantities). Even though it's relatively expensive, it is far, far less than you would pay in a restaurant. Serve it with freshly steamed leaf spinach . . . it's wonderful!

Nutritional Profile

PER SERVING	CLASSIC	MINIMAX
Calories	1032	473
Fat (g)	72	15
Calories from fat	63%	28%
Cholesterol (mg)	430	66
Sodium (mg)	2360	359
Fibre (g)	21	3

■ *Classic compared:* Fillet of Beef Meurice

Time Estimate

Hands On Unsupervised									
Minutes	10	20	30	40	50	60	70	80	90

Cost Estimate

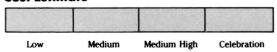

Low	Medium	Medium High	Celebration

Serves 2

INGREDIENTS

RICE PILAF
12 fl oz/340 ml beef stock (recipe page 210)
4 tablespoons/60 ml uncooked long grain rice, rinsed
2 tablespoons/30 ml uncooked pearl barley
2 tablespoons/30 ml uncooked wild rice
1 bay leaf
1 sprig tarragon
1 stalk parsley
1 tablespoon/15 ml Dijon mustard
1 teaspoon/5 ml fresh tarragon, chopped

FILLET OF BEEF
1 teaspoon/5 ml extra light olive oil with a dash
of sesame oil
¼ teaspoon/1.25 ml black pepper, freshly ground
8 oz/227 g fillet of beef
1 tablespoon/15 ml shallots, chopped
2 fl oz/57 ml de-alcoholized white wine
6 fl oz/170 ml beef stock (recipe page 210)
1 tablespoon/15 ml cornflour mixed with 2 table-
spoons/30 ml de-alcoholized white wine
2½ fl oz/70 ml strained yogurt (recipe page 210)
1 teaspoon/5 ml fresh tarragon, chopped

NOW COOK

■ *The Rice Pilaf:* In a medium saucepan, heat the
beef stock and add the long grain rice, pearl barley
and wild rice. Lay the bay leaf, tarragon and parsley
on top. Cook uncovered in a 375°F/190°C/Gas Mark 5
oven for about 45 minutes. When done, remove the
herbs. Add the mustard and chopped tarragon and
stir thoroughly.

■ Lightly grease two individual ramekins with olive
oil. Pack the rice into the dishes. To keep it warm,
place the ramekins in a pan filled with 1 inch/2.5 cm
of water. Put the pan on top of the stove over low heat.

■ *The Beef:* Pour the oil on a plate and sprinkle with
the black pepper. Dredge the meat through the oil so
that both sides are glazed.

■ Put the meat into a medium-sized sauté pan on
medium heat and brown both sides. Remove it and
place it back on the glazing plate.

■ Add the shallots to the same pan. Add the
de-alcoholized white wine to de-glaze the pan. Add
the beef stock and boil to reduce by half.

■ Mix the cornflour paste with the strained yogurt.
Add the reduced beef stock and return the mixture
to the sauté pan, stirring to thicken. Add the beef
to warm through, then sprinkle with the chopped
tarragon.

■ *To Serve:* Unmould the rice on to warm plates, top
with a portion of the steak and coat with the sauce.

Helpful Hints and Observations

SILVER SKIN – This is the fine, silvery membrane
or sheath that encases the fillet on at least one side.
This must come off in order to prevent the meat
from bunching. What happens is that the membrane
shrinks and toughens when it comes in contact with
the hot pan and squeezes the meat out of shape. In
this otherwise ultra-tender meat, it means having to
chew hard and swallow when you least expect it! So,
regardless of its eventual ragged shape or the apparent
weight loss on expensive meat, cut it off! By the way,
the trim is always useful for adding a soupçon of extra
flavour to any good beef stock.

About the Ingredients

MUSTARDS – The Romans started mustard on the
road to fame. The most commonly used mustards
are made from the white mustard plant, the black
mustard and the wild mustard. English mustard is
usually a mixture of black and white with turmeric
added. French mustards are made with a combination
of white and black mustard seeds, with different herbs
added. Dijon mustard is mixed with verjuice, an acid
juice extracted from large, unripened grapes.

SCOTTISH BEEF COLLOPS

The cuisine of Scotland can be broadly divided into two groups: cottage and castle. The castle food owes its influence to the French and Italian royal courts and it is from these courts that the term collops comes. The French word *escalopes* means thin slices. The same in Italian is *scaloppine.*

I've tried to use one pot to prepare the whole dish, therefore it isn't the most attractive serving piece. You can wrap a colourful cloth around the outside or simply serve on to individual plates in the kitchen. Beautifully cooked tiny peas with a little mint would be a great addition, or finely shredded carrot, lightly steamed, with a little nutmeg.

Nutritional Profile

PER SERVING	CLASSIC	MINIMAX
Calories	730	285
Fat (g)	41	9
Calories from fat	51%	28%
Cholesterol (mg)	183	42
Sodium (mg)	794	62
Fibre (g)	3	3

■ *Classic compared:* Scottish Beef Collops

Time Estimate

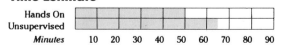

Hands On									
Unsupervised									
Minutes	10	20	30	40	50	60	70	80	90

Cost Estimate

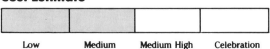

Low	Medium	Medium High	Celebration

Serves 6

INGREDIENTS

1¼ lb/570 g silverside of beef
2 teaspoons/10 ml extra light olive oil with a dash of sesame oil
1¼ pints/680 ml onions, peeled and chopped
4 oz/113 g mushrooms, finely chopped
2 tablespoons/30 ml plain flour
2 pickled walnuts, finely chopped
2 tablespoons/30 ml fresh thyme, chopped
½ pint/285 ml beef stock (recipe page 210)
1½ lb/680 g potatoes, peeled and sliced ¼ inch/0.75 cm thick
4 oz/113 g mushrooms, thinly sliced

GARNISH
1 tablespoon fresh parsley, chopped
Carrot shavings

FIRST PREPARE

■ Cut the beef into ¼-inch/0.75-cm slices across the grain, at a slight diagonal. You should end up with about 48 slices.

NOW COOK

■ In a low-sided casserole, heat half the oil and sauté the onions until they are soft and slightly brown. Place the onions on a plate and set aside.

■ Lightly rinse the casserole and place it back on the burner. Add the remaining oil and cover the bottom with half the beef slices, allowing them to brown fully. Re-position the browned beef to one side and brown the rest of the beef.

■ Add the cooked onions and the chopped mushrooms. Sprinkle with the flour and spoon the mixture into a bowl. Stir in the walnuts and thyme.

■ Rinse the sides and bottom of the casserole with the beef stock, removing any browning residue. Pour into a bowl and reserve.

■ Spread half the beef mixture over the bottom of the casserole. Layer with half the sliced mushrooms, followed by half the sliced potatoes. Repeat with layers of the remaining beef mixture and sliced mushrooms, topped with the remaining potatoes. Pour the reserved stock over the casserole, cover and cook at 350°F/180°C/Gas Mark 4 for 40 minutes.

■ Garnish with the parsley and carrot shavings.

About the Ingredients

PICKLED WALNUTS – If they aren't available at the local grocer's, you can make a substitute. Use 6 medium pitted black olives, marinated in 2 oz/57 g cider vinegar and 1 tablespoon/15 ml molasses for 3 hours. A slightly different texture but very similar flavour.

STEAK DIANE

$\mathcal{B}$ack in the 1960s and '70s, there was hardly a gourmet restaurant that didn't have table-side cooking . . . with flames. Steak Diane was an all-time favourite, being both simple and partially incinerated! I've doused the conflagration, lessened the portion size and reduced the fat. Oh, it's still simple!

In this recipe we've done all the presentation for you: the steak is served with pan-grilled tomatoes, steamed green beans and glazed red-skinned potatoes. It makes a pretty picture – and such an easy and well-appreciated dish!

Nutritional Profile

PER SERVING	CLASSIC	MINIMAX
Calories	1036	389
Fat (g)	74	17
Calories from fat	64%	39%
Cholesterol (mg)	406	81
Sodium (mg)	905	599
Fibre (g)	8	7

■ *Classic compared:* Steak Diane

Time Estimate

Hands On									
Unsupervised									
Minutes	10	20	30	40	50	60	70	80	90

Cost Estimate

Low	Medium	Medium High	Celebration

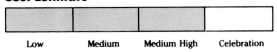

Serves 2

INGREDIENTS

8 oz/227 g beef fillet or topside
⅛ teaspoon/0.6 ml salt, freshly ground
¼ teaspoon/1.25 ml pepper, freshly ground
4 oz/113 g red potatoes
8 oz/227 g green beans, topped and tailed
Fine dusting of nutmeg, salt and pepper
¼ teaspoon/1.25 ml lemon juice, freshly squeezed
1 teaspoon/5 ml extra light olive oil with a dash
of sesame oil
½ oz/14 g butter
1 garlic clove, peeled and finely chopped
2 shallots, peeled and finely chopped
4 fl oz/113 ml fresh parsley, chopped
2 small Italian plum tomatoes, sliced
2 tablespoons/30 ml Worcestershire sauce
6 fl oz/170 ml beef stock (recipe page 210)

FIRST PREPARE

■ Tenderize the beef fillet by pounding it, with your fist, if you feel aggressive, or with a mallet if you're in a gentler mood. It should end up less than ¼ inch/1 cm thick. Sprinkle with the freshly ground salt and pepper.

■ Quarter and steam the potatoes for about 14 minutes. Add the green beans to the steamer and dust with nutmeg, salt and pepper. Steam for another 6 minutes. Separate the potatoes and beans. Sprinkle the lemon juice on the beans and set aside.

NOW COOK

■ Heat the oil in a large skillet. Drag both sides of the fillet through the oil, then brown it quickly, for no more than 30 seconds on each side. Set aside in the pan to keep warm.

■ Heat the butter in another skillet. Sauté the garlic and shallots for 2 minutes. Drop in half of the parsley and the tomato slices. Keep the tomato slices to one side of the pan and turn them to warm both sides. Remove them from the pan and keep warm.

■ Add the Worcerstershire sauce and beef stock. Cook until reduced by one-third. Add the beef fillet, the remaining parsley and the potatoes, making sure they are all coated with the sauce.

■ *To Serve:* Transfer the beef and potatoes to very hot plates. Put the tomatoes on one side and the green beans on the other.

Helpful Hints and Observations

TOPSIDE OF BEEF – Topside is much cheaper than fillet but also much tougher, and it needs special treatment. If you wish to use topside, marinate it in red wine with red wine vinegar, overnight if possible, and always in a glass or ceramic container. Dry the marinated beef with paper towels and pound it with a deeply indented meat mallet. It will never be as tender as fillet, but it has great flavour.

About the Ingredients

WORCESTERSHIRE SAUCE – Sir Marcus Sandys, a native of Worcestershire, asked his local grocers, Lea & Perrins, to make up a sauce resembling one he had discovered in the East Indies. The precise recipe remains a secret but the label admits to malt and spirit vinegar, molasses, sugar, salt, anchovies, tamarind, shallots, garlic, spices and flavouring.

RED WINE VINEGAR – Somewhere, in a vat, wine's complex molecules are breaking down, down, down, into . . . vinegar! Of course, vinegar doesn't have to be made from wine. Fermented apples are the source for cider vinegar; grains or potatoes for malt vinegar. But in this case, red wine's robust, hearty flavour is the perfect addition. Because vinegar is low in calories, it's a good choice as seasoning in the Minimax kitchen, where I'm constantly on the lookout for 'bright notes' of sour and bitter to replace the 'velvet notes' that come from the taste of fat.

KAREWAI STEAK PISCATELLA

C̲an this steak compete with the American favourite: Prime Rib with Baked Potato and Hollandaise Sauce? This is a legitimate question which Joe Piscatella, best-selling author of Don't Eat Your Heart Out, *answers with 'Yes!' Such success can go to one's head.*

Look for the ultimate in green. Broccoli works well, but then so do mangetout or sugar peas: when just cooked they have that wonderful, crisp texture that goes well with a dish like this.

Nutritional Profile

PER SERVING	CLASSIC	MINIMAX
Calories	1111	505
Fat (g)	75	15
Calories from fat	60%	28%
Cholesterol (mg)	327	84
Sodium (mg)	901	79
Fibre (g)	4	5

■ *Classic compared:* Prime Rib, Baked Potato and Hollandaise

Time Estimate

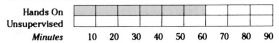

Cost Estimate

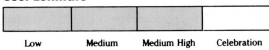

Low   Medium   Medium High   Celebration

Serves 4

INGREDIENTS

5 pints/2.8 l water
12 fl oz/340 ml orzo pasta
1 teaspoon/5 ml extra light olive oil with a dash of sesame oil
2 cloves garlic, peeled and chopped
1 large onion, peeled and thinly sliced
A 12-oz/340-g tin no-salt tomato sauce
8 fl oz/227 ml de-alcoholized red wine
1 tablespoon/15 ml good red wine vinegar
Black pepper, freshly coarse-ground
1 lb/450 g flank steak
5 tablespoons/75 ml fresh basil, chopped

NOW COOK

■ Cook the orzo in 2½ pints/1.4 l of boiling water for 8 minutes. Time the cooking to coincide with the steak's completion. Drain the orzo through a strainer. Place the strainer over hot water in a pot and cover with a lid to keep it warm.

■ Heat the olive oil in a saucepan and add the garlic and onion. Fry until the onion is soft – about 4 minutes.

■ Add the tomato sauce to the frying onion and stir in half the de-alcoholized wine. Add the red wine vinegar.

■ Spread the coarsely ground pepper on a large chopping board. Place the flank steak on top of the pepper and press so that the pepper sticks to the steak.

■ Put the steak into a hot skillet. Cook for 4 minutes on each side. The steak should be nice and brown on the outside, medium rare on the inside.

■ Pour the remaining wine over the steak. Scrape up the brown steak residue in the pan with a spatula. Add half the tomato sauce and 1 tablespoon/15 ml of the basil. Continue to cook and reduce the sauce. It will be very hot and will begin to darken in colour. Sprinkle 3 tablespoons/45 ml of the basil on top.

■ Put the orzo into the remaining tomato sauce. Add the other tablespoon/15 ml of basil.

■ Remove the steak from the tomato-onion sauce on to a chopping board with a gutter to catch the juices. Carve the steak across the grain in thin, diagonal pieces.

■ Serve the reduced steak juices as gravy on the side. De-glaze the steak pan with a swish of de-alcoholized wine, and pour this into the gravy as well.

■ Serve the sliced steak with the gravy, and the orzo in sauce on the side.

Helpful Hints and Observations

PASTA SHAPES – The eye does wonderful things to the other senses. In this case it's what the pasta looks like that creates such a difference. Please try different shapes, sizes and colours – it's good food and provides visual interest to distract the 'taste memory' that may be clamouring for noodles cooked Alfredo-style with eggs, cream and cheese – whoopee!

CARVING FLANK STEAK – Traditionally this cut is carved in thin, diagonal slices across the grain of the meat. I have suggested a 1-lb/450-g piece because it would come from a smaller, less fatty animal. It is enough to feed four people with at least two thin slices per head.

TOMATO SAUCE – I know this may seem odd but it's a unique flavour and colour when it's cooked in a hot pan. The colour deepens and the spices add to the overall flavour. It really is worth the effort to try it and see for yourself!

About the Ingredients

FLANK STEAK – This cut of meat has taken a 'bad rap' in the past. Flank steak is extremely lean and comes from the underside of the cow. Most recipes call for rolling and stuffing, then braising, a slow method of cooking reserved for tougher cuts of meat. On the contrary, we quickly fry this cut and achieve a wonderful

tenderness! The grain runs horizontally and if cut improperly it can be a bit too chewy. Take care to slice at an angle, making a thin cut across the grain.

ORZO – A pasta that derives its name from its shape. In Italy, if you asked for orzo you would get barley. Orzo pasta is semolina flour pressed into the shape of barley.

GOULASH

𝒜 Hungarian favourite, not with the traditional covering of sour cream or filled with sausage, dumplings and cottage cheese – but a deliciously satisfying meal to serve to those you love. Let your taste buds be dazzled, if such a thing is physiologically possible!

When Treena and I were first married and I was an Air Force officer, she worked making sandwiches at 50 cents an hour. We saved her money and made casserole dinners for our friends. This was one of our favourites. Try serving it with plain boiled noodles, and plenty of green peas sprinkled with fresh mint.

Nutritional Profile

PER SERVING	CLASSIC	MINIMAX
Calories	789	433
Fat (g)	55	14
Calories from fat	63%	30%
Cholesterol (mg)	153	85
Sodium (mg)	642	172
Fibre (g)	4	8

■ *Classic compared:* Goulash

Time Estimate

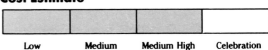

Hands On
Unsupervised — 95 Minutes

Minutes 10 20 30 40 50 60 70 80 90

Cost Estimate

Low	Medium	Medium High	Celebration

Serves 4

INGREDIENTS

1 teaspoon/5 ml extra light olive oil with a dash
of sesame oil

2 onions, peeled and finely chopped

2 garlic cloves, peeled, crushed and chopped

1½ lb/700 g silverside of beef, trimmed of fat and
cut into 2-inch/5-cm pieces

A 6-oz/170-g tin no-salt tomato paste

1¼ pints/700 ml fat-free beef stock (recipe page 210)

2 large potatoes, peeled and cut into ½-inch/1.25-cm
cubes

2 sweet green peppers, de-seeded and cubed

2 tablespoons/30 ml Hungarian paprika (slightly hot)

½ teaspoon/2.5 ml black pepper, freshly ground

1 teaspoon/5 ml caraway seeds

7 Italian plum tomatoes, peeled, de-seeded and
chopped

NOW COOK

■ Heat the olive oil in a large, heavy-bottomed saucepan (10 × 3½ inches/25 × 9 cm deep) and fry the
onions and garlic until translucent. Do not brown.
Turn out into a bowl and set aside.

■ Drop the cubed meat into the hot pan, making
sure all the pieces have a chance to touch the hot
surface – this will ensure that the meat sears and
browns properly.

■ Stir in the tomato paste. You'll see the sugar in
the paste start to caramelize and turn brown. This
is called the Maillard reaction. Now stir the onions
and garlic back into the pan.

■ Pour in the beef stock, cover and simmer for 90
minutes. Of course, you could do the recipe up to
this point the day before. If this is the case, make
sure you skim off any accumulated fat before you
proceed.

■ Add the potatoes, green peppers, half the paprika, the black pepper and the caraway seeds. Cover
and simmer until the potatoes are tender, about 30
minutes.

■ Before you serve, stir in your ruby-red tomato
pieces until just heated through. Sprinkle with the
remaining paprika. Stir and serve!

Helpful Hints and Observations

SILVERSIDE OF BEEF – I recommend silverside for
this Goulash rather than the traditional chuck steak.
It's not as fatty, but also not as juicy. However, the
bigger you cut the pieces, the more succulent the

final taste. So decide on the size pieces you want to
suit your preference.

LESS BEEF CAN MEAN MORE – I've also drastically
cut the amount of beef in this dish to 6 oz/170 g per
serving. It makes a big difference in the cholesterol
content, but as you'll see, not to your guests' ultimate
taste satisfaction.

BROWNING THE MEAT – It really helps to give the
meat enough heat, time and space to be properly
browned. Get the pan very hot and dry the meat
completely with paper towels. Drop each piece in
separately to give it enough space to roll on to its
side and brown before you add the next piece. The
point here is that normally meat never browns – it
sits there and simmers in its own juices (meat is 70%
water) rather than developing the essential 'scorched'
taste that adds depth of flavour without fat.

PAPRIKA – Usually added in two stages, one early
and the second immediately before serving.

About the Ingredients

HUNGARIAN PAPRIKA – The most esteemed of all
paprikas! Varying in degree of 'hotness', paprika is
made by drying and then grinding the flesh of red
chilli
peppers. To achieve the hotness, a suitable amount of
the pepper seed is added. If you have a sweet paprika
at home, add some cayenne pepper to it and you will
have a good substitute.

TOMATO PASTE – Provides a wonderful colour and
depth to any dish. It is made by extracting the liquid
and pulp of tomatoes and concentrating them to no
less than 24% solids. Tomato sauce and purée are
usually about 10–12% solids. Tomato paste can be
added to soups, sauces and casseroles, but make sure
you buy the no-salt variety (really no salt added). Best
purchased in the small 6-oz/170-g size.

SILVERSIDE – Usually bought as a small boned joint
for pot-roasting, this cut of beef comes from a section
below the rump, called the round. Other cuts that
come from the round are topside and leg. Silverside
is not as well marbled as, say, sirloin of beef – a
favourite of long standing for the traditional roast.
Because of this the texture is not as 'buttery', but
it does have an excellent flavour and an attractive
appearance. Remember, the more marbling, the more
fat, making silverside an excellent Minimax choice for
roasting and carving. Choose a silverside that is well
coloured and firm to the touch. Silverside can of
course be cubed and used in soups and stews, as in
this recipe.

BEEF CHILLI

Here it is, and I know that everyone has their favourite! Mine has only 11 grams of fat and 393 calories, which, when compared to a 'Grand Prize' recipe, which had 44 grams of fat and 663 calories, was a major drop. But the Minimax version also has substantial flavour and good fibre at 10 grams per serving.

I found some small bean pots that hold ½ pint/285 ml when filled to the brim. I filled these pots almost to the top, set them on a colourful plate and served crusty bread and a tossed salad on the side.

Nutritional Profile

PER SERVING	CLASSIC	MINIMAX
Calories	663	393
Fat (g)	44	11
Calories from fat	60%	26%
Cholesterol (mg)	129	59
Sodium (mg)	1185	381
Fibre (g)	8	10

■ *Classic compared:* Grand Prize Chilli

Time Estimate

Hands On Unsupervised									
Minutes	10	20	30	40	50	60	70	80	90

Cost Estimate

Low	Medium	Medium High	Celebration

Serves 6

INGREDIENTS

1½ lb/680 g silverside of beef

1 tablespoon/15 ml extra light olive oil with a dash of sesame oil

1 large onion, peeled and finely chopped

2 garlic cloves, peeled and diced

2 red chilli peppers, de-seeded and chopped

A 6-oz/170-g tin no-salt tomato paste

1 teaspoon/5 ml cayenne pepper

1 tablespoon/15 ml powdered cumin

12 fl oz/340 ml cold water

12 fl oz/340 ml de-alcoholized red wine

4 fl oz/113 ml bulgur wheat

1 teaspoon/5 ml baking powder

Two 15-oz/425-g tins pinto beans, drained, to give 1¼ pints/700 ml beans

6 tablespoons/90 ml spring onions, finely minced

6 teaspoons/30 ml mild Cheddar cheese, grated

FIRST PREPARE

■ Cut half of the beef into ¼-inch/0.75-cm cubes. Cut the remaining beef into strips and grind it coarsely. Use the bread trick to make sure you've ground all the meat (see page 71).

NOW COOK

■ Here's a new way of browning meat. Pour the oil over the cubed meat and stir until completely coated. This will prevent the meat from simmering in its own juices. Now drop it into a very hot, high-sided casserole pan and cook each cube on all sides for 5 minutes. Notice the cubes are nice and brown! Also note the dark brown residue on the bottom of the pan. Scrape it up to provide a wonderful depth of taste. When the cubes are brown, stir in the ground beef and cook until all the pink is gone.

■ Add the onion, garlic and chilli pepper. Stir in the tomato paste. Now you will see the Maillard reaction: a darkening colour change in the tomato paste that is the source of a deep, smoky taste. Stir in the cayenne pepper and the cumin.

■ Take the pan off the heat and stir in 8 fl oz/227 ml of the cold water. Scrape any residue off the bottom of the pan. Stir in 8 fl oz/227 ml of the de-alcoholized wine. Breathe deeply: what an aroma! Put the pot back on very low heat, cover and simmer for approximately 1 hour, or until the meat chunks are tender.

■ Put the bulgur in a 1½-pint/1-l container. In a small saucepan, boil together the remaining water and the remaining wine and then pour them on to the bulgur. Let it stand until the bulgur has absorbed all the liquid – about 5 minutes.

■ After the beef has simmered for 1 hour, mix in the cooked bulgur and baking powder. Stir in additional liquid, either water or wine, to your desired consistency. I prefer wine, feeling that wine added to the end of a dish is like the last spray of perfume before a woman leaves her room.

■ Put the pinto beans in a strainer and place over a pan with steaming water. Cover and steam until the beans are warm – about 15 minutes.

■ *To Serve:* Place 4 fl oz/113 ml of the beans in each serving dish and smother them with 4 fl oz/113 ml of the chilli. Dust each with 1 tablespoon/15 ml of minced spring onions and 1 teaspoon/5 ml of cheese.

About the Ingredients

HOMEMADE CHILLI POWDER – Cayenne and cumin are the two essential ingredients for any chilli powder. Instead of buying prepared chilli powder, try mixing these two spices at home to make your own. They can be combined in varying amounts to suit your own taste.

GRATED CHEESE – Cheddar is an excellent cooking cheese as it doesn't turn stringy and a little of its flavour goes a long way. It is a semi-hard cheese and grates well, but you may like to experiment with some of the less widely available hard cheeses if you live near a supplier. As well as the popular Parmesan, try Italian Asiago, Caciocavallo, Pecorino and Provolone (a smoked cheese). The Greeks have Kefalotyri, which is used in several national dishes, and from Switzerland you may come across Sbrinz and Sapsago (which has the aroma and green colour of dried clover). Bergkäse is a mild hard cheese from Austria.

SANCOCHO

One-pot cooking makes so much sense, and this great Puerto Rican dish is such a good example. At the heart of it must be a good meat broth and lots of fresh vegetables. In this recipe the meat is more a condiment than the star attraction.

One-pot cooking also means one-pot serving! There is enough going on here to simply serve Sancocho from a good-looking earthy casserole dish with a swiftly flashing ladle!

Nutritional Profile

PER SERVING	CLASSIC	MINIMAX
Calories	1265	353
Fat (g)	46	11
Calories from fat	33%	27%
Cholesterol (mg)	225	55
Sodium (mg)	2283	215
Fibre (g)	15	5

■ *Classic compared:* Sancocho Especial

Time Estimate

Hands On								
Unsupervised								

| Minutes | 10 | 20 | 30 | 40 | 50 | 60 | 70 | 80 | 90 |

Cost Estimate

Low	Medium	Medium High	Celebration

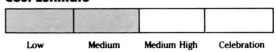

Serves 6

INGREDIENTS

1 tablespoon/15 ml extra light olive oil with a dash of sesame oil

1 large onion, peeled and diced

1 tablespoon/15 ml fresh garlic, minced

1 sweet green pepper, de-seeded and cut in ½-inch/1.5-cm cubes

2 sweet red peppers, de-seeded and cut in ½-inch/1.5-cm cubes

12 oz/340 g silverside of beef, trimmed and cut in ½-inch/1.5-cm cubes

8 oz/227 g pork shoulder, trimmed and cut in ½-inch/1.5-cm cubes

2 oz/57 g ham, finely cubed

¾ pint/450 ml beef stock (recipe page 210)

4 oz/113 g fresh yam, peeled and cut in ½-inch/1.5-cm cubes

4 oz/113 g fresh pumpkin meat, peeled and cut in ½-inch/1.5-cm cubes

4 oz/113 g potatoes, peeled and cut in ½-inch/1.5-cm cubes

4 oz/113 g unpeeled Jerusalem artichoke or peeled cassava root, cut in ½-inch/1.5-cm cubes

1 large plantain, cut in ½-inch/1.5-cm slices

¾ pint/450 ml cooked maize kernels

2 tablespoons/30 ml arrowroot mixed with 4 tablespoons/60 ml water

1 tablespoon/15 ml fresh coriander leaves, finely chopped

¼ teaspoon/1.25 ml black pepper, freshly ground

BOUQUET GARNI

3 sprigs fresh coriander leaves

1 bay leaf

1 teaspoon/5 ml marjoram

1 teaspoon/5 ml black peppercorns, cracked

3 whole cloves

NOW COOK

■ Heat the oil in a large stockpot and sauté the onion, garlic and peppers for 5 minutes. Remove the vegetables and set aside.

■ Increase the heat and add the beef, pork and ham to the stockpot. When the meat is browned, return the vegetables to the pot.

■ Pour in the beef stock, add the bouquet garni, cover and bring to the boil, then simmer gently for 45 minutes.

■ Add the yam, pumpkin and potato. Cover and simmer for 30 minutes.

■ Add the Jerusalem artichoke, plantain and corn and simmer for another 10 minutes. Remove the stockpot from the heat, add the arrowroot paste, return to the heat and stir until thickened. Mix in the chopped coriander leaves and the black pepper. Remove the bouquet garni before serving, of course.

Helpful Hints and Observations

JERUSALEM ARTICHOKE vs CASSAVA – I have suggested Jerusalem artichoke instead of the classic cassava because cassava is high in calories (262 per 100 g) and carbohydrate but low on protein, vitamins and minerals. If you decide to use cassava it must be added to the pot at the same time as the yam, pumpkin and potato.

OVERNIGHT IMPROVES THE FLAVOUR – As with most casseroles, Sancocho improves if kept under refrigeration overnight. The flavours seem to melt together.

BOUQUET GARNI – Cut a piece of muslin or cheesecloth about 4 inches/10 cm square. Place the herbs and spices in the middle, bring all four corners of the muslin together and tie securely into a small pouch. Hit it several times with the back of a knife to bruise the herbs and spices, helping them to release their volatile oils.

About the Ingredients

PLANTAIN – In appearance the plantain is very similar to a banana, only it's larger and not as sweet. The starchy plantain is used as a vegetable in Central America and the Caribbean. Indeed, plantains are served with almost any main course – pork, beef, chicken, or fish. They must be cooked before eating. You can buy them when they're an unripe green colour – they will ripen at room temperature at home.

JERUSALEM ARTICHOKE – Small, knobbly, edible tubers, very similar to root ginger in appearance, these are on sale in winter and spring. They have a sweet, nutty flavour and a crunchy texture when raw, and are good as dips or in salads. As a cooked vegetable they can become mushy, but simmered gently, unpeeled, for 8 to 10 minutes, they remain al dente. They are rich in phosphorus and potassium. They are not related to artichokes and have nothing to do with Jerusalem! The name is an adaptation of the Italian *girasole*, meaning 'sunflower', which the plants resemble.

COTTAGE PIE

Like any great 'food of the people' dish, this English classic has many local variations. Mine reduces the meat and adds bulgur wheat, but in my judgement does no disservice to the original's flavour . . . in fact, it seems better than most!

The Cottage Pie has such an attractive golden-brown appearance that you can dish it up at the table. You'll need to add at least one fresh vegetable on the side. One of our favourites is freshly steamed Swiss chard, with perhaps half an orange-fleshed sweet potato.

Nutritional Profile

PER SERVING	CLASSIC	MINIMAX
Calories	653	464
Fat (g)	35	12
Calories from fat	49%	23%
Cholesterol (mg)	109	47
Sodium (mg)	584	325
Fibre (g)	7	8

■ *Classic compared:* Cottage Pie

Time Estimate

Hands On									
Unsupervised									

Minutes 10 20 30 40 50 60 70 80 90

Cost Estimate

Low	Medium	Medium High	Celebration

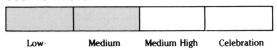

Serves 6

INGREDIENTS

1½ lb/680 g potatoes
½ teaspoon/2.5 ml salt, freshly ground
⅛ teaspoon/0.6 ml white pepper, freshly ground
8 fl oz/227 ml buttermilk
Dusting of nutmeg
4 teaspoons/20 ml extra light olive oil with a dash of sesame oil
1 onion, peeled and finely diced
1 medium carrot, peeled and finely diced
1 garlic clove, peeled and finely chopped
1 tablespoon/15 ml fresh parsley, chopped
1 tablespoon/15 ml fresh thyme, chopped
1 tablespoon/15 ml fresh marjoram, chopped
16 fl oz/450 ml beef stock (recipe page 210)
4 tablespoons/57 ml bulgur wheat
1 tablespoon/15 ml soy sauce
¾ lb/340 g extra lean ground beef
3 tablespoons/45 ml no-salt tomato paste
1 tablespoon/15 ml horseradish, freshly grated
1 tablespoon/15 ml arrowroot mixed with 4 fl oz/113 ml beef stock

NOW COOK

■ Bake the potatoes at 350°F /180°C/Gas Mark 4 for 1 hour. When cool enough to handle, scoop out the flesh (you can save the skins for a snack – see Cynthia's Skins, page 177), place in a large bowl and stir in ¼ teaspoon/1.25 ml of the salt, the pepper, buttermilk and nutmeg. Continue stirring until you have creamy mashed potatoes. Set aside.

■ In a large low-sided pan, heat 1 tablespoon/15 ml of the olive oil and fry the onion, carrot and garlic until the onion becomes soft and slightly translucent.

■ Add the parsley, thyme and marjoram.

■ In a small saucepan, heat half the beef stock. Pour this over the bulgur wheat and stir in the soy sauce. Leave the bulgur to stand for 10 minutes to soften.

■ In a medium-sized wok or skillet, heat the remaining olive oil. Pinch the ground beef into 1-inch/2.5-cm chunks and drop them into the pan. Turn the chunks, allowing all sides to brown. Stir in the tomato paste and continue to cook until the tomato deepens in colour.

■ Put the ground beef mixture into the large pan with the vegetables.

■ Pour the remaining beef stock into the empty wok or skillet. Scrape up the residue. Pour stock and residue into the beef-vegetable mixture.

■ Add the bulgur wheat, horseradish and remaining salt, and stir thoroughly.

■ Bring to the boil, cover and simmer for 15 minutes.

■ Remove from the heat and stir in the arrowroot mixture. Pour the contents of the pan into a flameproof serving dish.

■ Pipe the mashed potatoes on top of the filling and spread the potatoes to cover the beef with an attractive ribbed top. Pop under the grill to brown for 3 minutes.

Helpful Hints and Observations

BAKED MASHED POTATOES – I make the best mashed potatoes by baking large, mature potatoes in their skins, then scooping out the centres, mashing them and adding buttermilk, salt, white pepper and nutmeg. The result is infinitely better than the waterlogged mush you often get from boiling potatoes. The baking process actually steams the extra water *out* rather than boiling water *in*. You don't really need to mash – I just use a ricer to remove any lumps. It looks like a large garlic press.

THE BASIC MINCED BEEF RECIPE – You can use the minced beef recipe given here for any number of recipes that call for a hamburger-style meat sauce. It has lots of flavour and is quite low in fat.

About the Ingredients

BULGUR – I know it looks a little strange but bulgur is actually just wheat kernels that have been boiled, dried and then cracked. It's very simple to prepare and, as you will taste from this recipe, bulgur also has a charming, nutty flavour. It's been a staple food of people in the Middle East for thousands of years. So, now that you've been introduced, get cooking with bulgur: in salads, soups, or just eaten by itself.

BEEF – The sixty million dollar question (from a cattleman's point of view): can you still enjoy beef on a low fat diet? The answer is demonstrated in this recipe: ¾ lb/340 grams of beef to feed 6 people! Most nutritionists will advise that 4 oz/113 g is the maximum serving portion. The other factor to consider: look at the percentage of fat written on pre-packed meat labels. Utilizing these two factors, most healthy people can keep small amounts of beef in their diet and experience its many nutritional benefits: iron, B vitamins and zinc, to name just a few!

STEAK AND OYSTER PIE

$\mathcal{N}$othing *represents the best of British food as well as beef-based pies with kidneys, mushrooms and oysters. Unfortunately in classic form, these pies are riddled with cholesterol; and the crust, when cooked on the meat, can be mostly sodden on the underside. I've set out to bring some relief!*

I've replaced the traditional butter in the crust with a polyunsaturated margarine. In a careful taste test, I found no discernible difference in flavour or texture (probably because of the extra flavour from the wheatgerm).

I serve the crust as a separate wedge – very crisp and delicious. Part of me says that it isn't right, because it isn't a pie: it's a stew with a piece of pastry. I just wanted you to know how I feel!

Nutritional Profile

PER SERVING	CLASSIC	MINIMAX
Calories	906	228
Fat (g)	48	9
Calories from fat	48%	37%
Cholesterol (mg)	395	58
Sodium (mg)	682	210
Fibre (g)	4	2

■ *Classic compared*: Steak, Kidney and Oyster Pie

Time Estimate

Hands On									
Unsupervised									
Minutes	10	20	30	40	50	60	70	80	90

Cost Estimate

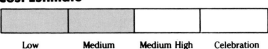

Low	Medium	Medium High	Celebration

INGREDIENTS

PIE CRUST

6 oz/170 g plain flour

4 tablespoons/57 ml wheatgerm

3 oz/85 g margarine, cut into 12 small pieces and well chilled

5 tablespoons/75 ml iced water

1 tablespoon/15 ml semi-skimmed milk

FILLING

1 teaspoon/5 ml extra light olive oil with a dash of sesame oil

2 onions, peeled and cut in chunks

2 carrots, peeled and cut in chunks

12 oz/340 g silverside of beef, cut in ½-inch/1.5-cm cubes

3 tablespoons/45 ml tomato paste

12 oz/340 g large mushrooms, wiped clean and sliced, stems included

¾ pint/450 ml beef stock (recipe page 210)

8 large shelled oysters (with reserved liquid from a jar or tin), drained and chopped

2 tablespoons/30 ml oyster sauce

2 tablespoons/30 ml arrowroot mixed with 4 table-spoons/60 ml water

Black pepper, freshly ground

Fresh parsley, chopped

BOUQUET GARNI

1 bay leaf

1 teaspoon/5 ml fresh thyme

1 tablespoon/15 ml fresh parsley

3 whole cloves

1 teaspoon/5 ml black peppercorns

TO MAKE THE PIE CRUST

NOTE: You can do this during the hour the filling is cooking.

■ Pre-heat the oven to 425°F/220°C/Gas Mark 7.

■ Sift the flour into a bowl and stir in the wheatgerm.

■ Pinch the chilled margarine pieces into the flour with the tips of your fingers.

■ Stir in the iced water until the mixture forms a stiff mass. Turn out on to a floured board and roll into an oblong shape. The less you handle it the better!

■ Fold the bottom third towards the centre and the top third on top. Give the dough a quarter turn, roll it out to an oblong again, and fold as before. Repeat this process once more.

■ Roll the pastry out to an 11-inch/28-cm diameter circle. Trim the rough edges. For a more attractive crust you can crimp the edge as in an oldfashioned apple pie.

■ Transfer to a baking tray. Lightly score eight wedges in the dough without cutting all the way through. Brush lightly with the milk. Prick to help release steam during the baking process.

■ Bake in the pre-heated oven for 12 to 15 minutes or until golden and crisp. Cool on a wire rack.

TO MAKE THE FILLING

■ Heat the oil in a large ovenproof casserole with a lid. Add the onions and carrots and sauté for about 1 minute on high heat. Transfer the vegetables to a bowl and set aside.

■ Add the meat to the casserole and brown on all sides. Stir in the tomato paste, scraping the bottom of the pan so that all the juices and residue are mixed together. Cook for 3 to 4 minutes.

■ Add the mushrooms to the carrots and onions. Stir two-thirds of this mixture into the meat.

■ Pour in the stock and reserved oyster juice all at once and stir. Add the bouquet garni and the oyster sauce. Cover and simmer for 1 hour.

■ Add the remaining mushrooms, carrots, onions and the oysters to the mixture. Remove the pot from the heat and stir in the arrowroot mixture. Return to the heat and stir until thickened. Season with black pepper.

ASSEMBLE AND SERVE

■ Spoon the filling into a high-sided 9-inch/23-cm pie dish. Place the pie crust on top and heat in a 400°F/205°C/Gas Mark 6 oven for 5 minutes.

■ Cut the pie crust into wedges and set each one over two large spoonfuls of the filling. Garnish with parsley.

Helpful Hints and Observations

UPPER CRUST? – The crust I've used has less fat than is usual by at least 4 oz/113 g. It is made very quickly (another benefit compared with the time-consuming puff pastry) and because of the wheatgerm addition, it is speckled in an attractive way and has a toasted, nutty flavour.

About the Ingredients

OYSTERS – They should look plump and cream-coloured in a clear liquor. Since they are to be cooked, buy the least expensive.

WHEATGERM – See page 181.

BLINCHATY PIROG

This is the Russian equivalent of the American Sloppy Joe or the British Mince on Toast. Language does have quite a romantic influence, doesn't it? I have substantially increased the mushroom content and played some other games . . . and . . . it works!

Serve it whole and cut it in wedges as you would a pie. You will need a pie server to save a spill en route! Fresh green beans (if in season) are wonderful with this and I'm fond of large grilled tomatoes to add colour as well as taste.

Nutritional Profile

PER SERVING	CLASSIC	MINIMAX
Calories	945	359
Fat (g)	62	12
Calories from fat	59%	30%
Cholesterol (mg)	339	63
Sodium (mg)	404	359
Fibre (g)	3	3

■ *Classic compared:* Meat Pirog

Time Estimate

	10	20	30	40	50	60	70	80	90

Hands On
Unsupervised
Minutes

Cost Estimate

Low	Medium	Medium High	Celebration

Serves 6

INGREDIENTS

CREPE BATTER

1 whole egg
1 egg yolk
½ pint/284 ml skimmed milk
4 oz/113 g plain flour
¼ teaspoon/1.25 ml salt
1 tablespoon/15 ml extra light olive oil with a dash of sesame oil

BEEF FILLING

1 tablespoon/15 ml extra light olive oil with a dash of sesame oil
4 fl oz/113 ml onion, peeled and chopped
2 garlic cloves, peeled and crushed
12 oz/340 g silverside of beef, coarsely ground
3 tablespoons/45 ml tomato paste
8 fl oz/227 ml water
8 fl oz/227 ml de-alcoholized dry red wine
1 tablespoon/15 ml arrowroot mixed with 1 tablespoon/15 ml water

MUSHROOM FILLING

1 tablespoon/15 ml extra light olive oil with a dash of sesame oil
12 oz/340 g mushrooms, finely chopped
3 spring onions, trimmed and chopped
1 teaspoon/5 ml cayenne pepper
1 tablespoon/15 ml lemon juice, freshly squeezed
8 oz/113 ml cooked rice
⅛ teaspoon/0.6 ml black pepper, freshly ground
2 oz/57 g low-fat cottage cheese
1 teaspoon/5 ml fresh dill, chopped

SAUCE

12 fl oz/340 ml strained yogurt (recipe page 210)
2½ fl oz/70 ml de-alcoholized white wine
1 tablespoon/15 ml dill, chopped

GARNISH

6 sprigs fresh dill

FIRST PREPARE THE CREPES

■ In a small bowl, mix the whole egg, egg yolk and milk. Sift the flour and salt into a medium bowl and make a well in the centre. Pour the egg mixture into the well and gradually stir it together with the flour until fully incorporated with no lumps. Strain through a sieve. Set the batter aside in a cool place and let it rest for 30 minutes. The resting will relax the starch cells in the batter and provide a more delicately finished crêpe.

■ Heat an 8-inch/20-cm sauté pan to medium. Pour the olive oil into the pan, swish it around, then pour it into the crêpe batter and mix thoroughly. This will help make the crêpe self-releasing.

■ Pour 2 fl oz/57 ml of crêpe batter into the sauté pan. Rotate the pan until the entire surface is covered.

■ When the edges of the crêpe start curling up and the top looks waxy, flip the crêpe over. Cook the other side until it turns light brown, just a minute or two, then turn it out on to a dish. Make four more, giving you a stack of five.

■ Pour 4 fl oz/113 ml of batter into a 10-inch/25-cm sauté pan. Cook in the same manner as the smaller crêpes and set aside.

NOW COOK

■ *Beef Filling*: Heat the olive oil in a large skillet, and brown the onion and garlic until the onion is translucent (approximately 2 minutes). Transfer to a plate. Clean out the skillet, leaving no trace of onion.

■ Add the beef to the skillet and brown. Stir in the tomato paste and cook until it has a dark brown colour, but is not burnt – about 4 minutes. Take off the heat and add the water to cool down the beef. This is done so that the wine, when added, won't evaporate too quickly. Put the pan back on high heat and add the wine, the cooked onion and garlic. Bring to the boil, then lower the heat to medium. Remove from the heat and add the arrowroot paste. Stir thoroughly and reheat to thicken.

■ *Mushroom Filling*: Put the olive oil and mushrooms in a 10½-inch/27-cm heated saucepan and sauté the mushrooms for approximately 5 minutes. Remove from the heat and add the spring onions, cayenne and lemon juice.

■ *To Assemble*: Mix the mushroom filling into the beef mixture. Add the cooked rice and the black pepper. At the last moment stir in the cottage cheese and distribute evenly.

■ Place one small crêpe on a plate. Cover with a thick layer of meat mixture. Place another of the smaller crêpes on top. Repeat these layers, finishing with a layer of meat. Cover with the larger crêpe. Garnish with the chopped dill.

■ *The Sauce*: Mix the yogurt with the de-alcoholized white wine and the chopped dill.

■ *To Serve*: Dollop a spoonful or two of the sauce on to a plate and place a wedge of the Pirog on it. Garnish with a sprig of dill and enjoy!

MOUSSAKA

*O*riginally this classic was made in Romania, but it has become one of the greatest examples of Greek 'food of the people'. I have made several changes in order to lower the health risks. As always, the taste values are less velvety without the oil and lamb fat, but the overall flavour is still there.

This dish is usually served at the table from the pan it's cooked in. I really enjoy a mixed wild rice and long grain rice pilaf with it (see page 79) and some perfectly cooked tiny green peas.

Nutritional Profile

PER SERVING	CLASSIC	MINIMAX
Calories	756	176
Fat (g)	64	6
Calories from fat	76%	30%
Cholesterol (mg)	231	60
Sodium (mg)	4934	461
Fibre (g)	4	2

■ *Classic compared:* Moussaka

Time Estimate

Hands On Unsupervised									
Minutes	10	20	30	40	50	60	70	80	90

Cost Estimate

Low	Medium	Medium High	Celebration

Serves 6

INGREDIENTS

1 teaspoon/5 ml extra light olive oil with a dash of sesame oil

8 fl oz/227 ml onion, peeled and finely diced

1 garlic clove, peeled and minced

12 oz/340 g ground lamb

3 tablespoons/45 ml low-salt tomato paste

4 tablespoons/57 ml bulgur wheat

1 teaspoon/5 ml dried oregano

8 fl oz/227 ml water

8 fl oz/227 ml de-alcoholized red wine

⅛ teaspoon/0.6 ml ground cinnamon

1 bay leaf

⅛ teaspoon/0.6 ml salt, freshly ground

¼ teaspoon/1.25 ml black pepper, freshly ground

A 13-oz/370-g aubergine, peeled and sliced

1 oz/28 g + 2 tablespoons/30 ml Parmesan cheese, freshly grated

SAUCE

8 fl oz/227 ml skimmed milk

⅛ teaspoon/0.6 ml nutmeg, freshly ground

⅛ teaspoon/0.6 salt, freshly ground

2 tablespoons/30 ml cornflour mixed with 4 tablespoons/60 ml water

1 egg yolk, lightly beaten

NOW COOK

■ In a large wok or frying pan, heat the oil and sauté the onion and garlic until the onion is soft and translucent. Turn out on to a plate and set aside.

■ In the same pan, brown the lamb. Add the tomato paste, bulgur, cooked onion and garlic, oregano and water. Stir, scraping any residue off the bottom of the pan and into the mixture for added depth of taste. Add the wine, cinnamon, bay leaf, salt and pepper.

■ Layer one-third of the aubergine slices on the bottom of a ceramic or glass soufflé dish. Cover with half the lamb and sprinkle with a third of the 1 oz/28 g of cheese. Repeat with one-third of the aubergine, the remaining lamb and one-third of the cheese, finishing with a layer of aubergine and the other third of the cheese.

■ *The Sauce*: In a 2½-pint/1.4-l saucepan, heat the milk. Sprinkle with the nutmeg and salt. Gradually stir in the cornflour paste and bring to the boil. Remove from the heat. Pour a little of the sauce into the beaten egg yolk, then stir it back into the sauce. This will prevent the egg yolk from curdling.

■ Pour the sauce over the Moussaka layers and sprinkle with the remaining Parmesan cheese. Bake in the oven at 350°F/180°C/Gas Mark 4 for 40 minutes. When done, the aubergine will separate from the sides of the soufflé pan, revealing the bubbling juices.

■ Slice the Moussaka into six even wedges and serve.

Helpful Hints and Observations

ON SALTING AUBERGINE – A great many recipes call for salting aubergine slices liberally and then pressing them to reduce both bitterness and excess water content. The slices are then cooked in oil or lamb fat.

I chose to buy a smaller-sized aubergine, not more than 3 inches/8 cm in diameter, and simply peeled it, sliced it and slipped it naked into the sauce – no salt, no oil, no bother and no bitterness! I did add the bulgur wheat to soak up any surplus liquid.

The result of these efforts is clear from the numbers: an incredible drop of 57 grams of fat, 580 calories and 4,473 mg of sodium – for each serving!

My local deli owner is Greek. The day after this recipe went on television he looked at me, bit his finger and shook his head in mock bewilderment – then he smiled!

About the Ingredients

AUBERGINE – Despite its other name, eggplant, not always egg-shaped: it can be round or even long. The colour ranges from purple-black through to white, although purple varieties are by far the most common. Buy aubergine with skin that's shiny and a stem-cap that's bright green. The skin should feel firm, not mushy. The smaller aubergines have less seeds and more tender skins.

ROGAN JOSH

This recipe was developed in co-operation with Mr Ranjan Dey, of the excellent New Delhi restaurant on Ellis Street in San Francisco.

The cuisine of Northern India is heavily influenced by the Aryan peoples of the northern borders. This is where the yogurt and lamb comes from. When you smell the combination of garlic, ginger and the sweet, warm spices, then you always know exactly where you are!

The classic way to dish up the lamb is with a good basmati rice, 8 oz/227 ml raw for three servings, and a variety of chutneys, chapatis (flat bread) and sliced fruits as side dishes.

Nutritional Profile

PER SERVING	CLASSIC	MINIMAX
Calories	1038	378
Fat (g)	63	13
Calories from fat	55%	31%
Cholesterol (mg)	204	80
Sodium (mg)	333	140
Fibre (g)	4	2

■ *Classic compared:* Rogan Josh

Time Estimate

Hands On
Unsupervised
Minutes 10 20 30 40 50 60 70 80 90

Cost Estimate

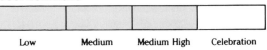

Low   Medium   Medium High   Celebration

Serves 6

INGREDIENTS

2 tablespoons/30 ml extra light olive oil with a dash of sesame oil

4 garlic cloves, peeled and finely diced

16 fl oz/450 ml onion, chopped

1 tablespoon/15 ml ginger root, freshly grated

½ teaspoon/2.5 ml cayenne pepper

¼ teaspoon/1.25 ml powdered nutmeg

½ teaspoon/2.5 ml turmeric

¼ teaspoon/1.25 ml mace

1½ teaspoons/7.5 ml paprika

1 teaspoon/5 ml garam masala

1½ lb/680 g lean leg of lamb, cut in 1-inch/2.5-cm cubes

1 tablespoon/15 ml ground coriander seeds

16 fl oz/450 ml peeled and chopped tomatoes

⅛ teaspoon/0.6 ml salt, freshly ground

1 tablespoon/15 ml cornflour combined with 2 tablespoons/30 ml water

6 fl oz/170 ml plain non-fat yogurt

6 fl oz/170 ml water

1 tablespoon/15 ml fresh coriander leaves, chopped

1¼ pints/700 ml steamed rice (see page 47)

NOW COOK

■ Heat half the olive oil in an 11-inch/28-cm wok. Stir in the garlic, onion, ginger and cayenne pepper. Sauté until the onion is slightly softened and appears translucent. Stir in the nutmeg, turmeric, mace, paprika and garam masala.

■ Put 13-inch/33-cm pan on high heat and add the remaining olive oil. Drop the lamb cubes in around the edges, allowing them to brown fully on one side (see *Helpful Hints*). Add the ground coriander seeds.

■ Stir in the sautéd onion mixture. Now add the tomatoes and the salt.

■ Blend in the cornflour paste, yogurt and water. Cover and simmer for 1 hour. Uncover and cook for another 30 minutes. Sprinkle with chopped coriander leaves. Serve each portion on 4 fl oz/113 ml of steamed rice.

Helpful Hints and Observations

SPICE SAUTE – A classic Indian method calls for the warm, citrus-like spice of coriander and the bite of cayenne pepper to be added to the oil before frying the meat. I've adapted this idea using much less fat. In a six-person dish, up to 6 fl oz/170 ml of oil or clarified butter (ghee) can be added. I've dropped this down to 2 tablespoons/30 ml.

ONE-SIDED SAUTE – I learned a completely new technique during the development of this dish. In India, the meat is never browned; instead they leave it open to receive maximum spice penetration. Because I struggle to lower fat levels, I need to brown the meat to replace the perception of depth of taste you get when plenty of fat holds the flavour longer. Eventually I settled for a one-side-only browning: I got my depth of taste, Mr Dey got his spice absorption, and a new technique that works well for all manner of casseroles was born!

NON-FAT YOGURT AND THE BREAKING PROBLEM – Whole yogurt, with its 3.5% fat content, can be added to hot dishes and stirred in without separating (what I call 'breaking'). When the fat is removed, yogurt moves apart into a million tiny flecks (I haven't counted them but it seems a fair estimate). To counter this I've added a small amount of cornflour as a binder. It seems to work and it's a lot better than resorting to more fat.

About the Ingredients

GARAM MASALA – The secret of India's great curries is here: there is no such thing as curry powder. Instead they mix their own blend of spices to create a specific curry taste for each individual dish. Garam masala is as close as you can get to the aromas of an Indian curry without blending your own spices. You might want to use it as a base, and then add your own finishing flourishes. Generally the basic ingredients of garam masala include coriander seeds, cumin seeds, cloves, cinnamon and black pepper. Blend your own if you can't find it commercially available.

MACE – This fragrant spice might sound unfamiliar but it is actually part of a familiar friend. It is ground from the dried outer covering of the nutmeg!

PORK TENDERLOIN WITH GLAZED PEARS

*A*nother dish from my 'galloping' days and, remarkably, it wasn't too bad! I've adjusted it a bit in order to further reduce the fat and I'm delighted at having found a new technique that gives fresh fruit a light pickled spice.

The colours of the dish are really wonderful. They don't need anything in the reds or oranges to fight the plump, pale, saffron-tinted pears. So I'd recommend just adding some freshly steamed French beans with a hint of nutmeg.

Nutritional Profile

PER SERVING	CLASSIC	MINIMAX
Calories	472	485
Fat (g)	14	13
Calories from fat	26%	25%
Cholesterol (mg)	125	109
Sodium (mg)	197	301
Fibre (g)	2	2

■ *Classic compared:* Pork Tenderloin with Glazed Pears

Time Estimate

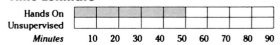

Hands On									
Unsupervised									
Minutes	10	20	30	40	50	60	70	80	90

Cost Estimate

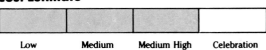

Low	Medium	Medium High	Celebration

Serves 4

INGREDIENTS

2 butterflied pork tenderloins, 8 oz/227 g each
⅛ teaspoon/0.6 ml salt
¼ teaspoon/1.25 ml black pepper, freshly ground
¾ pint/450 ml water
7 tablespoons/105 ml brown sugar
⅛ teaspoon/0.6 ml saffron
½ teaspoon/2.5 ml allspice berries
½ teaspoon/2.5 ml cloves
2 fl oz/57 ml cider vinegar
2 pears, preferably Comice, peeled, halved lengthwise and cored
2 tablespoons/30 ml extra light olive oil with a dash of sesame oil
1 oz/28 g back bacon, trimmed of all fat and diced
1 tablespoon/15 ml honey

NOW COOK

■ Pound the butterflied pork tenderloins until they are ½ inch/1.5 cm thick. Season with salt and pepper.

■ In a medium saucepan, over medium heat, dissolve 4 tablespoons/60 ml of the brown sugar in the water. Add the saffron, allspice berries, cloves and vinegar. Poach the pears in this syrup, turning them so that the 'cup side' is uppermost. This is done so that if there is oxidation, it occurs on the side not seen in the final dish! The poaching process should take about 15 minutes. Remove the pears to a small bowl. Pour the poaching liquid over them and set aside.

■ Heat the olive oil in a small saucepan and fry the bacon for approximately 5 minutes. Brush the oil from the pan over the pork tenderloins and on the base of the grill pan. Sprinkle half the bacon bits on top of the tenderloins. Place under the grill for 6 minutes. Turn the pork, brush with more oil and sprinkle with the remaining bacon bits. Place under the grill for 4 minutes longer.

■ Strain the pears and reserve the poaching liquid. In a skillet over medium heat, mix the honey and the remaining brown sugar. Add 2 fl oz/57 ml of the pear poaching liquid. Bring to the boil, then simmer until reduced to a thin glaze. Add the pears and coat with the glaze.

■ *To Serve*: Cut each tenderloin into ½-inch/1.5-cm slices. Fan a quarter of the tenderloin on each plate and place a glazed pear half in the middle. Brush with the remaining glaze.

Helpful Hints and Observations

TO BUTTERFLY PORK – Make an incision along the pork tenderloins, cutting lengthwise, not quite all the way through, and then open out – or ask your butcher to do this for you!

RE-USING THE SPICED VINEGAR – Simply pour the entire mixture into a sealable plastic bag or container and deep freeze for future use. Make sure you label it just in case you think it could be the fish fumet you made and froze and use it to poach scallops . . . come to think of it, that could work!

BACON BITS SEND SIGNALS – I found that the bacon bits begin to explode on the tenderloin surface at just the stage when the meat is ready to be turned. Imagine that . . . a natural timer!

About the Ingredients

PEARS – I like Comice pears for this recipe. They're the chubby, roundish green pears that are rather sensitive to blemishes and bruise marks. At the greengrocer's, choose pears that are firm but not hard. When are they ready? When the area around their stem gives just slightly under pressure. Remember, when you cook pears it may be better if they're slightly under-ripe.

VINEGARS – When you go to your supermarket, you should see quite an array of vinegars. These vinegar varieties vary distinctly in taste: rich, mellow, or sharp. I prefer the fragrant, light qualities of white wine vinegar in this recipe. Don't be alarmed if you take a wine vinegar home and over time see an eerie, cloudy residue. This is something all vinegars do, and for some obscure reason, it's called 'mothering'. A gentle shake and it's dispersed.

PORK TENDERLOIN – The fresh pork you buy in the shops today is different – it's not as fatty! Pork breeders are actually feeding their pigs differently to get leaner meat. The tenderloin cut I use in this recipe is the tenderest part of the pork. At the butcher's, look for pork that is pink to pinkish-white and firm to the touch.

HAWK'S PRAIRIE ENCHILADA

Chef Richard Wright of the Hawk's Prairie Inn, located just off Highway 5 near Olympia, Washington, has been creating special low-fat dishes for over ten years. I wanted to honour him and his work with a recipe made up from a list of his favourite ingredients.

Obviously this dish borrows from the Mexican style and so it helps to create an attractive, colourful setting. If you enjoy this type of dish, you could get some simple bold table-top china to help in the celebration. Olé!

Nutritional Profile

PER SERVING	CLASSIC	MINIMAX
Calories	685	532
Fat (g)	35	17
Calories from fat	46%	28%
Cholesterol (mg)	84	44
Sodium (mg)	2028	371
Fibre (g)	11	9

■ *Classic Compared:* Hawk's Prairie Enchilada

Time Estimate

Hands On										
Unsupervised										

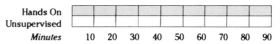

| Minutes | 10 | 20 | 30 | 40 | 50 | 60 | 70 | 80 | 90 |

Cost Estimate

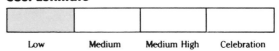

Low	Medium	Medium High	Celebration

Serves 6

INGREDIENTS

2 fl oz/57 ml de-alcoholized Chardonnay wine
4 tablespoons fresh basil, chopped
8 fl oz/227 ml strained yogurt (recipe page 210)
Black pepper, freshly ground, to taste
2 heads broccoli
1 lb/450 g smoked ham hocks
2 pints/1.25 l water
8 fl oz/227 ml dried pinto beans
8 fl oz/227 ml wild rice
1 teaspoon/5 ml extra light olive oil
1 large red onion, peeled and cut in ¼-inch/0.75-cm cubes
2 red chilli peppers, de-seeded and chopped
2 garlic cloves, peeled and chopped
2 Italian plum tomatoes, cored and cut in ¼-inch/0.75-cm cubes
12 warm wholewheat tortillas

FIRST PREPARE

■ *For the Sauce*: Add the de-alcoholized Chardonnay wine and half the basil to the strained yogurt. Season with pepper to taste and set aside.

■ Chop the broccoli into individual florets. Trim off the outer skin of the stalks and cut into small pieces.

NOW COOK

■ In a pressure cooker, place the ham hocks and water. Be sure the lid vent is clear of any food particles! Pressure cook for 30 minutes. Remove and discard the ham hocks, skim off the surface fats and add the pinto beans to the pressure cooker. Bring it to the boil. Put the lid on and when the top starts to flutter, begin timing for 5 minutes, then open, add the rice, and cook for 20 minutes more, a total of 25 minutes.

■ In another casserole pan, heat the olive oil. Add the onion, chopped broccoli stalks, chilli peppers and garlic. Cook until the onion is soft, about 5 minutes.

■ Add the cubed tomatoes and broccoli florets. Cover and cook gently for 6 minutes.

■ Add the remaining basil to the cooking vegetables.

■ *To Serve:* Spoon the rice and beans into a warm tortilla and roll up. Serve with the yogurt-wine sauce and the vegetables on the side. You can add a spoonful of the yogurt-wine sauce to help combine the beans with the wild rice, but it isn't absolutely necessary.

Helpful Hints and Observations

■ YOGURT-WINE SAUCE – This is a great idea! I had been looking for an effective alternative to the standard dollop of sour cream and began with the strained yogurt concept, adding the de-alcoholized wine and flavourings. The result was excellent and it made me think of all kinds of sauces that could be developed in this manner. Why not have a go at it yourself?

■ PRESSURE COOKING – I'm delighted to have found a safe and efficient pressure cooker. It has removed all my old apprehensions about the method and it does make the full range of beans and 'whole' rices much more attractive in this speed-conscious world. Imagine: 25 minutes from scratch!

■ HAM HOCK STOCK – It's important to remember to skim the stock before using it to cook the beans and rice. The flavour is wonderful but you really don't need the fats that are released in cooking. You can shred the lean ham meat and add this to the dish. Add another 20 calories per portion if you do.

About the Ingredients

WILD RICE – See page 79.

RED CHILLI PEPPERS – These are the fruit of a piquant type of Capsicum, a group of vegetables native to the New World and first discovered by explorers some time in the 15th century. Sweet or bell peppers, also called pimentos, belong to the same group. Chilli peppers are small and cone-shaped – and hot, especially the seeds. When selecting a chilli, choose one that is firm and glossy. Green in most cases means milder; red means hotter.

HAM HOCKS – A smoked pork product. When boiled, they lend their flavour to soups, stocks and bean dishes.

LOBSCOUSE

Lobscouse originated in the 18th century, when it meant a sailor's meal of meat stewed with vegetables and hard-tack biscuits. More recently a shortened form of the name, Scouse, has come to mean Liverpudlian. Lobscouse itself may be derived from the Dutch lapskous *or the Danish* lapskaus. *Many changes have been made to this recipe since the days of the old clipper ships, but one thing remains the same: it's a wonderful rib-sticking family meal in the depths of winter!*

This is another 'food of the people' dish that gets cooked all at once in one pot. You might like to add some freshly cooked sweet green peas for extra colour, but it isn't strictly necessary.

Nutritional Profile

PER SERVING	CLASSIC	MINIMAX
Calories	592	271
Fat (g)	35	8
Calories from fat	52%	26%
Cholesterol (mg)	78	32
Sodium (mg)	1116	253
Fibre (g)	5	5

■ *Classic compared:* Creamed Pork and Peas

Time Estimate

Hands On		
Unsupervised		
Minutes	10 20 30 40 50 60 70 80 90

Cost Estimate

Low	Medium	Medium High	Celebration

Serves 6

INGREDIENTS

1 tablespoon/15 ml extra light olive oil with a dash of sesame oil

12 oz/340 g lean pork shoulder, cut into ½-inch/1.5-cm cubes

1 large onion, peeled and diced

2 carrots, peeled and sliced

1½ lb/680 g potatoes, peeled and diced into 1-inch/2.5-cm cubes

1 tablespoon/15 ml fresh mint, chopped

1 tablespoon/15 ml fresh thyme, chopped

½ teaspoon/2.5 ml salt, freshly ground

4 fl oz/113 ml yellow split peas

4 fl oz/113 ml green split peas

1¼ pints/680 ml chicken stock (recipe page 210)

3 bay leaves

½ teaspoon/2.5 ml black pepper, freshly ground

8 fl oz/227 ml celery leaves

NOW COOK

■ In a flameproof casserole pot, heat the oil and fry the pork until browned.

■ Scatter the onion over the pork; do not stir. This allows the pork to continue to brown on the bottom of the pot and the onion to steam.

■ Add the carrots and potatoes on top of the onion. Sprinkle in the mint, thyme and salt. Add the yellow and green peas and mix thoroughly, scraping the residue off the bottom of the pan.

■ Pour in the stock, push the bay leaves under the surface and add pepper to taste. Bring to the boil, cover and simmer for 90 minutes.

■ Garnish with the celery leaves.

Helpful Hints and Observations

THE DRY MEAT BENEFIT – It's always a good idea to dry off surface juices from meat, because it enhances the browning process.

About the Ingredients

SPLIT PEAS – Split peas are a wonderful variation on the usual bean theme: you don't have to soak them before cooking. Simply simmer them slowly for 40 or 50 minutes. Have you ever used the yellow split pea before? A refreshing colour change, I think, especially in spring, perhaps, in a kitchen filled with daffodils . . .

MINT – Legend has it that mint was created when an envious Greek deity changed her rival into a plant so that mortals would tramp over her forever. Well I'm afraid that's backfired somewhat because mint is now a valued addition to many recipes. Fortunately, the cool, clean flavour of mint leaves can easily come from your garden. Indeed, mint grows like a weed. So if you haven't started your Minimax herb garden yet, mint might be a marvellous plant with which to start.

TOLTOTT KAPOSZTA *(Hungarian Stuffed Cabbage)*

This is Hungarian 'food of the people' fare. It's fairly simple to fix and makes an occasion out of very plain food. The centre of the cabbage is relatively small so the rest of the filling winds up as a sauce.

I always take the whole cabbage to the table and cut wedges out of it, coating each slice with the meat sauce. Sour cream is traditionally served. I sidestepped this with 2 fl oz/57 ml of strained yogurt added to the sauce. How about whipped potatoes on the side? Or a hunk of dark rye bread?

Nutritional Profile

PER SERVING	CLASSIC	MINIMAX
Calories	372	226
Fat (g)	26	5
Calories from fat	62%	22%
Cholesterol (mg)	203	37
Sodium (mg)	727	295
Fibre (g)	1	9

■ *Classic compared:* Stuffed Cabbage

Time Estimate

Hands On									
Unsupervised									
Minutes	10	20	30	40	50	60	70	80	90

Cost Estimate

Low	Medium	Medium High	Celebration

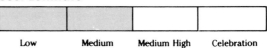

Serves 6

INGREDIENTS

12 oz/340 g pork loin, cut into 2-inch/5-cm cubes

8 fl oz/227 ml onion, peeled and chopped

2 garlic cloves, peeled and chopped

8 oz/227 g mushrooms, coarsely chopped

8 fl oz/227 ml pork or chicken stock (recipe page 210)

2 fl oz/57 ml bulgur wheat

1 medium-sized cabbage head, trimmed, with damaged leaves removed

1 tablespoon/15 ml extra light olive oil with a dash of sesame oil

3 tablespoons/45 ml low-salt tomato paste

1 tablespoon/15 ml + 2 teaspoons/10 ml paprika

½ teaspoon/2.5 ml caraway seeds

⅛ teaspoon/0.6 ml salt, freshly ground

¼ teaspoon/1.25 ml black pepper, freshly ground

2 fl oz/57 ml strained yogurt (recipe page 210)

1 tablespoon/15 ml fresh parsley, chopped

2 tablespoons/30 ml cornflour mixed with 2 tablespoons/30 ml water

Parsley to garnish

FIRST PREPARE

■ Mince the pork, onion, garlic and mushrooms in a meat grinder (remember the bread trick on page 71).

■ Bring the pork or chicken stock to the boil, add the bulgur wheat and simmer 5 minutes. Remove from the heat and set aside for later use in the sauce.

■ In a large saucepan, cover the whole cabbage with water, bring to the boil and cook for 30 minutes. Remove the cabbage from the pan and cool it quickly with cold water. Drain.

NOW COOK

■ Heat the olive oil in a medium-sized wok or large frying pan and add the ground pork mixture. When there is no pink left in the pork meat, add the tomato paste. Sprinkle in 1 tablespoon/15 ml of the paprika and caraway seeds. Remove from the heat, stir in the salt and pepper and the cooked bulgur and set aside.

■ Place the cabbage core-side down on a board. Peel back the leaves without pulling them off at the core. Pull back as many cooked leaves as possible leaving a round inner head about 4 inches/10 cm in diameter. Hollow out the top of this inner head. Fill the hollow with one-third of the pork filling or until packed solid. Set the leftover pork filling aside. Carefully re-fold the cabbage leaves into their original order and position. Wrap securely in muslin or cheesecloth.

■ Place some marbles in the bottom of a large stockpot or flameproof casserole. Put a steamer insert on top of the marbles. Add water to just above the base of the steamer. Place the wrapped cabbage on the steamer and cover. Cook on high heat for 30 minutes. If you hear marbles clanking against the pot, you know it's time to add more water!

■ While the cabbage cooks, put the pork filling back on low heat, cover and simmer. Add additional stock if needed to keep it from sticking.

■ When the cabbage is done, lift it out of the pan with a couple of wooden spoons. Place it in a bowl just large enough to hold it, with the core facing upwards. Cut the muslin or cheesecloth away from the cabbage and fold it over the sides of the bowl. Cover the bowl with a plate and holding it firmly, turn it upside down. Remove the bowl, strip off the muslin or cheesecloth and you've got a big, steamed cabbage sitting right-side up!

■ Add the strained yogurt, the remaining paprika and parsley to the filling. Remove from the heat, stir in the cornflour paste until thickened and return to the heat to boil for about 20 seconds.

■ *To Serve:* Slice the cabbage in wedges like a cake and serve in a small pool of sauce. Garnish with parsley.

Helpful Hints and Observations

THE STEAMER INSERT – By insert I mean one of those stainless steel expanding steamers that open up their multiple leaves to just fit the pot. They stand on short legs and help to keep large re-heated dishes, like this one, off the bottom.

About the Ingredients

CABBAGE – Talk about foods of the people, cabbage is eaten just about everywhere on earth! And why not? It's a good source of fibre, vitamin C and other vitamins and minerals. When you buy a cabbage, first get the feel of it in your hands. It should feel heavy. Now look at it: its leaves should be crisp and its colour strong and unblemished. Kept in the refrigerator it should last about 2 weeks.

CARAWAY – This spice pervades the roof of your mouth with a cloud of freshness. A tiny, crescent-shaped speck, you've probably seen it scattered on top of breads and cakes.

PANCIT LUGLUG PALABOK *(Pork and Prawns in a Red Sauce with Rice Noodles)*

This is a popular dish in the Philippines. It uses readily available ingredients and the simple two-pan method is almost as quick as a stir-fry. I've added finely diced red pepper and coriander leaves to help with the colour and texture.

As with any noodle and sauce dish, the noodles are served in a deep bowl and the sauce is placed on top. In the Philippines, the garnish is a salad of hard-boiled egg, celery leaves, finely shredded lettuce and lemon wedges, but I prefer to serve mine perfectly plain.

Nutritional Profile

PER SERVING	CLASSIC	MINIMAX
Calories	432	304
Fat (g)	19	8
Calories from fat	40%	25%
Cholesterol (mg)	143	89
Sodium (mg)	300	92
Fibre (g)	2	1

■ *Classic compared:* Pancit Luglug Palabok

Time Estimate

Hands On									
Unsupervised									
Minutes	10	20	30	40	50	60	70	80	90

Cost Estimate

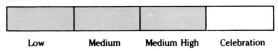

Low	Medium	Medium High	Celebration

Serves 6

INGREDIENTS

1¼ pints/680 ml water
12 oz/340 g uncooked prawns, shells on
12 oz/340 g boneless pork loin chop, trimmed of all visible fat
1 teaspoon/5 ml extra light olive oil with a dash of sesame oil
4 garlic cloves, peeled and chopped
1 teaspoon/5 ml annatto powder
1 teaspoon/5 ml fish sauce
2 tablespoons/30 ml arrowroot mixed with 4 tablespoons/60 ml water
2 spring onions, chopped
1 sweet red pepper, finely chopped
1 tablespoon/15 ml fresh coriander leaves, chopped
8 oz/227 g firm tofu, cut into tiny dice
¼ teaspoon/1.25 ml black pepper, freshly ground
12 oz/340 g rice noodles

FIRST PREPARE

■ Pour the water into a medium saucepan and bring to a boil. Add the prawns and simmer for 5 minutes. Strain, reserving the water. Plunge the prawns into ice-cold water, then peel them. Simmer the shells in the reserved water for 15 minutes to make a stock. Strain off ¾ pint/425 ml to use later. Coarsely grind the prawns (don't forget the bread trick, page 71).

■ Coarsely grind the pork loin chop.

NOW COOK

■ Heat the oil in a large skillet or wok. Fry the garlic and pork quickly – about 2 to 3 minutes. Add the ground prawns and fry until just warmed – about 1 minute.

■ Stir in the reserved prawn stock, the annatto powder and the fish sauce. Remove the pan from the heat, stir in the arrowroot paste and stir until thickened. Add the spring onions, red pepper, coriander leaves, tofu and black pepper to taste and heat through.

■ Cook the rice noodles in boiling water until soft – about 3 minutes. You should stir them once, at the beginning, the moment they become flexible. This will help to keep them separated during the cooking process. Drain well.

■ Serve the prawn mixture on top of the rice noodles.

Helpful Hints and Observations

PRAWN STOCK – There is a constant temptation to somehow leave stocks out of recipes. After all, they take time and in our modern lifestyles, time is so precious that something that appears so trivial can easily be replaced by tap-water.

In my food style, water just won't cut the mustard (so to speak!). You see, I've already subtracted so much fat that it reduces the 'depth' of taste. Stock is essential to give an added dimension to the taste, as well as aroma.

Less fat means less risk in recipes . . . but without creative alternative tastes we are likely to be defeated before we start. So please, in both this and all other dishes, do try to make the stocks and make them well . . . and don't forget to 'springboard' by adding in your own thoughts and favourite ingredients. I'm absolutely delighted to be a catalyst for your new inventions.

PS Let me know when you do – I'm eager to live in a two-way street and learn from you!

About the Ingredients

ANNATTO POWDER – Made from the small, reddish seeds of the annatto tree, it gives a lovely colour to many dishes.

FISH SAUCE – There's nothing fishy about its taste, despite the fact that it's extracted from fish. Fish sauce is used as ubiquitously in Thailand as soy sauce is in China and Japan. You might want to sample several brands because they vary in saltiness. See page 23 for how it's made.

RICE NOODLES – These are noodles made from rice flour and water. Look for them in clear plastic packages in Oriental foodstores. You may also see them under the name 'rice sticks' or 'rice vermicelli'.

Pancit Luglug Palabok (Pork and Prawns)
in a Red Sauce with Rice Noodles) 121

VEAL BUCO WITH RISOTTO

*H*ere *it is: one of my all-time favourites. I can almost dream about it! I ate the classic Osso Buco with Risotto Milanese the other day and couldn't finish it – TOO RICH – wonderful, to be sure, but much more than I can manage after a decade of change. So I made some alterations and dealt with my dreams.*

The rice looks wonderful in a bright red bowl; the veal in a green casserole! No matter really, on the plate together they are handsome enough. Whole green beans or fresh asparagus go well.

Nutritional Profile

PER SERVING	CLASSIC	MINIMAX
Calories	1183	574
Fat (g)	59	19
Calories from fat	45%	30%
Cholesterol (mg)	312	135
Sodium (mg)	2283	959
Fibre (g)	5	5

■ *Classic compared:* Osso Buco

Time Estimate

Hands On									
Unsupervised									

Minutes   10   20   30   40   50   60   70   80   90

Cost Estimate

Low	Medium	Medium High	Celebration

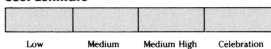

Serves 4

INGREDIENTS

1 tablespoon/15 ml extra light olive oil with a dash of sesame oil

8 fl oz/227 ml celery, diced

8 fl oz/227 ml carrot, peeled and diced

2 garlic cloves, peeled and mashed

1 lb/450 g boned hind knuckle of veal, trimmed of fat and cut into 1-inch/2.5-cm pieces

½ pint/285 ml tomato puree

¼ teaspoon/1.25 ml salt, freshly ground

¼ teaspoon/1.25 ml black pepper, freshly ground

2 fl oz/57 ml de-alcoholized Chardonnay wine

8 fl oz/227 ml veal stock (recipe page 210)

8 oz/227 g mushrooms, quartered

½ teaspoon/2.5 ml grated lemon rind

1 tablespoon/15 ml fresh parsley, chopped

1 tablespoon/15 ml capers

¼ teaspoon/1.25 ml baking powder

1 tablespoon/15 ml arrowroot mixed with 2 table-spoons/30 ml water

BOUQUET GARNI

4 sprigs thyme

2 bay leaves

6 stalks parsley

RISOTTO

1 tablespoon/15 ml extra light olive oil with a dash of sesame oil

1 medium onion, peeled and very finely diced

8 fl oz/227 ml uncooked Italian risotto rice

A pinch powdered saffron

16 fl oz/455 ml good quality chicken stock (recipe page 210)

4 fl oz/113 ml de-alcoholized Chardonnay wine

Freshly ground salt to taste

Freshly ground black pepper to taste

2 tablespoons/30 ml fresh parsley, finely chopped

2 oz/57 g Parmesan cheese, finely grated

NOW COOK

■ In a flameproof casserole, heat the olive oil and sauté the celery, carrot and garlic for 5 minutes. Remove the cooked vegetables and set aside.

■ In the same casserole, increase the heat to high and add the meat one piece at a time. If you put all the meat in at once, liquid is released and the meat simmers instead of browning. Keep turning the meat until all surfaces are lightly browned. Browning adds more depth of flavour.

■ Return the cooked vegetables to the casserole and stir in the tomato purée. Add the bouquet garni, salt, black pepper, wine and veal stock and bring to the boil. Cover, reduce the heat and simmer gently for about 70 minutes.

■ *The Risotto:* In a large saucepan, heat the oil and sauté the onion for 2 minutes. Add the rice, stirring until it's well coated. Scatter the saffron evenly over the rice and stir. In a small bowl, mix the chicken stock and wine. Pour in enough to just cover the rice and stir, over low heat, until it is absorbed. Continue to add the rest of the liquid, stirring until all of it has been absorbed. Remember, to achieve the proper creamy consistency, the rice must be stirred. Finally, fold in the salt, pepper, parsley and cheese.

■ After the veal is cooked, remove the bouquet garni, stir in the mushroom quarters and simmer uncovered for 5 minutes.

■ Just before serving, stir in the lemon rind, chopped parsley, capers and baking powder. Remove the casserole from the heat, add the arrowroot paste, return to the heat and stir until thickened.

Helpful Hints and Observations

BONE OR NO-BONE – The classic is made with sections of veal shin, the meat quite tender, and the bone filled with marrow – a highly saturated fat with ample cholesterol problems of its own! The shin meat can be cut off, the bones used for stock and the marrow discarded. The shin has good connective tissue content so it cooks well and becomes almost as succulent as the original. The result is easier to cook ... but Osso Buco it is not.

RISOTTO – Here is another problem child. The classic, made in the Milan style, is filled with butter and cheese ... very rich indeed! I've used Italian rice with cheese, saffron, stock and wine. It's attractive and not as rich.

About the Ingredients

SAFFRON – See page 61.

ITALIAN RICE – The rice sold under this name is usually arborio rice, a short, roundish-grain rice from Northern Italy, opaque in the centre and transparent around the edges. It is especially suited to risotto because, when properly cooked, it is neither too hard nor too soft. It will give your risotto both a creamy and slightly crunchy texture. You can generally find arborio rice in an Italian delicatessen; supermarkets usually sell it as Italian risotto rice.

VEAL HAMPSHIRE

Treena and I visited the small Canadian city of Victoria on Vancouver Island off the west coast, and found a very pleasant little restaurant in Oak Bay called The Hampshire Grill. This is one of their special dishes that we have since worked on together.

Add a sprig of fresh mint for garnish. Easy if it's growing all over your garden patio, like mine!

Nutritional Profile

PER SERVING	CLASSIC	MINIMAX
Calories	473	386
Fat (g)	22	12
Calories from fat	41%	28%
Cholesterol (mg)	260	154
Sodium (mg)	531	450
Fibre (g)	2	3

■ *Classic compared:* Veal Calvados

Time Estimate

	Minutes	10	20	30	40	50	60	70	80	90
Hands On Unsupervised										

Cost Estimate

Low	Medium	Medium High	Celebration

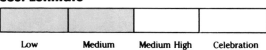

Serves 6

INGREDIENTS

3 lb/1.35 kg boneless loin of veal

STUFFING

1 onion, peeled and diced
1 sweet green pepper, cored, de-seeded and diced
1 sweet red pepper, cored, de-seeded and diced
8 fl oz/227 ml mushrooms, chopped
¾ pint/450 ml raw spinach leaves
1 tablespoon/15 ml extra light olive oil with a dash of sesame oil
8 fl oz/227 ml breadcrumbs
1 tablespoon/15 ml fresh thyme
⅛ teaspoon/0.6 ml salt, freshly ground
¼ teaspoon/1.25 ml black pepper, freshly ground
⅛ teaspoon/0.6 ml allspice
1 tablespoon/15 ml Dijon mustard
1 oz/28 g back bacon, cut into fine strips
½ medium apple, peeled, cored and sliced

FRUIT SAUCE

16 fl oz/450 ml veal stock (recipe page 210)
1 tablespoon/15 ml orange juice, freshly squeezed
8 fl oz/227 ml apple juice
1 tablespoon/15 ml arrowroot mixed with 2 table-spoons/30 ml water
⅛ teaspoon/0.6 ml black pepper, freshly ground

FIRST PREPARE

■ Butterfly the veal (see page 113) and pound it until it is ½ inch/1.25 cm thick.

■ Grind the onion, peppers and mushrooms in a meat grinder. Drain to separate the juices from the vegetables, reserving the juice. (I tried to use it as a super vitamin drink but it tasted awful – so it gets added to the stuffing later on!)

■ Steam the spinach for 2 to 3 minutes. Put it into a cheesecloth, press out the excess juice and discard it.

NOW COOK

■ In a low-sided stewpot, heat the oil and fry the ground onion, peppers and mushrooms until the onion appears translucent. Add the breadcrumbs and the reserved grinding juices, stirring constantly so that the ingredients bind together. Add the thyme, salt, pepper and allspice.

■ Place the veal on a chopping board and spread it with the mustard. Spoon the cooked vegetables on top. Next, lay the pressed spinach over the vegetables. The bacon slices are next, topped with the apple slices.

Fold or roll the veal, so that the filling is encased by the meat.

■ Wrap the veal in butcher's net (see *Helpful Hints*). Place the meat on a trivet in a roasting pan and roast at 375°F/190°C/Gas Mark 5 for 1 hour.

■ *The Sauce:* Drain off any surplus fats from the low-sided stewpot and blot the surface with a little paper towel. Deglaze the stewpot with the veal stock. Turn the stock into a small saucepan along with the orange juice and apple juice and boil to reduce it by one-third. Remove from the heat, add the arrowroot paste, return to the heat and stir until thickened. Season with the pepper.

■ Remove the veal from the oven and let it sit for about 20 minutes. Carve the veal into slices and serve them on a pool of the fruit sauce.

Helpful Hints and Observations

ELASTIC BUTCHER'S NET – This really is the easiest way to hold a rolled piece of meat or boned poultry (even baked double fillets of salmon) together. It can be purchased from the meat department at your local supermarket. Here's how to use it. Next time you use a 30-oz/850-g tin, cut off both ends, wash and dry it thoroughly, brush it with oil and store the elastic net over one end of the tin, allowing 2 inches/5 cm more at each end than the size of the meat you want to wrap. Slip the meat into the tin and shake it through into the net. It will come out at the other end completely surrounded by the net.

About the Ingredients

SPINACH – Fresh spinach should look crisp and have unblemished green leaves. Wash it several times as dirt seems to cling stubbornly to its stems. It doesn't keep very well – about 2 to 4 days – so refrigerate it and use it as soon as possible.

VEAL SUTTON

This was another of our very special 'celebrity from the street' encounters, where we go out to find some real people who are struggling with the issue of food styles. In New York, we found Brie Sutton and asked her to tell us her favourite foods. I created a dish using the ingredients she liked the most.

This is a very simple, yet almost tropical dish, served in a nest of rice. The papaya and avocado balls glisten under the slightly spicy curry sauce and go wonderfully with the veal – nice choices, Brie Sutton!

Nutritional Profile

PER SERVING	CLASSIC	MINIMAX
Calories	1384	521
Fat (g)	134	18
Calories from fat	87%	30%
Cholesterol (mg)	614	74
Sodium (mg)	1342	183
Fibre (g)	3	8

■ *Classic compared:* Veal Savoyarde

Time Estimate

Hands On
Unsupervised

Minutes 10 20 30 40 50 60 70 80 90

Cost Estimate

Low	Medium	Medium High	Celebration

INGREDIENTS

1 lb/450 g bottom round of veal, trimmed
1 papaya, halved lengthwise and seeded
1 avocado, halved and the stone removed
4 tablespoons/60 ml lime juice, freshly squeezed
1 tablespoon/15 ml fresh coriander leaves, chopped
1 pint/570 ml beef stock (recipe page 210)
4 tablespoons/57 ml wild rice
8 fl oz/227 ml long grain rice
2 tablespoons/30 ml garam masala
4 fl oz/113 ml onion, peeled and chopped
1 tablespoon/15 ml + 1 teaspoon/5 ml extra light olive oil with a dash of sesame oil
⅛ teaspoon/0.6 ml salt, freshly ground
¼ teaspoon/1.25 ml black pepper, freshly ground
2 shallots, peeled and finely sliced
2 teaspoons/10 ml curry powder
8 fl oz/227 ml papaya nectar
2 fl oz/57 ml water
1 tablespoon/15 ml cornflour mixed with 2 table-spoons/30 ml papaya nectar

GARNISH
4 sprigs of coriander

FIRST PREPARE

■ Carefully remove any silver skin from the veal. Cut the veal across the grain, at a 45° angle, into ten ¼-inch or 1-cm slices. Tenderize and pound the veal to increase the size of each piece by about a third.

■ Scoop the papaya and avocado into small balls using a melon baller. Place them in a bowl and stir in the lime juice and coriander.

NOW COOK

■ Put the beef stock in a large pot and bring to the boil. Add the rices, garam masala and chopped onion and return to the boil. Turn the heat to the lowest possible point and cook, covered, until all the water has been absorbed by the rice. Test the rice after 15 minutes – if it's soft but not mushy, turn off the heat and let the rice stand, covered, for 5 more minutes.

■ Pour 1 tablespoon/15 ml of the olive oil on a plate. Rub the veal slices in oil on each side and sprinkle with the salt and pepper.

■ In a large skillet, heat the remaining olive oil and sauté the shallots and the curry powder. Add the papaya nectar, pour into a small bowl and set aside.

■ Rinse the skillet and place it back on the burner over medium heat. Place in it as many veal slices as will fit without overlapping. Brown the veal and set aside. Continue browning the rest of the veal slices in this manner. Depending on your skillet size, it may take two or three lots.

■ Add the water to the same skillet and drop in the papaya and avocado balls. Pour the curried papaya nectar through a sieve and into the skillet. Add the veal. Gradually stir in the cornflour paste and cook until thickened and heated through.

■ *To Serve:* Put 8 fl oz/227 ml of the rice on each plate and spoon the veal and sauce over it. Garnish with a coriander sprig.

Helpful Hints and Observations

THIN SLICES . . . SMALL PANS – Very thin slices of meat, poultry, or fish cook rapidly, but are seldom used because people say 'I don't have a large enough pan'. Indeed, veal slices, like the ones used in this dish, usually take up half an average skillet. I have found the perfect cooking method for these thin slices is to cook them a few pieces at a time, without crowding the pan, about 30 seconds on each side, and then set aside. Just before serving, you can return them to a skillet sauce to heat through. This is such an easy and interesting way to cook that I hope you'll give it a go and then make up a dish with a few of your own favourite foods.

About the Ingredients

SHALLOTS – See page 57.

PAPAYA – Walking down the supermarket aisle you might not look twice at this large, pear-shaped fruit. Green with overtones of yellow and orange, papaya might not look exciting on the outside, but just under its skin lurks a source of hidden power – it's loaded with vitamins A and C and potassium! A ripe papaya should feel just slightly yielding when pressed. It will last about a week if you store it in the refrigerator.

AVOCADO – With a green, leathery hide, this small oval fruit looks most like an alligator egg! But like papaya, under the skin an avocado hides its treasure: creamy smooth, nutty flesh. Choose avocados that feel heavy in your hand and have no blemishes. You'll know they're ripe when they yield gently to pressure. If you buy them very hard, put them in a paper bag, and they'll ripen beautifully.

VEAL WEYERHAEUSER

$\mathcal{I}$*'ve grown increasingly disenchanted with the idea of snow-white veal, called provimi or milk-fed veal. It seems to me that the colour benefit is far outweighed by the apparent suffering caused these young animals. This recipe shows that grass-fed veal can work just as well!*

This is an elegant dish that rivals Chinese techniques for last-minute speed cooking. Crisp cooked, bright green snow peas are wonderful on the side.

Nutritional Profile

PER SERVING	CLASSIC	MINIMAX
Calories	1384	455
Fat (g)	134	15
Calories from fat	87	31
Cholesterol (mg)	614	76
Sodium (mg)	1342	277
Fibre (g)	3	4

■ *Classic compared:* Veal Savoyarde

Time Estimate

Hands On
Unsupervised
Minutes   10 20 30 40 50 60 70 80 90

Cost Estimate

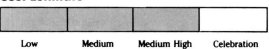

Low   Medium   Medium High   Celebration

Serves 4

INGREDIENTS

MIXED RICE PILAF

1 tablespoon/15 ml extra light olive oil with a dash of sesame oil

1 large Spanish onion, peeled and chopped

1 large garlic clove, peeled and chopped

8 fl oz/227 ml mixed rices (see *Helpful Hints*)

16 fl oz/455 ml chicken stock (recipe page 210)

2 bay leaves

1 sprig fresh thyme

1 sprig fresh parsley

4 oz/113 g small green peas

4 oz/113 g large mushrooms, cut into ½-inch/25-cm slices

VEAL AND SAUCE

1¼ lb/570 g grass-fed veal loin, yielding 1 lb/450 g boned and trimmed meat

2 tablespoons/30 ml extra light olive oil with a dash of sesame oil

1 sweet green pepper, cored, de-seeded and finely chopped

1 sweet red pepper, cored, de-seeded and finely chopped

1 sweet yellow pepper, cored, de-seeded and finely chopped

8 fl oz/227 ml veal stock (recipe page 210)

2 tablespoons/30 ml cornflour

2 fl oz/57 ml de-alcoholized dry white wine

2 fl oz/57 ml evaporated skimmed milk

Black pepper, freshly ground

¼ teaspoon/1.25 ml salt, freshly ground

1 tablespoon/15 ml fresh basil, chopped

FIRST PREPARE THE PILAF

■ Heat the oil in a casserole pan and fry the onion and garlic until the onion is translucent. Add the rice and stir until well coated. Add the stock and lay the herbs on top. Cook uncovered in a 375°F/190°C/Gas Mark 5 oven for 30 minutes. When it's done, remove the herbs, stir in the peas and the mushrooms and return to the oven to heat through – about 5 minutes.

NOW COOK THE VEAL

■ Trim all visible fat and silver skin from the veal. You can use the bones to make the veal stock for this recipe (see *Helpful Hints*). Cut the trimmed veal into 20 even-sized pieces, just over ¼ inch/0.75 cm thick.

■ Heat half the oil in a large frying pan and quickly fry the veal pieces for about 30 seconds on each side. Place the cooked veal on a plate and keep it warm while cooking the remaining pieces.

■ Put the remaining oil into the same frying pan and fry the peppers for 1 minute. Add the veal stock and bring it quickly to the boil. Scrape the meat residues off the bottom of the pan in order to blend all the flavours. Remove the pan from the heat.

■ In a small bowl, mix together the cornflour, wine and evaporated milk. Add to the veal and stir until thickened.

■ Add the cooked veal to the sauce and heat through. Season with the pepper, salt and basil. Serve with the Mixed Rice Pilaf.

Helpful Hints and Observations

THE PERFECT PILAF MIX – I recommend 4 fl oz/113 ml mixed long grain rice, 2 fl oz/57 ml pearl barley and 2 fl oz/57 ml wild rice.

VEAL STOCK – Since you will pay quite a price for the veal I suggest you ask your butcher for some veal bones to make the stock.

SWEDISH MEATBALLS

The classic version is almost irresistible – until you add up the fat! 'Well,' you might argue, 'it's a matter of tradition. . . er. . . it's our cultural heritage!' So rather than chuck it all out I tried to put three and three and three together and came up with nine meatballs coated in cream sauce . . . that are not all they seem to be!

This dish must take the prize for plate appeal: the wreath of red cabbage filled with cream-coated potatoes, mushrooms and meatballs. Nothing else is needed.

Nutritional Profile

PER SERVING	CLASSIC	MINIMAX
Calories	707	489
Fat (g)	51	11
Calories from fat	65	21
Cholesterol (mg)	197	39
Sodium (mg)	900	370
Fibre (g)	4	18

■ *Classic compared:* Swedish Meatballs

Time Estimate

Hands On									
Unsupervised									
Minutes	10	20	30	40	50	60	70	80	90

Cost Estimate

Low	Medium	Medium High	Celebration

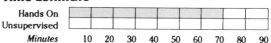

Serves 6

INGREDIENTS

10 fl oz/285 ml boiling water
4 fl oz/113 ml bulgur wheat
6 oz/170 g lean veal shoulder
6 oz/170 g lean pork shoulder
1¼ pints/680 ml water
18 small red new potatoes
8 oz/227 g mushrooms 1 inch/2.5 cm across (about the same size as the potatoes and meatballs)
4½ teaspoons/22.5 ml extra light olive oil with a dash of sesame oil
2 fl oz/57 ml shallots, finely chopped
1 tablespoon/15 ml fresh dill, chopped
¼ teaspoon/1.25 ml nutmeg, freshly ground
1 egg white
½ teaspoon/2.5 ml salt, freshly ground
2 fl oz/57 ml de-alcoholized white wine
1 medium onion, peeled and finely sliced
2 pints/1.15 l red cabbage, finely sliced
8 fl oz/227 ml pickled beetroots from a jar, drained, cut into thin strips with the juice reserved
¼ teaspoon/1.25 ml black pepper, freshly ground
3 tablespoons/45 ml fresh parsley, chopped

SAUCE
2 tablespoons/30 ml cornflour
8 fl oz/227 ml strained yogurt (recipe page 210)
8 fl oz/227 ml tinned low-salt chicken broth
1 tablespoon/15 ml fresh dill, chopped
¼ teaspoon/1.25 ml cayenne pepper

GARNISH
Fresh parsley, chopped

FIRST PREPARE

■ Pour the boiling water on top of the bulgur and let it stand for 15 minutes. Strain and set aside. Put the veal and pork through a fine blade grinder into a large bowl (see page 71 for the bread trick).

■ Put a steamer platform in a large pot and bring the 1¼ pints/680 ml water to the boil. Put the potatoes on the platform, cover and steam for 20 minutes. Add the mushrooms, cover and steam for 4 minutes more.

■ *For the Sauce:* In a medium-sized bowl, mix the cornflour and strained yogurt. Stir in the chicken broth, dill and cayenne pepper with a wire whisk until all the lumps are gone.

NOW COOK

■ In a small pan heat ½ teaspoon of the oil and sauté the shallots until slightly translucent.

■ In a large bowl combine the cooked shallots with the cooked bulgur, dill, nutmeg and ground meat. Stir in the egg white and half the salt. Make the meatballs by taking a rounded tablespoon of the mixture and squeezing and rolling it between lightly water-moistened hands. You should have eighteen.

■ In a large non-stick skillet, heat 3 teaspoons/15 ml of the oil and brown the meatballs, shaking the skillet frequently to prevent them from sticking. Cook for approximately 10 minutes.

■ Add the steamed potatoes and mushrooms, pour in the wine and the chicken stock-yogurt sauce and stir until thickened.

■ In another skillet, heat the remaining oil and fry the onion and cabbage until the onion is slightly translucent. Add 4 fl oz/113 ml of the reserved beetroot juice, the remaining salt and the pepper. Cover and cook for 10 minutes. Sprinkle with the parsley.

■ *To Serve:* Make a wreath of the cabbage mixture on each individual plate, garnished with the strips of pickled beetroots. Into the centre spoon three meatballs, three potatoes and three mushrooms. Coat with the sauce and garnish with chopped parsley.

Helpful Hints and Observations

APPEARANCES ARE IMPORTANT! – Somehow a serving of only three small meatballs per head sends the wrong visual signal. Moderation is wonderful but – ONLY THREE MEATBALLS? In this case we supplemented the 'meat in a minor key' with the same sized potatoes and button mushrooms. Even though they are obviously not meatballs their number and shape lends enough support and, frankly, they make a delicious combination of flavours, especially with the beetroot and cabbage.

VENISON WITH SPICED PEARS

$\mathcal{V}$enison comes from the hunter's bag or a properly regulated game farm. It is hard to say which is more expensive when you add in all the trappings enjoyed by the modern hunter. Whichever, it isn't cheap, but it's extra lean and very tasty. This recipe can be made using well-trimmed pork loin as a delicious alternative.

Serve with boiled potatoes dusted with fresh mint and a little parsley, small green peas with a touch of brown sugar, and half a small baked sweet potato, served perfectly plain – sounds great, doesn't it?

Nutritional Profile

PER SERVING	CLASSIC	MINIMAX
Calories	421	152
Fat (g)	17	3
Calories from fat	37%	15%
Cholesterol (mg)	132	59
Sodium (mg)	253	100
Fibre (g)	3	3

■ *Classic compared:* Marinated Saddle of Venison

Time Estimate

Hands On Unsupervised	3 Hours, 30 Minutes
Minutes	10 20 30 40 50 60 70 80 90

Cost Estimate

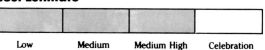

Low	Medium	Medium High	Celebration

Serves 6

INGREDIENTS

VENISON
1¼ lb/570 g loin of venison
1 teaspoon/5 ml extra light olive oil with a dash
of sesame oil
3 tablespoons/45 ml tomato paste
2 large carrots, peeled and chopped into 1-inch/2.5-cm
chunks
2 medium leeks, cleaned and chopped into 1-inch/2.5-
cm chunks
1 tablespoon/15 ml fresh thyme
8 fl oz/227 ml de-alcoholized red wine
1 sprig fresh rosemary
8 juniper berries
1 tablespoon/15 ml arrowroot mixed with 2 table-
spoons/30 ml water

MARINADE
4 fl oz/113 ml de-alcoholized red wine
4 fl oz/113 ml cider vinegar
4 sprigs fresh rosemary

PEAR POACHING LIQUID
4 fl oz/113 ml de-alcoholized red wine
4 fl oz/113 ml cider vinegar
6 whole cloves, freshly ground
6 allspice berries
A 3-inch/8-cm cinnamon stick
2 pears, peeled, halved and cored
8 fl oz/227 ml water, or amount needed to cover

GARNISH
Sprigs of fresh rosemary

FIRST PREPARE

■ Trim away the excess fat and silver skin from the
venison. Mix the marinade ingredients together in a
glass or ceramic bowl. Place the trimmed venison in
the marinade and marinate overnight in the refrigerator.
■ Remove the venison from the marinade and blot
dry with paper towels. Reserve the marinade. Wrap
the venison in butcher's net, as described on page
125.

NOW COOK

■ Pre-heat the oven to 375°F/190°C/Gas Mark 5. Pour
the reserved marinade into a small saucepan, bring to
the boil and set aside.
■ *The Poaching Liquid:* In a medium-sized saucepan,
heat the wine and vinegar. Mix in the cloves, allspice
berries and cinnamon stick. Add the pear halves,
cover with the water and poach for approximately
30 minutes.
■ Heat the oil in a low-sided flameproof casserole
and fry the tomato paste, carrots and leeks until the
tomato darkens in colour. Put the wrapped venison
into the pan and brown, rolling to brown the entire
outer surface. Add the thyme and wine.
■ Pour the boiled marinade over the venison. Add
the rosemary sprig and juniper berries and cover. Put
in the pre-heated oven to braise for 40 minutes.
■ Transfer the cooked venison on to a carving dish.
Pour the casserole juices through a strainer into a
small heated saucepan. Remove the saucepan from
the heat, add the arrowroot paste, return to the heat
and stir until thickened.
■ *To Serve:* Cut the stockinette away from the
venison and discard. Slice the meat into ¼-inch/1-cm
slices. Arrange the slices in the centre of a serving tray
and surround with the pear halves. Pour the thickened
sauce over the venison and garnish with rosemary
sprigs.

Helpful Hints and Observations

MARINADE – A marinade is a great flavour booster
but it can also be a trap for bacteria! I always bring
marinades to the boil to kill off these unfriendly
fellows before adding the strained mixture to the
cooking liquid for an added bite.
■ COATING SAUCE BEFORE SERVING – Sometimes
sauce is best poured on to a plate first and then the
meat placed on top. In this case it is reversed. Venison
tends to look dry and needs the glossy arrowroot
sauce to appear as succulent as it is!

About the Ingredients

VENISON – The venison available commercially is
from deer raised on game farms. The deer are fed a
special diet to promote growth and health. In many
countries it is illegal to purchase wild game because
it is not inspected for disease. Farm-raising these
animals ensures both quality and availability.
JUNIPER BERRIES – These 'berries' are actually a
cone from an evergreen tree that can grow up to 40
ft/12 m in height and is found in all temperate zones,
from Africa to North America. Juniper berries (cones)
take 2 years to ripen, changing colour from light green
to a deep purple blue. They are used to impart their
flavourful perfume in the making of gin.

MINIMAX SEED BREAD

This is a robust bread: full of flavour and texture and good nutrient density. It toasts well and makes excellent sandwiches. If that isn't enough, it needs only one proving and very little kneading!

Serve toasted Minimax Seed Bread with 'proper tea' (see Helpful Hints). I like Earl Grey tea, which is light in flavour but creates a wonderful aroma as its volatile oils are released.

Nutritional Profile

PER SERVING	CLASSIC	MINIMAX
Calories	187	183
Fat (g)	3	6
Calories from fat	15%	29%
Cholesterol (mg)	8	0
Sodium (mg)	833	245
Fibre (g)	2	5

■ *Classic compared:* Flower Pot Bread

Time Estimate

Hands On									
Unsupervised					2 Hours				
Minutes	10	20	30	40	50	60	70	80	90

Cost Estimate

Low	Medium	Medium High	Celebration

Makes an 18- to 20-Slice Loaf

INGREDIENTS

12 oz/340 g 100% wholewheat flour
Extra light olive oil mixed with a dash of sesame oil (for the tin)
1 envelope active dry yeast
1 tablespoon/15 ml sugar
18 fl oz/513 ml warm (105°F/41°C) water
1 teaspoon/5 ml salt
6 fl oz/170 ml Minimax Seed Mix (*see* page 205), very coarsely cracked in an electric coffee grinder

FIRST PREPARE

■ Make sure all ingredients are warm. Tip the flour into a large bowl and put it, with all your utensils, in the coolest part of your oven. Light the oven, turn it to the very lowest setting possible, and leave the door open. Don't cook the equipment!

■ Use a piece of paper towel dipped in the olive oil mixture to grease a 10 × 5 × 4 inch/25 × 13 × 10 cm loaf tin.

NOW COOK

■ Dissolve the active dry yeast and the sugar in 4 fl oz/113 ml of the warm water. Measure the temperature with a cooking thermometer to ensure the best results. Stir well and let the mixture rest in a warm place for about 10 minutes to develop a froth.

■ In a large bowl, mix the flour, salt and Minimax Seeds. Add the frothy yeast and start kneading with an electric dough hook or by hand. Swish 14 fl oz/400 ml of the warm water around the now empty yeast bowl, and add it to the dough. This water will contain any remaining yeast. Knead until the dough is silky, about 3 minutes.

■ Transfer the dough to the prepared loaf tin and cover loosely with plastic wrap. Let it rise, or 'prove', for about 1 hour in a warm place. It will rise only slightly.

■ Pre-heat the oven to 400°F/205°C/Gas Mark 6. Bake the bread on the middle rack for 35 to 40 minutes.

■ Take the tin out of the oven and remove the loaf. Return bread to the oven rack *upside down*. Bake for another 10 minutes to crisp the bottom. It should sound hollow when tapped.

■ Please note that this recipe does not produce a 'tall' loaf. It never rises above the level of the loaf tin. Place the loaf on a wire rack and let it cool completely before slicing.

Helpful Hints and Observations

'PROPER TEA' – Pour very hot water into a china or earthenware teapot, to warm it. Fill the kettle with fresh water. When it starts to sing, empty the pot and put in roughly 1 tea-bag or 1 flat teaspoon/15 ml loose tea per ½ pint/284 ml capacity – more or less, according to how strong you like your tea. As soon as the water boils, pour it into the pot, replace the lid, cover the pot with a 'cosy' or cloth and leave to brew for 3–4 minutes. You can, of course, hurl a tea-bag into a cold cup, pour three-times-boiled water on it and mash it around with a spoon. This produces 'fast tea', which is a different drink altogether!

OUR DAILY BREAD –
Once a known commodity, a staple, attractive, homely thing upon which we could rely. Nowadays we can expect much of our daily bread to be treated to a barrage of chemical additives. The reason for this is logical enough: it reduces the effect of

human error on the eventual product. Note, please, that it permits the error to continue, but it fixes up the mistakes. What man lacks in genuine honest skill he makes up for with chemical manipulation! The best comment I ever heard about bread sums up the whole thing wonderfully: 'If mould won't grow on it, neither will you.' So now it's up to you. Either find a quality source of bread or summon up all your creative resolve and try mine – with proper tea, of course!

BANANA SPICE BREAD

ℋere's another well-known favourite where our standards have been set by wonderful, thick, fragrant, spicy slabs of meltingly soft fruit bread. No need for added butter . . . it's built in! Can it be done another way? Well yes, but our standards need to change. This isn't fat plus fat plus sugar, but it is thick, fragrant and spicy!

You may want a 'touch' of whipped butter or extra light margarine on the Banana Spice Bread, but please, don't undo all we've tried to achieve: a snacking bread that doesn't bite first . . . especially where it shows!

Nutritional Profile

PER SERVING	CLASSIC	MINIMAX
Calories	489	187
Fat (g)	25	5
Calories from fat	47%	26%
Cholesterol (mg)	71	18
Sodium (mg)	338	157
Fibre (g)	2	3

■ *Classic compared:* Kona Inn Banana Bread

Time Estimate

Hands On									
Unsupervised									
Minutes	10	20	30	40	50	60	70	80	90

Cost Estimate

Low	Medium	Medium High	Celebration

Serves 12

INGREDIENTS

⅛ teaspoon/0.6 ml + 2 oz/57 g margarine
1 teaspoon/5 ml + 4 oz/113 g plain flour, sifted
4 oz/113 g wholewheat flour
2 teaspoons/10 ml bicarbonate of soda
2 oz/57 g sun-dried whole bananas or sun-dried papaya chunks
5 tablespoons/75 ml light brown sugar
1 egg
4 fl oz/113 ml buttermilk
3 ripe bananas, mashed
1 teaspoon/5 ml vanilla essence
1 teaspoon/5 ml powdered cinnamon
1 teaspoon/5 ml ground allspice
2 tablespoons/30 ml flaked almonds

FIRST PREPARE

■ Pre-heat oven to 350°F/180°C/Gas Mark 4.

■ Grease a 9 × 5 × 3 inch/23 × 13 × 8 cm loaf tin with the ⅛ teaspoon/0.6 ml of margarine. Dust with the 1 teaspoon/5 ml of plain flour and shake out the surplus.

■ Sift the remaining plain flour, the wholewheat flour and the bicarbonate of soda into a large bowl.

■ Cut the bananas or papaya into ¼-inch/0.6-cm chunks. Toss them in the flour, making sure all the chunks are completely separate and well coated.

NOW COOK

■ In a large mixing bowl, cream the brown sugar and the 2 oz/57 g of margarine. Beat in the egg and buttermilk. Add the mashed bananas, vanilla essence, cinnamon and allspice. Beat with an electric mixer on low speed until all the ingredients are combined.

■ Gradually beat in the flour mixture with the electric mixer on low – don't overwork it, please!

■ Spread the batter into the greased and floured loaf tin. Drop the pan on to the counter top to remove any excess air bubbles. Sprinkle flaked almonds over the top, and poke them under the surface.

■ Pop in the oven for about 1 hour.

■ Remove when a thin-bladed knife inserted into the middle of the loaf comes out clean. Cool on a baking rack.

Helpful Hints and Observations

THE WET AND THE DRY – Try to see the two mixtures as importantly different tasks.

The Wet – Always start by dissolving the sugar in the fat. This is called 'creaming' and it's essential. An electric mixer helps but it can be done by hand with a wooden spoon. Just beat until the mixture lightens in colour and the sugar loses some of its grittiness. It takes longer with brown sugar, but you get more flavour. Then whisk in the egg until it has absorbed the sweetened fat. Now you can add the remaining wet items just as you please. Finally, pop in the only dry ingredients – the spices.

The Dry – You have two flours. For added nutrition and texture they must be double sifted along with the bicarbonate of soda (and ½ teaspoon/2.5 ml of salt, if you feel you really must).

Wet Meets Dry – Always tip the flours into the smooth batter using a dough hook or spoon rather than a whisk, which will clog up!

About the Ingredients

SUN-DRIED BANANAS –
Not the prettiest of fruit, but the taste is unbeatable! Look for these in the dried fruit section of your grocer's. The dried banana is different from banana chips, which are fried in oil. When you bite one you'll see how densely  the banana taste has been concentrated by drying. It's interesting to note that the nutrient value of the banana isn't affected by the drying process.

BROWN SUGAR – Simply made by adding a small amount of molasses to refined white sugar. It is about 96% sucrose.

SMOKED CHICKEN PASTA JACKIE

$\mathcal{H}$ere's another dish created for a 'celebrity from the streets'. This time we asked Jackie Bylund from Bellevue, Washington, for a list of her favourite foods. She included Fettucine Alfredo (a very rich pasta concoction with egg yolks, cream and cheese), smoked chicken and sweet red peppers (pimentos). Now you can see how this dish got its name!

Typically, it's a simple matter of serving the pasta, topped with chicken and sauce, in a large soup bowl with a good salad on the side and a hunk of crusty bread to give the pasta a nudge . . . if it's being difficult!

Nutritional Profile

PER SERVING	CLASSIC	MINIMAX
Calories	668	506
Fat (g)	39	9
Calories from fat	53%	15%
Cholesterol (mg)	201	134
Sodium (mg)	81	233
Fibre (g)	3	5

■ *Classic compared:* Fettucine Alfredo with Chicken

Time Estimate

Hands On									
Unsupervised									
Minutes	10	20	30	40	50	60	70	80	90

Cost Estimate

Low	Medium	Medium High	Celebration

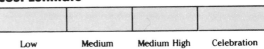

INGREDIENTS

HERB POWDER
1 tablespoon/15 ml fresh rosemary
1 tablespoon/15 ml fresh thyme
3 large sage leaves, roughly chopped
12 black peppercorns
1/8 teaspoon/0.6 ml salt, freshly ground

SMOKE
2 tablespoons/30 ml brown rice
1 Earl Grey tea-bag
1 tablespoon/15 ml brown sugar
4 whole cloves
1 teaspoon/5 ml extra light olive oil with a dash
of sesame oil
2 whole skinless and boneless chicken breasts,
1 lb/450 g each
12 oz/340 g fettucini noodles
2 tablespoons/30 ml Parmesan cheese, freshly grated

SAUCE
8 fl oz/227 ml strained yogurt (recipe page 210)
1 whole pimento (4 oz/113 g)
4 fl oz/113 ml chicken stock (recipe page 210)
4 fl oz/113 ml de-alcoholized white wine
2 tablespoons/30 ml cornflour mixed with 4 table-
spoons/60 ml de-alcoholized white wine
1 tablespoon/15 ml fresh chives, snipped
1 tablespoon/15 ml fresh parsley, chopped
2 oz/57 g pimento, diced

FIRST PREPARE

■ *The Herb Powder:* Put all the herbs and spices in
a small coffee mill or grinder and whiz until you have
a powder. Set aside.

NOW COOK

■ Shape a piece of aluminium foil into a 7-inch/18-cm
saucer. Thicken with four more pieces, moulding as
you go. This will be your smoke container.

■ *The Smoke:* Gently pour the brown rice, the
contents of the tea-bag, the sugar and cloves into the
foil smoke container. Place the filled container in the
bottom of a stockpot and turn the burner on high. Use
only a heavy, solid cast aluminium or solid cast iron
stockpot – never one made of bonded metals. Cover
tightly (see *Helpful Hints*) and allow the smoke to build
up heat for 3 to 5 minutes.

■ Pour the oil on a plate and sprinkle with the herb
powder mix. Wipe the chicken in the oil and herbs so
that both sides are evenly coated. Arrange the chicken
on a stainless steel expanding steamer platform. Place
carefully in the stockpot over the smoke mixture,
cover tightly and smoke for 10 minutes. Remove the
chicken.
*HINT: Wrap the smoke mixture in its foil saucer,
pop it into a bag and put it outside in the trash as
soon as possible. This will prevent smoke from filling
your kitchen!*

■ *The Sauce:* Purée the strained yogurt, whole
pimento, chicken stock and wine in a food processor
or blender. Pour it into a saucepan and bring to the
boil. Stir in the cornflour paste, chives, parsley and
diced pimento.

■ Cook the pasta in boiling water for about 2 minutes
if the pasta is fresh, about 11 minutes for dried. Drain
in a colander set over a large serving bowl. When the
hot water has warmed the bowl, discard the water.

■ Pour half the sauce into the heated bowl. Stir
in the pasta and Parmesan cheese. Place a portion
of the sauced pasta on each plate and top with half
a chicken breast sliced diagonally into thick chunks.
Serve the remaining sauce on the side.

Helpful Hints and Observations

TIGHT LIDS OR SMOKE ALARM! – I have perfectly
fitting, heavy glass lids on my cookware. If you are
using a large pot without such a good lid, you'll need
to find a way to create a good seal. This can be done
with a large, damp, piece of old towelling, aluminium
foil, or even some flour and water mixed to a stiff
dough and made into a long sausage, to be squeezed
between the lid and pan after the early smoke has been
created.

About the Ingredients

PIMENTO – You can call this red pepper or
(if you really want to dazzle your audience)
Capsicum frutescens! The term pimento usually
refers to fully ripened, cooked, sweet red peppers.
You've probably used pimento in one of its dried
and powdered forms: cayenne pepper, chilli powder,
paprika and red pepper. Look for bottled pimentos in
the condiment section of your grocer's. If you can't
find bottled pimentos, roasted red peppers are a fine
substitute.

PASTA ALLA MARINARA

There is so much truly excellent dried and freshly made pasta on the market that it might not seem necessary to make your own. However, for some wonderful reason, there are people who love to do it for themselves and who gain a great deal by converting their energy into a skilled gift of love. So for all you 'make it from scratch' people out there, here's a recipe for your very own Minimax pasta in a simple sauce.

I enjoy tossing my pasta in the sauce and serving it in a deep pasta bowl. Because of the fat factor, I seldom serve the classic bowl of grated Parmesan cheese on the side.

Nutritional Profile

PER SERVING	CLASSIC	MINIMAX
Calories	983	452
Fat (g)	44	6
Calories from fat	40%	12%
Cholesterol (mg)	822	107
Sodium (mg)	1743	189
Fibre (g)	4	8

■ *Classic compared:* Tortellini

Time Estimate

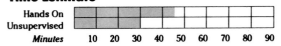

Hands On								
Unsupervised								
Minutes	10	20	30	40	50	60	70	80	90

Cost Estimate

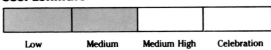

Low   Medium   Medium High   Celebration

Serves 4

INGREDIENTS

PASTA

6 oz/170 g plain flour

6 oz/170 g semolina flour

2 large eggs

¼ teaspoon/1.25 ml salt

7 tablespoons/105 ml water

4 fl oz/113 ml loosely packed fresh herb leaves (Use your favourite. I recommend oregano. Also, use more or less depending on your taste.)

SAUCE

1 teaspoon/5 ml extra light olive oil with a dash of sesame oil

1 medium onion, peeled and finely sliced

1 garlic clove, peeled and chopped

1 tablespoon/15 ml fresh oregano leaves

A 28-oz/800-g tin whole Italian plum tomatoes

1 tablespoon/15 ml cornflour combined with 2 tablespoons/30 ml water

FIRST PREPARE THE PASTA

■ In a food processor combine the two flours, eggs and salt. Process at high speed, gradually incorporating the water. When slightly tacky, remove the dough and put it on a smooth surface.

■ Knead the dough until it becomes very smooth – about 2 to 3 minutes. Roll the dough into a 6-inch/15-cm long cylinder shape and let it rest for 30 minutes.

■ Cut the dough into quarters and using a rolling pin or pasta machine, roll each piece into a very thin sheet. You should be able to see the shadow of your hand through the thin dough. Cut sheets into manageable working pieces – about 12–15 inches/30–38 cm long.

■ Fold the sheets of pasta in half lengthwise, creasing the folded edge to mark the centre, then open the pasta sheet again. Line one side of the sheet with the herb leaves. Fold the pasta back along the crease, covering the herbs. Using a rolling pin or pasta machine, seal the two edges.

■ Cut the pasta into bite-sized pieces, incorporating a herb leaf in each piece. You could also leave it in sheets and use it for lasagna, ravioli, or tortellini!

NOW COOK THE SAUCE

■ In a medium saucepan on medium heat, add the olive oil, onion and garlic. Sweat these ingredients until the onion is translucent and they've released their volatile oils.

■ Add the oregano and cook for 1 minute to incorporate its flavour. Add the tomatoes and cook for 5 minutes more. Pour into a blender and whiz until it's reached a thick consistency.

■ Return the sauce to the saucepan and re-heat. When it's hot add the cornflour paste and stir constantly until thickened – about 1 minute.

■ Add the pasta to a large pot of boiling water and cook for 2 to 3 minutes. Strain and serve tossed with the sauce!

Helpful Hints and Observations

ALL THAT GLISTENS ISN'T FAT! – When you remove fat from a sauce you lessen the sparkle. The pasta starch seems to take over and cloud the sauce. Therefore, I always add either cornflour for opaque or dairy sauces, or arrowroot for totally clear sauces and gravies. In either case, the proportion is 1 tablespoon/15 ml starch mixed to a creamy consistency with 2 tablespoons/30 ml of cold liquid to thicken 8 fl oz/227 ml of thin liquid. When these starches clear, they produce a glistening surface on the sauce that looks like a rich fatty gloss.

Now here's a look at this year's Designer Pasta...

DESIGNER PASTA? – The idea of putting fresh herbs into pasta is perfect justification for making your own from scratch – it really is different and delicious!

SPAGHETTI ALLA CARBONARA

$\mathcal{M}$y first brush with this great classic 'food of the people' was appropriately in Rome. It was served in the Golden Room at the Hosteria Dell'Orso, and prepared on a golden lamp, with a golden spoon and fork . . . well . . . you've got the picture.

I've left the flavours intact and want you to sample what is a great supper dish, made in 10 minutes, enjoyed for years.

Since this is a supper dish, it really needs nothing more than a good hunk of well-made bread. Have fun and don't forget the candle in the Chianti bottle and a red checked tablecloth!

Nutritional Profile

PER SERVING	CLASSIC	MINIMAX
Calories	900	413
Fat (g)	38	13
Calories from fat	38%	28%
Cholesterol (mg)	379	124
Sodium (mg)	1399	632
Fibre (g)	5	5

■ *Classic compared:* Spaghetti alla Carbonara

Time Estimate

Hands On
Unsupervised

Minutes   10 20 30 40 50 60 70 80 90

Cost Estimate

Low   Medium   Medium High   Celebration

Serves 4

INGREDIENTS

2 eggs

⅛ teaspoon/0.6ml salt, freshly ground

¼ teaspoon/1.25 ml black pepper, freshly ground

8 oz/227 g spaghetti

3 teaspoons/15 ml extra light olive oil with a dash of sesame oil

4 oz/113 g back bacon, fat removed and diced

2 tablespoons/30 ml pine nuts

2 tablespoons/30 ml fresh parsley, chopped (see *Helpful Hints*)

2 tablespoons/30 ml fresh chives, snipped

1 oz/28 g Parmesan cheese, freshly grated

3 sun-dried tomato halves, ground to yield 1 tablespoon/15 ml (see *Helpful Hints*)

NOW COOK

■ Break the eggs lightly with a fork. Sprinkle with the freshly ground salt and pepper.

■ Drop the spaghetti into boiling water and cook for 10 minutes until al dente. Drain in a colander set over a large serving bowl. Pour the water out of the bowl, leaving it nicely heated.

■ While the spaghetti is cooking, heat 1 teaspoon/5 ml of the oil in a large skillet. Add the bacon and the pine nuts. Sauté until lightly browned, then transfer into the heated bowl.

■ Add the remaining oil to the heated skillet. Scrape the residue off the bottom of the pan and pour into the heated bowl.

■ Stir the beaten eggs, parsley, chives, cheese and sun-dried tomatoes into the bowl. Add the spaghetti and toss to cover with the egg mixture, which will be cooked by the spaghetti's heat. Season with additional salt and pepper to taste.

Helpful Hints and Observations

A DASH OF SESAME? – You might easily wonder what quantity constitutes a dash. We make up our special signature oil with 16 parts extra light olive oil to 1 part toasted sesame seed oil, and store it in the refrigerator. If you don't make it in bulk, we suggest a dash. I think the nutty aroma of the sesame imparts a hint of butter to the otherwise highly scented olive oil. By the way, 'extra light' refers to the aroma, not the fat content, which is the same as in any other olive oil.

TO GRIND DRIED TOMATOES – Put them through a clean coffee grinder or a mini-mill.

CHOPPED PARSLEY – To produce freshly cleaned, beautifully coloured parsley, simply wrap the chopped herb in the corner of a towel, rinse under cold water and wring it out.

IN THE PINK? – According to Jane Brody, nitrates and nitrites have been used as curing agents for meat for more than 2,000 years. Why? Primarily for the pink colour they add to things like ham and hot dogs. Unfortunately when you cook the meat, a cancer-causing chemical can be formed. This is a controversial issue, of course. But if you think, like me, 'Why expose myself to unnecessary risk?', then read your meat label before buying. Nitrates and nitrites must be listed if they are present. I do, on occasion, use very small amounts of back bacon and ham hocks for their essential flavour, largely because I'm against outright exclusion. But note: in very small amounts . . . occasionally.

RADIATORE IN TOMATO SAUCE

$\mathcal{M}$ost people think a radiatore is the thingummy jig between the headlights of their car! But it's actually an unusual spiral pasta, cooked here in a remarkable way. Instead of being hurled into massive amounts of water, the pasta is cooked from its raw state in its finishing sauce – a most extraordinary taste and texture!

Like most pasta, this is really good served 'as it is'. You may want to add a few pieces of freshly stir-fried chicken if you absolutely must get your teeth into something fleshy.

Nutritional Profile

PER SERVING	CLASSIC	MINIMAX
Calories	1122	378
Fat (g)	59	9
Calories from fat	47%	20%
Cholesterol (mg)	165	7
Sodium (mg)	1562	76
Fibre (g)	7	7

■ *Classic compared*: Spaghetti Kareena

Time Estimate

Hands On									
Unsupervised									
Minutes	10	20	30	40	50	60	70	80	90

Cost Estimate

Low	Medium	Medium High	Celebration

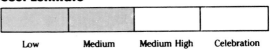

Serves 4

INGREDIENTS

10 Italian plum tomatoes
8 fl oz/227 ml water
1 tablespoon/15 ml extra light olive oil with a dash of sesame oil
1 sweet red pepper, de-seeded and chopped
2 garlic cloves, peeled and chopped
8 fl oz/227 ml de-alcoholized white wine
1 branch fresh basil (at least 6 leaves)
8 oz/227 g radiatore
1 tablespoon/15 ml fresh oregano, chopped
1 tablespoon/15 ml fresh parsley, chopped
4 tablespoons/60 ml mild Cheddar cheese, grated
4 teaspoons/20 ml pine nuts

FIRST PREPARE

■ Make a tomato purée, using either the following traditional method or the quicker one described in *Helpful Hints*. Remove the stalk end of the tomatoes and drop them into a pot of boiling water. In a few moments you'll see the skins start to peel back. Drain the tomatoes and plunge them into cold water. You should be able to pick them up quite easily. Peel off the skins and cut out the seeds, reserving both. Put the tomato flesh into the work bowl of your food processor. Use the pulse switch and process into a smooth purée. Or you can push it through a wire mesh sieve with the back of a spoon.

NOW COOK

■ In a small saucepan add the water to the tomato skins and seeds and bring to the boil.

■ In a large saucepan, heat the olive oil with the chopped pepper and garlic.

■ To the frying garlic and pepper add the tomato purée, the de-alcoholized wine and the branch of fresh basil. Stir in the radiatore.

■ Drain the tomato skins and seeds through a small strainer into the large pan. Press out all the juice you can. This gives you extra tomato taste. And don't throw those skins out yet! Pour them into your potted plants (not over them, that would look sordid, but under, to enrich the soil).

■ Turn the heat to low and put the lid on the saucepan. Cook for 4 minutes if you have fresh pasta, 8 minutes for dried pasta. This will cook the pasta 'verde verde', or just a little bit less than 'al dente'. You'll see that most of the sauce is absorbed into the radiatore.

■ Remove the basil branch. Add the oregano and parsley and stir.

■ Place in a serving bowl and sprinkle with the grated cheese and pine nuts.

Helpful Hints and Observations

MORE THAN ONE WAY OF SKINNING A TOMATO! – A new machine makes this quite a bit simpler. Quarter the tomatoes and hurl them into a saucepan on medium heat until they're just heated through – only a few minutes. Then pour them into the top of a special 'separator'. When you turn the handle, the tomatoes will be processed so that the skin and seeds come out one end and the tomato purée comes out the other! Not only is this method much less time-consuming than the oldfashioned way, it is also a good aerobic activity!

About the Ingredients

RADIATORE – A dry pasta shaped like an oldfashioned radiator. The wonderful shape, all the ins and outs, holds the sauce and keeps it on the pasta, not the plate. If you can't find this pasta at your local supermarket, try an Italian delicatessen.

PINE NUTS – Also called pignoli in Italian, pine nuts are actually the seeds of certain pine trees. The most prized are grown in Portugal. After harvesting, pine cones are dried to crack and separate the scales. Then the hard shell is cracked and the seed is released. Raw pine nuts have a 'piney' flavour and some cooks say a turpentine smell. They are wonderful roasted. Place them on a baking sheet at 400°F/205°C/Gas Mark 6 for 6 to 8 minutes. Look for pine nuts near the home baking section of your local supermarket, or in any health food shop. For the best value, purchase them in bulk and store them airtight in the refrigerator.

TORTELLINI IN BUTTER BEAN SAUCE

My favourite pasta suddenly got better! I'm really delighted with this recipe which has only one real drawback: it takes time to make the little pasta packages, unless you press the entire family into service! Of course, then it's not only easy, it's fun!

This dish is wonderful garnished with 2 tablespoons/30 ml of freshly grated Parmesan cheese and 1 tablespoon/15 ml of fresh snipped chives. Serve with a colourful herbed salad in the summer (or in a well-heated winter home), or perhaps freshly cooked green beans seasoned with a touch of fresh garlic and nutmeg.

Nutritional Profile

PER SERVING	CLASSIC	MINIMAX
Calories	983	566
Fat (g)	44	7
Calories from fat	40	11
Cholesterol (mg)	822	146
Sodium (mg)	1743	520
Fibre (g)	4	8

■ *Classic compared:* Tortellini

Time Estimate

Hands On	3 Hours
Unsupervised	
Minutes	10 20 30 40 50 60 70 80 90

Cost Estimate

| Low | Medium | Medium High | Celebration |

Serves 4 as Main Course

INGREDIENTS

FILLING

8 oz/227 g boneless skinless turkey thighs, trimmed of fat

1 oz/28 g back bacon, trimmed of fat

5 large sage leaves, finely chopped

¼ teaspoon/1.25 ml black pepper, freshly ground

⅛ teaspoon/0.6 ml salt, freshly ground

PASTA

6 oz/170 g plain flour

6 oz/170 g semolina flour

2 eggs

¼ teaspoon/1.25 ml salt, freshly ground

7 tablespoons/105 ml water

SAUCE

6 fl oz/170 ml whey from strained yogurt (recipe page 210)

12 fl oz/340 ml butter beans (from a 15-oz/425-g tin), drained

16 fl oz/455 ml homemade chicken stock (recipe page 210)

4 fl oz/113 ml evaporated skimmed milk (see page 197)

1 teaspoon/5ml fresh tarragon, chopped

1 teaspoon/5 ml fresh sage, chopped

½ teaspoon/2.5 ml cayenne pepper

⅛ teaspoon/0.6 ml salt, freshly ground

1 tablespoon/15 ml cornflour mixed with 2 tablespoons/30 ml evaporated skimmed milk

FIRST PREPARE THE FILLING

■ In a meat grinder, coarsely grind the turkey thighs and the bacon, ending with a slice of wholewheat bread. (When you see the bread come through the grinder you know you've ground all the turkey – the bread is not part of the filling.) Spread the meat over a chopping board and sprinkle with the sage, pepper and salt. Scrape and smooth together to combine all the ingredients, form into a ball and set aside.

THEN PREPARE THE PASTA

■ In a food processor combine the two flours, eggs and salt. Process at high speed, gradually incorporating the water. When slightly tacky, remove the dough and put it on a smooth surface.

■ Knead the dough until it becomes very smooth – about 2 to 3 minutes. Roll the dough into a 6-inch/15-cm long cylinder shape and let it rest for 30 minutes.

■ Cut the dough into quarters and, using a rolling pin or pasta machine, roll each piece into very thin sheets. You should be able to see the shadow of your hand through the thin dough. Cut the sheets into manageable working pieces – about 12–15 inches/30–38 cm long.

■ Working with one sheet at a time, lay it on a cutting board. Cut out 2-inch/5-cm diameter circles. You should have 48 circles from this recipe. Cover them with a damp cloth, as they should not dry out before they are moulded.

■ Using a small pastry brush, lightly brush the pasta circles with water. Put ¼ teaspoon/1.25 ml of the filling in the centre of each circle – don't overfill. Fold the pasta in half, in the shape of a half moon. Crimp the folded-over edge tightly so it's completely sealed. Fold the half moon ends over towards each other, slightly twisting one end under the other in a graceful swirl (it's supposed to look like a navel!). Set aside on a plate with a little semolina flour underneath to keep it separate.

NOW COOK THE SAUCE

■ In a food processor, purée the yogurt whey, butter beans, chicken stock and skimmed milk until smooth. Pour into a large non-stick wok or high-sided frying pan. The pan needs to be large because you will be tossing the tortellini in the sauce. Add the tarragon, sage, cayenne pepper and salt. Bring to the boil and simmer until it has a thin consistency.

■ Just before adding the tortellini, stir in the cornflour paste, bring to the boil and stir until the sauce has thickened.

AND FINALLY COOK THE TORTELLINI

■ Put 6½ pints/3.6 l water in a large saucepan and bring to the boil. Toss in the tortellini and boil until al dente, or just tender to the tooth – about 3 minutes. Taste to see if the texture suits your palate.

■ Drain the cooked tortellini in a colander. Spoon them into the sauce and toss until well coated. (You can then freeze the stock to use again.)

■ Bring to the table and dazzle your dinner guests!

Helpful Hints and Observations

BUTTER BEAN SAUCE – See page 45.

TORTELLINI METROPOLITAN

$\mathcal{I}$ must admit to being a tortellini fan. It began, for me, in Bologna, when I first ate these little pasta parcels bathed in a cream sauce with sliced white truffles! Recently I ate tortellini at the extraordinarily creative Metropolitan Diner in Victoria, British Columbia, owned and run by brothers Ford and Matthew MacDonald with the able assistance of their mother, Leslie. It's well worth a special visit.

At the Metropolitan Diner they serve this as an appetizer, but I've stretched it to go the distance as a main dish. Chef MacDonald and I have also collaborated to bring the nutritional numbers in to line for special needs. It's still a lovely dish!

Nutritional Profile

PER SERVING	CLASSIC	MINIMAX
Calories	508	311
Fat (g)	32	10
Calories from fat	56%	28%
Cholesterol (mg)	164	58
Sodium (mg)	303	679
Fibre (g)	3	3

■ *Classic compared:* Spinach Tortellini

Time Estimate

Hands On									
Unsupervised									
Minutes	10	20	30	40	50	60	70	80	90

Cost Estimate

Low	Medium	Medium High	Celebration

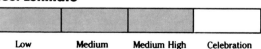

INGREDIENTS

6½ pints/3.6 l water
2 packets spinach tortellini with cheese filling (9 oz/255 g each)

SAUCE

1 teaspoon/5 ml extra light olive oil with a dash of sesame oil
1 tablespoon/15 ml onion, finely chopped
1 teaspoon/5 ml garlic, peeled and minced
3 tablespoons/45 ml cornflour
8 fl oz/227 ml strained yogurt (recipe page 210)
8 fl oz/227 ml evaporated skimmed milk (see page 197)
2 fl oz/57 ml de-alcoholized white wine (I prefer a somewhat sweet variety)
1 oz/28 g Swiss cheese, shredded
1 tablespoon/15 ml Parmesan cheese, freshly grated
1 teaspoon/5 ml fresh tarragon, chopped
1 tablespoon/15 ml cashew pieces, toasted

GARNISH

1 tablespoon/15 ml lime juice, freshly squeezed
1 tablespoon/15 ml cashew pieces, toasted
1 teaspoon/5 ml fresh tarragon, chopped
1 teaspoon/5 ml fresh chives, snipped
⅛ teaspoon/0.6 ml salt, freshly ground

NOW COOK

■ Bring the water to the boil, add the spinach tortellini, bring back to the boil and cook for 8 minutes. Drain the tortellini and set aside.

■ Heat the olive oil in a saucepan and sauté the onion and garlic.

■ In a bowl, combine the cornflour with the strained yogurt. Add the evaporated milk and the wine.

■ Remove the saucepan from the heat and add the cornflour-yogurt mixture. Return to the heat, bring to the boil and stir until the sauce has thickened.

■ Add the Swiss and Parmesan cheeses, tarragon and cashews to the sauce.

■ Pour the sauce into a large skillet. Add the tortellini and toss until well coated.

■ Spoon the tortellini on to a plate and garnish with the lime juice, toasted cashews, tarragon, chives and salt.

Helpful Hints and Observations

THE SAUCE IS CONTROVERSIAL! – Some of the world's most popular sauces are those that have a dense, white, creamy finish (Alfredo sauce is a good example). Unfortunately they are also loaded with saturated fat and impossible to re-create Minimax style without adding strange, reconstructed non-fat emulsions. This sauce recipe is the best I've been able to design. It retains some of the characteristics of the original, but with much less fat – a drop of 20 grams of saturated fat per serving. The most important issue here is 'Do I like it?', and *not* 'How does it compare to my Fettucini Alfredo?'

About the Ingredients

CASHEWS – If you saw a cashew tree, would you know where to find the nuts? Cashew trees have a red and yellow fruit, and the cashews grow on the bottom. But nut pluckers beware: cashew shells have two layers and between them is a caustic black liquid that can cause skin blisters if you try to crack the shell by hand. Shoppers buying cashews in their local market should be wary for another reason. Read the label of commercially toasted cashews: very high in oil, salt, sugar and preservatives. I recommend buying them raw and toasting them at home. Stored in a tightly covered container they will keep in the refrigerator for up to 6 months.

TARRAGON – Described as sweet, clean, bold and full-bodied when used fresh, it's been used for years by chefs in the classic French sauces, such as béarnaise and hollandaise. It seems to have a natural ability to enhance strong-flavoured foods such as duck, lamb, seafood, beetroots, greens and mushrooms. If you have to use dried tarragon, be careful: the drying process emphasizes tarragon's liquorice taste while suppressing its other, more subtle qualities. This hardy perennial herb is a good one to grow in your garden. Make sure you get French tarragon – this is one place the Russian tarragon can't compete.

HARD HAT PIZZA

Scott Keck was minding his own business and hard at work on the construction of a new building when our cameras caught him! His favourite foods were: beef, tomato, sweet potato and crisp greens. I put them together into a crustless pizza and put him on the spot to taste it publicly on the television show.

He liked it! And once again the old adage was proven wrong: men aren't simply meat and potato eaters to the exclusion of every new idea!

This is another all-in-one meal. One quarter-slice is ample with the sauce served on the side.

Nutritional Profile

PER SERVING	CLASSIC	MINIMAX
Calories	814	316
Fat (g)	53	9
Calories from fat	58%	25%
Cholesterol (mg)	187	57
Sodium (mg)	417	107
Fibre (g)	3	7

■ *Classic compared:* Steak and Fries

Time Estimate

Hands On									
Unsupervised									
Minutes	10	20	30	40	50	60	70	80	90

Cost Estimate

Low	Medium	Medium High	Celebration

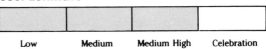

Serves 4

INGREDIENTS

1½ large yams (preferably garnet yams)
8 oz/227 g silverside of beef
10 large Savoy cabbage leaves, core removed
¼ teaspoon/1.25 ml nutmeg, freshly grated
¼ teaspoon/1.25 ml black pepper, freshly ground
4 Italian plum tomatoes, sliced lengthwise
4 basil leaves, thinly sliced
Freshly ground salt and pepper to taste

SAUCE

1 teaspoon/5 ml extra light olive oil with a dash
of sesame oil
1 garlic clove, peeled and chopped
8 fl oz/227 ml no-salt tomato sauce
1 tablespoon/15 ml fresh basil leaves, chopped
1 tablespoon/15 ml fresh parsley stalks, chopped
⅛ teaspoon/0.6 ml nutmeg, freshly grated
¼ teaspoon/1.25 ml black pepper, freshly ground
4 fl oz/113 ml de-alcoholized white wine
1 tablespoon/15 ml arrowroot mixed with 2 table-
spoons/30 ml de-alcoholized white wine
1 Italian plum tomato, finely diced
½ teaspoon/2.5 ml baking powder
1 tablespoon/15 ml fresh parsley, chopped
½ teaspoon/2.5 ml horseradish sauce

FIRST PREPARE

■ Bake the yams for 1 hour at 350°F/180°C/Gas Mark
4. Remove from the oven, allow to cool and slice 1
inch/2.5 cm thick.

■ Roast the beef at 350°F/180°C/Gas Mark 4 for
25 minutes. The meat thermometer should measure
140°F/60°C. Remove the roast from the oven, let it cool
for 15 minutes and then slice it into fine strips.

NOW MAKE THE PIZZA

■ Place the cabbage leaves in a steamer and steam
for 2 to 3 minutes. Make a bed of five leaves on a
large ovenproof plate. The leaves should fully cover
the base of the plate and have a slight overhang.

■ Lay the yam slices over the leaves, sprinkle with
the nutmeg and pepper and cover with two cabbage
leaves.

■ Layer tomato slices on top of the cabbage and
sprinkle with the basil, salt and pepper. Cover with
the remaining cabbage leaves.

■ Trim the overhanging leaves and place an inverted
ovenproof plate on top. Your pizza is now ready to go
into the oven!

■ Place the covered pizza in the oven and cook
at 350°F/180°C/Gas Mark 4 for 20 minutes.

■ While the pizza cooks, make the sauce. Heat the
oil in a large saucepan and cook the garlic, tomato
sauce, basil, parsley stalks, nutmeg and pepper. Add
the wine and cook for 15 minutes over medium heat.

■ Remove from the heat, add the arrowroot paste,
put back on the heat and add the diced tomato and
strips of beef. Stir in the baking powder, parsley and
horseradish sauce.

■ When the pizza is cooked, remove it from the
oven and flip the top plate. Firmly lift the plates
into a vertical position and squeeze them together so
that most of the flavourful pizza juices dribble into the
sauce. Stir the sauce to mix thoroughly.

■ *To Serve:* Slice the pizza into quarters and serve
on individual plates. Spoon a quarter of the sauce on
to each serving.

About the Ingredients

SAVOY CABBAGE – Next to the pale green flat leaves
of the common domestic cabbage, Savoy is the fancy
cousin: yellowish-green, loose crinkly leaves. It is not
as strong tasting as the domestic variety. At the
greengrocer's, look for fresh crisp leaves. Stay away
from wilted or thin-leaved cabbage.

PIZZA POLESE

*I*ncredibly popular, the classic pizza has an almost no-fault crust, especially when compared to the rich, fatty pie crust used for quiche and some fruit pies. Instead, it's the pizza toppings that can go overboard – our version tries to keep you in the boat!

Slice as you would any pizza. I love to serve a colourful salad, including, if possible, some rocket.

Nutritional Profile

PER SERVING	CLASSIC	MINIMAX
Calories	419	271
Fat (g)	26	10
Calories from fat	57%	32%
Cholesterol (mg)	47	68
Sodium (mg)	1356	240
Fibre (g)	3	3

■ *Classic compared:* Pepperoni Pizza

Time Estimate

Hands On Unsupervised									
Minutes	10	20	30	40	50	60	70	80	90

Cost Estimate

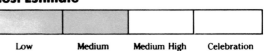

Low	Medium	Medium High	Celebration

INGREDIENTS

CRUST

1 clove garlic
2 loosely-packed tablespoons/30 ml oregano leaves
1 tablespoon/15 ml packed rosemary leaves
6 oz/170 g plain flour
1 egg
1 tablespoon/15 ml water
1 tablespoon/15 ml extra light olive oil with a dash of sesame oil
1 teaspoon/5 ml salt
½ oz/14 g compressed yeast
1 tablespoon/15 ml hot water to blend yeast
Dusting of semolina flour

TOPPING

2 skinless and boneless chicken breasts, 4 oz/113 g each
1 sweet red pepper, cored, de-seeded and finely diced
12 fl oz/340 ml Italian plum tomatoes, de-seeded and diced
1 tablespoon/15 ml fresh oregano leaves, chopped
1 tablespoon/15 ml fresh parsley, chopped
½ teaspoon/2.5 ml black pepper, freshly ground
4 teaspoons/20 ml capers
6 slices of Mozzarella cheese (⅛ inch/0.5 cm thick)
4 good quality anchovy fillets, soaked in a little milk to remove the saltiness, soaking milk reserved, quartered lengthwise

PREPARE THE CRUST

■ Put the garlic, oregano and rosemary into a small food grinder or pepper mill and process to a fine, moist 'dust'.

■ Pre-heat the oven to 500°F/260°C/Gas Mark 10. Put the flour in a large bowl. Make a well in the centre and pour in the egg, water, oil, salt and ground herb mixture. In another small bowl, break the compressed yeast into small pieces, add the hot water and stir until completely dissolved. Pour into the flour-well.

■ Gradually start incorporating the flour and egg mixture together. Stir gently up against the sides of the well, mixing in a little flour at a time. The dough will be fairly stiff. When it's hard to stir, use your hands to form the dough into a ball. Turn it out on to a board and continue kneading until the dough feels springy. It will be slightly tacky but should come off your hands after you press into it. Form it into a ball, put it back in the bowl, cover it with a towel and leave it in a warm place for 30 minutes, or until doubled in size.

■ Turn the proved dough out on to a board. Knead it just a couple more times then roll it out to fit a 14-inch/35-cm pizza pan. The dough should be fairly thin, about ⅛ inch/5 cm thick.

■ Prepare the pizza pan with a light dusting of semolina flour. Press the dough to fit the shape of the pan and let it sit for 15 minutes before baking. Bake in the pre-heated oven for 8 minutes or until light brown.

PREPARE THE TOPPING

■ On the coarsest setting, grind the chicken.

■ In a small bowl, mix the ground chicken, red pepper, tomatoes, oregano, parsley, black pepper and 3 teaspoons/15 ml of the capers.

NOW ASSEMBLE

■ Flip your cooked pizza crust over so that the browned, crisp side is now on the bottom. Spread the filling over the crust, leaving a ½-inch/1.5-cm crust edge.

■ Place the Mozzarella slices around the edge of the filling. Sprinkle the remaining capers on top and decorate with a crisscross of anchovy fillets.

■ Bake in the pre-heated oven for 8 more minutes.

■ When the pizza comes out of the oven, brush the exposed crust very lightly with the reserved anchovy soaking milk.

Helpful Hints and Observations

SEASONED PIZZA DOUGH – Whenever you move in to take fat out of a dish it really does help to make every attempt to replace the taste loss with aroma, colour and texture (A.C.T.). In this case, I added some classic Mediterranean herbs (oregano and rosemary) to the dough.

THIN CRUST, OVERTURNED – I prefer a crust on the thin side (even though the classic pizza crust from Napoli is quite thick). The overturning technique allows for a pre-bake, after which the crusted bottom becomes the top and the layers of garnish don't prevent the surface from cooking.

About the Ingredients

ANCHOVY FILLETS – Oh, come on, try them just once! You will be in for a marvellous, salty, tangy titbit with every bite.

CAPERS – See page 59.

GHIVETCH

In Romania, this meatless vegetable dish is often used to celebrate the arrival of the summer vegetables. I use it as a 'vegetables only' dish to alternate with meat proteins. It keeps well in the refrigerator for 4 to 5 days and can be served hot or cold.

I like to serve Ghivetch as a 'wedge of salad', ice-cold in summer with cold meats – it really is wonderful! You can, by the way, serve it hot, by the glorious spoonful, directly from the bowl. As a first course, Ghivetch can be served as a 'terrine of vegetables' with wholewheat toast and a little of Treena's Vinaigrette on the side (see page 39).

Nutritional Profile

PER SERVING	CLASSIC	MINIMAX
Calories	278	298
Fat (g)	13	7
Calories from fat	41%	21%
Cholesterol (mg)	0	0
Sodium (mg)	229	211
Fibre (g)	11	14

■ *Classic compared:* Ghivetch

Time Estimate

Hands On Unsupervised	4 Hours, 30 Minutes
Minutes	10 20 30 40 50 60 70 80 90

Cost Estimate

Low	Medium	Medium High	Celebration

Serves 8

INGREDIENTS

16 fl oz/454 ml boiling water

¼ teaspoon/1.25 ml bicarbonate of soda

1 bunch spinach, washed and de-stemmed (Savoy cabbage can be used when in season)

16 fl oz/454 ml boiling chicken stock (recipe page 210)

8 fl oz/227 ml bulgur wheat

FIRST LOT

1 tablespoon/15 ml extra light olive oil with a dash of sesame oil

1 onion, peeled and chopped

1 garlic clove, peeled and chopped

1 large carrot, peeled and sliced ⅛ inch/0.3 cm thick on the diagonal

1 sweet green pepper, de-seeded and chopped

1 tablespoon/15 ml lemon juice, freshly squeezed

SECOND LOT

2 tablespoons/30 ml extra light olive oil with a dash of sesame oil

1 large potato, peeled and cut into ½-inch/1.25-cm cubes

1 lb/450 g aubergine, cut into ½-inch/1.25-cm cubes

1 large courgette, cut into ½-inch/1.25-cm cubes

1 tablespoon/15 ml fresh dill, chopped

Juice of ½ lemon

½ teaspoon/2.5 ml black peppercorns, cracked

¼ teaspoon/1.25 ml grated nutmeg

1 tablespoon/15 ml fresh chives, chopped

2 tablespoons/30 ml fresh parsley, chopped

6 fl oz/170 ml green beans, topped and tailed

1 teaspoon/5 ml salt

¼–½ pint/140–280 ml chicken stock

THIRD LOT

12 fl oz/340 ml peas

1 lb/450 g tomatoes, de-seeded and diced

2 tablespoons/30 ml fresh basil, chopped

8 fl oz/227 ml mushrooms, quartered

SAUCE

8 fl oz/227 ml chicken stock

Grated rind of 1 lemon

2 tablespoons/30 ml lemon juice, freshly squeezed

¼ teaspoon/1.25 ml turmeric

1 tablespoon/15 ml arrowroot mixed with 1 tablespoon/15 ml water

1 teaspoon/5 ml fresh dill, chopped

FIRST PREPARE

■ In a large saucepan, add the baking soda to the boiling water, then the spinach leaves. Blanch for a moment, then plunge the leaves immediately into iced water. When they are bright green, remove the leaves, line a large serving bowl with them and set aside.

■ In a large saucepan, add the boiling chicken stock to the bulgur and let it stand for 5 minutes.

NOW COOK

■ *First Lot:* Heat the olive oil in a large, heavy frying pan. Add the remaining First Lot ingredients and cook for about 2 minutes. Turn into a stockpot large enough to hold all three lots of vegetables.

■ *Second Lot:* In the empty frying pan, heat half the olive oil. Add the potato and courgette and fry until brown on the edges. Add to the vegetables in the stockpot and stir together.

■ Pour the remaining oil into the empty pan, followed by the remaining Second Lot ingredients and the cooked bulgur. Cover and simmer for 35 minutes. Add a little chicken stock as necessary to keep the mixture moist and prevent the bulgur 'catching'. Tip the contents of the pan into the stockpot.

■ *Third Lot:* Add the Third Lot ingredients to the vegetables in the stockpot.

■ Fill the spinach-lined serving bowl with the vegetable mixture. Press down firmly. Place a plate on top of the mixture and push down hard. Remove any extra liquid that collects on the plate. Chill the Ghivetch.

■ *The Sauce:* In a small saucepan, mix the chicken stock, lemon rind, lemon juice and turmeric.

■ Stir the arrowroot paste into the sauce to thicken it. Add the dill.

■ *To Serve:* Unmould the vegetables on a serving dish. Serve the sauce on the side.

Helpful Hints and Observations

ALTERNATE 'VEGETABLES ONLY' DAYS – See page 157.

OVEN COOKING – The classic Ghivetch is often cooked in an oven, uncovered, for at least 1½ hours. We've reduced the time by two-thirds in an effort to preserve colour, texture and nutrition. Do watch the stove-top heat. Keep it low, stir well and use a heavy-based pot with a tightly fitting lid.

About the Ingredients

BULGUR – See page 103.

TURMERIC – See page 15.

GOLDEN THREADS STIR-FRY

*J*ust for the record, this dish is the brain child of my Senior Food Associate, Robert Prince. Since it was his own from concept, I wanted to make sure he got the credit for at least this, his first step, in a hopefully long, creative journey as part of our team.

What a great natural invention: the so-called vegetable spaghetti has a unique internal thread-like structure – and bright golden colour! The classic uses a sausage filling, but we've kept the meat out for another wonderful vegetable dish. With one brimming bowl per head it will serve six. We like some freshly steamed broccoli on the side.

Nutritional Profile

PER SERVING	CLASSIC	MINIMAX
Calories	192	194
Fat (g)	12	6
Calories from fat	57%	27%
Cholesterol (mg)	31	3
Sodium (mg)	474	258
Fibre (g)	4	10

■ *Classic compared:* Sausage and Squash Bake

Time Estimate

Hands On	
Unsupervised	
Minutes	10 20 30 40 50 60 70 80 90

Cost Estimate

Low	Medium	Medium High	Celebration

INGREDIENTS

1 vegetable spaghetti (4½ lb/2 kg)
1 tablespoon/15 ml extra light olive oil with a dash of sesame oil
2 garlic cloves, peeled and crushed
2 medium carrots, peeled and cut into matchsticks
1 sweet red pepper, de-seeded and cut into matchsticks
1 sweet green pepper, de-seeded and cut into matchsticks
2 fl oz/57 ml chicken stock (recipe page 210)
1½ tablespoons/23 ml fresh basil, finely chopped
4 tablespoons/60 ml Parmesan cheese, freshly grated
Black pepper, freshly ground
1 tablespoon/15 ml arrowroot mixed with 2 tablespoons/30 ml chicken stock

GARNISH

½ oz/14 g cracked hazelnuts
1 sprig fresh basil

FIRST PREPARE

■ Prick the vegetable spaghetti on one side to let it 'breathe'. Place it on a baking sheet and bake at 325°F/160°C/Gas Mark 3 for 80 minutes. Remove and plunge it in iced water to prevent overcooking by retained heat.

■ Put the vegetable spaghetti on one side and cut off a long lid. Scoop out the seeds, carefully scraping the spaghetti-like threads out of the shell. Put these golden threads on a plate and set aside.

■ Put the empty shell on a serving dish. If the shell won't stay in place, scoop out some of the pulp from the sides, and put it on the dish as a base to hold the shell stable.

NOW COOK

■ Heat the olive oil in a wok and fry the crushed garlic.

■ Add the carrots, peppers and chicken stock, then gradually stir in the reserved golden spaghetti threads.

■ Sprinkle with the basil and half of the grated cheese and stir lightly to mix.

■ Add some freshly ground pepper. Now remove from the heat and add the arrowroot paste. Return the wok to the heat and stir until thickened.

■ Tip the mixture into the prepared shell and garnish with the remaining cheese, the hazelnuts and the basil sprig.

Helpful Hints and Observations

PRICK IT OR STAND BACK! – There are stories of this kind of baked vegetable building up a moist heat internally in the seed cavity and suddenly exploding – with messy consequences. A couple of vent holes will completely cure this problem.

ALTERNATE 'VEGETABLES ONLY' DAYS – Just another reminder of how an attractive 'vegetables only' dish can replace the traditional flesh protein foods on an occasional basis. Not only is this a healthy idea, reducing calories, fat and cholesterol, it also saves you money on your food budget and tastes delicious! At one time Treena and I used to alternate one day on, one day off, beginning with Monday for vegetables and allowing the weekend to be 'fleshy' days. Don't be too rigid on this . . . keep variety coming and the family reception will be increasingly flexible and appreciative.

About the Ingredients

VEGETABLE SPAGHETTI – This is probably a case of grow your own – or you could experiment with pumpkin as a substitute, if you like it. (You can use the shell afterwards for a Hallowe'en lantern!) If you do produce or track down the original, make sure that its skin is hard, with no soft spots, decay, cracks, or bore holes. And do try vegetable spaghetti as a substitute for pasta with your favourite sauce – it's delicious!

HAZELNUTS – Buy them in the shell or not in the shell: your goal is the same, a wonderful, sweet-tasting nut meat. Do beware of commercially roasted hazelnuts that could contain high amounts of salt, fat, etc. If you want your nuts roasted, just buy them raw, throw them on a baking sheet and bake at 350°F/180°C/Gas Mark 4, for 5 to 10 minutes if shelled, 20 to 25 minutes if still in the shell.

ARROWROOT – There is a legend that this name originated because the Indians considered the sap obtained from the roots capable of healing wounds caused by arrows. The fact is that arrowroot's name is from the American Indian word for flour-root, *araruta*. In any case, this versatile starch is leached from the tubers of several kinds of tropical plants, refined and packaged. It is a lot less expensive when you buy it in bulk from a wholefood shop. Easily digestible, arrowroot can be used as a thickener in many soups, sauces and puddings, and numerous sweet dishes. I usually keep it for clear or dark sauces, soups and gravies. Dairy products thicken better with cornflour used in the same way.

PANJABI KALI DAL

The New Delhi Restaurant must be spelled, rather than spoken, otherwise it sounds like a 'new deli' and that doesn't do justice to this exotic San Francisco eatery. Treena and I have never had such delicious dal (lentil stew) and we've eaten Indian food on four continents.

Dal is usually served as a side dish with either poultry or meat and sometimes as an appetizer. It is full of flavour and even though it doesn't look wonderful, it is extremely nutritious.

Nutritional Profile

PER SERVING	CLASSIC	MINIMAX
Calories	156	93
Fat (g)	11	5
Calories from fat	62%	48%
Cholesterol (mg)	0	0
Sodium (mg)	139	13
Fibre (g)	3	2

■ *Classic compared:* Panjabi Kali Dal

Time Estimate

Hands On Unsupervised		
	2 Hours, 30 Minutes	
Minutes	10 20 30 40 50 60 70 80 90	

Cost Estimate

Low	Medium	Medium High	Celebration

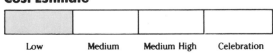

Serves 6

INGREDIENTS

2 fl oz/57 ml dried red kidney beans
2 fl oz/57 ml yellow split peas
4 fl oz/113 ml chickpeas
2 tablespoons/30 ml extra light olive oil with a dash of sesame oil
1 teaspoon/5 ml garam masala
½ teaspoon/2.5 ml cayenne pepper
1 teaspoon/5 ml paprika
½ teaspoon/2.5 ml turmeric
1 teaspoon/5 ml ground coriander seeds
1 teaspoon/5 ml ginger root, freshly grated
2 garlic cloves, peeled and finely diced
1 tablespoon/15 ml fresh coriander leaves, chopped
2 fl oz/57 ml strained yogurt (recipe page 210)
1 tablespoon/15 ml lemon juice, freshly squeezed

BOUQUET GARNI

4 bay leaves
4 whole green cardamom pods
2 whole black cardamom pods
A 2-inch/5-cm cinnamon stick
4 whole cloves
1 teaspoon/5 ml whole cumin seeds

GARNISH

Fresh coriander sprigs

NOW COOK

■ Pour the kidney beans, yellow split peas and chickpeas into a large stockpot. Just cover with water, bring to the boil and simmer for 2 minutes. Remove from the heat, cover and let stand for 1 hour. Drain and rinse well.

■ In a small, high-sided casserole, heat half the olive oil. Add the garam masala, cayenne, paprika, turmeric and ground coriander seeds. Mix to make a curry paste.

■ Stir the strained beans and lentils into the curry paste. Add 1¼ pints/680 ml of water and the bouquet garni. Bring to the boil, cover and simmer for 1 hour. Remove the bouquet garni.

■ In a small sauté pan, heat the remaining olive oil and sauté the ginger root and garlic. Combine with the beans and stir in the coriander leaves.

■ Take out one-third of the beans and set aside. Scoop the rest into a food processor and purée. Mix the whole beans back into the purée. Add the strained yogurt and lemon juice.

■ Garnish with a sprig of coriander and serve with pitta bread.

Helpful Hints and Observations

WASH WELL! – In many Western nations we are so used to clean food in ultra-sealed containers that we sometimes doubt instructions that say 'wash several times'. It is a very wise precaution to do this when using beans and lentils. You might also want to pick over these pulses and discard any that look tight and shrivelled. Some might even be stones!

I'm washing the lentils.

About the Ingredients

DAL – Pulses, that is, lentils, split peas and beans, are called *dal* in Hindustani. There are all sorts of varieties and colours. Split peas, like lentils, are one of the easiest pulses to use because they do not require pre-soaking. Keep them in an airtight container – they will last indefinitely.

BLACK AND GREEN WHOLE CARDAMOM – These ingredients are seed pods belonging to the ginger family. The seeds in the pods are where the aroma comes from. Ground cardamom in the tin or jar is not as aromatic because the ground seeds are mixed with ground pod. Look for the whole pods in the special foods department of your supermarket or in Asian foodstores.

STIR-FRIED SALAD VINAIGRETTE

$\mathcal{I}$ often suggest you add a crisp, well-dressed herbal salad as a side dish, so I thought it was time that I gave you an example. Several years ago I invented an idea called a split salad and we've used it ever since as it avoids over-use of dressing and slimy greens!

This idea can be used with many, many variations. Do try to make it with your own favourite vegetables and herbs.

Nutritional Profile

PER SERVING	CLASSIC	MINIMAX
Calories	263	141
Fat (g)	27	5
Calories from fat	93%	34%
Cholesterol (mg)	0	0
Sodium (mg)	73	57
Fibre (g)	2	5

■ *Classic compared:* Vinaigrette Sauce

Time Estimate

Hands On		
Unsupervised	4 Hours	
Minutes	10 20 30 40 50 60 70 80 90	

Cost Estimate

Low	Medium	Medium High	Celebration

Serves 4

INGREDIENTS
VINAIGRETTE DRESSING

4 fl oz/113 ml rice wine vinegar

2 fl oz/57 ml extra light olive oil with a dash of
sesame oil

2 tablespoons/30 ml brown sugar

¼ teaspoon/1.25 ml cayenne pepper

2 tablespoons/30 ml lime juice, freshly squeezed

3 thin slices fresh ginger root

2 garlic cloves, finely chopped

6 fresh basil leaves, finely sliced

6 fresh mint leaves, finely sliced

SALAD

1 tablespoon/15 ml extra light olive oil with a dash
of sesame oil

½ small Spanish onion, peeled and finely sliced

1 garlic clove, peeled and finely chopped

2 large carrots, peeled and sliced diagonally

5 spring onions, trimmed and sliced

4 oz/113 g green beans, trimmed and sliced in half
lengthwise

2 oz/57 g Florence fennel, finely sliced

4 thin slices fresh ginger root, finely chopped

4 oz/113 g sweet red pepper, cored, de-seeded and
cut into fine matchsticks

4 oz/113 g sweet green pepper, cored, de-seeded
and cut into fine matchsticks

2 stalks celery, sliced diagonally

4 oz/113 g Jerusalem artichoke, scrubbed and sliced

4 oz/113 g cucumber, finely sliced

12 leaves of assorted salad greens, rinsed and dried
with paper towels or a salad spinner

FIRST PREPARE THE VINAIGRETTE

■ In a blender combine the vinegar, olive oil, brown
sugar and cayenne pepper. Add the lime juice, ginger,
garlic, basil and mint and mix on high speed for 45
seconds. Strain into a bowl.

NOW MAKE THE SALAD

■ Heat the olive oil in a medium-sized casserole
and fry the Spanish onion, garlic and carrots. Add the
spring onions, green beans, fennel, ginger, peppers,
celery and artichoke and cook until just warmed
through.

■ Remove the warmed vegetables and place in a
large bowl. Add the cucumber and set aside.

■ Pour the vinaigrette into the casserole, dredging

the residue from the bottom and edges. Heat the vinaigrette slightly and then pour it over the vegetables.
Marinate for about 4 hours.

■ Strain the vegetables over a bowl, catching the
excess vinaigrette. You should have about 4 fl oz/113
ml of excess vinaigrette.

■ Place the salad greens in a bowl, pour in the
excess vinaigrette and toss well. Add the marinated
vegetables and serve!

Helpful Hints and Observations

STIR-FRIED SALAD? – It must seem rather odd to
toss the hard salad items in oil, but I do this to
get the maximum flavour from the volatile oils of the
vegetables which can only be fully released at frying
temperatures.

About the Ingredients

ASSORTED SALAD GREENS – The class of vegetable
called 'greens' is not only a festival of greens, blues,
whites and reds, it's also loaded with vitamins A and
C. And some greens – like kohlrabi, broccoli, turnips
and kale – are thought to be cancer-preventers. Take
your time at the greengrocer's and look at the
varieties available. Select greens that have fresh,
vibrant colours. The leaves should not look wilted or
have blemish spots. Since greens grow so close to the
ground, wash them well.

CELERY – Long green stalks of celery are a familiar
sight in any supermarket or greengrocer's. The
stalks are usually harvested from year-old plants. If the
plants are allowed to grow for 2 years they go to seed,
which is where we get the spice, celery seed. Choose
celery that is firm, with no yellow or wilted leaves. If
you store it in an airtight container it will stay fresh
for up to 2 weeks. But don't separate the stalks until
you're ready to use them – once separated they wilt
more quickly. If your celery is a bit soft, cutting off
the stalks and putting them in a jug of cold water in
the refrigerator will restore their crispness.

GINGER – If you haven't already, you should add this
ingredient to your Minimax larder! Fresh ginger is a
tan, knobby, underground stem that can be found in
many supermarkets. Its taste is completely different
from that of powdered ginger. It adds zest, zing and
zoom to your dishes. Fresh ginger should be hard
and its skin tight. If the skin is shrivelled, the flavour
of the ginger will be weakened. Most recipes call for
you to peel ginger before using it. In the Orient, they
just slice off the scarred tips and use it skin and all!
Fresh ginger keeps very well in the refrigerator, in a
dry, airtight plastic bag.

MUESLI and KERRMUSH

$\mathcal{I}$ have been eating these cereals since 1978. I alternate between the Kerrmush and the Muesli, according to either the weather or boredom! My Welsh 'dinner' guest on television was terrorized by porridge as a child – this recipe helped to change his mind. If it changes yours, you will have taken the largest single step toward a more creative food-style. Most breakfasts are either smothered in fat or don't exist at all. Kerrmush and Muesli are low in fat, and provide lots of good energy until lunch.

Muesli must be served cold and the surface scattered with fresh fruit, such as straw-berries, rasp-berries, or even slices of kiwi.

One bowlful with a toasted wholewheat muffin does the trick for me until lunchtime.

MUESLI

Serves 1

INGREDIENTS

2 tablespoons/30 ml rolled oats
1 tablespoon/15 ml raisins
½ Granny Smith apple, grated
1 tablespoon/15 ml fresh lemon juice
1 tablespoon/15 ml runny honey
2 tablespoons/30 ml plain, non-fat yogurt
1 tablespoon/15 ml Minimax Seed Mix (see page 205),
ground until just broken
Fruit of your choice

FIRST PREPARE

■ Soak the oats and raisins in water overnight.

NOW ASSEMBLE

■ Drain the oats and raisins.

■ Mix the grated apple with the lemon juice, oats and raisins.

■ Mix together the honey and yogurt, and stir into the oat mixture.

■ Sprinkle with Minimax Seed Mix, garnish with small pieces of bright fruit, and serve.

Nutritional Profile

PER SERVING	CLASSIC	MINIMAX
Calories	186	278
Fat (g)	7	5
Calories from fat	33%	16%
Cholesterol (mg)	15	1
Sodium (mg)	238	58
Fibre	3	5

■ *Classic compared:* Muesli

Time Estimate

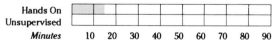

Hands On									
Unsupervised									
Minutes	10	20	30	40	50	60	70	80	90

Cost Estimate

Low	Medium	Medium High	Celebration

KERRMUSH

Serves 4

INGREDIENTS

8 fl oz/227 ml rolled oats
4 tablespoons/60 ml raisins
1 pint/568 ml skimmed milk
4 tablespoons/60 ml Minimax Seed Mix (see page 205)
4 teaspoons/20 ml runny honey

NOW COOK

■ Simmer the oats, raisins and milk until just cooked – about 10 minutes. Stir and remove from the heat.

■ Sprinkle with the Minimax Seed Mix, either whole, or partly or fully ground. I use a small electric coffee bean grinder to do this fresh each day.

■ Drizzle the honey on top and serve hot.

About the Ingredients

ROLLED OATS – This grain is oat groats that have been heated to soften them, then rolled or literally flattened. Rolled oats will cook more quickly than oat groats, which can take up to 2 hours.

Nutritional Profile

PER SERVING	CLASSIC	MINIMAX
Calories	211	248
Fat (g)	9	5
Calories from fat	37%	19%
Cholesterol (mg)	28	3
Sodium (mg)	281	92
Fibre (g)	2	3

■ *Classic compared:* Oatmeal

Time Estimate

Hands On									
Unsupervised									
Minutes	10	20	30	40	50	60	70	80	90

Cost Estimate

Low	Medium	Medium High	Celebration

CREMPOG *(Welsh Pancakes)*

Jn Wales there is a charming seasonal custom of cooking Crempog (pancakes) for the children who go from house to house in search of the best buttered, best sugared, softest fudge syruped . . . well . . . it's charming!

My changes have kept the Welsh-styled soft soda pancake and used the seasonal apples and plums of the area to make a most unusual dessert. No cream is needed: this is full of its own flavours.

Nutritional Profile

PER SERVING	CLASSIC	MINIMAX
Calories	885	271
Fat (g)	49	3
Calories from fat	50%	9%
Cholesterol (mg)	180	37
Sodium (mg)	590	196
Fibre (g)	2	3

■ *Classic compared:* Crempog

Time Estimate

Hands On
Unsupervised

Minutes   10 20 30 40 50 60 70 80 90

Cost Estimate

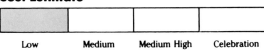

Low   Medium   Medium High   Celebration

Serves 4

INGREDIENTS

PANCAKE BATTER

6 oz/170 g plain flour

1 egg, lightly beaten

6 fl oz/170 ml non-fat plain yogurt

8 fl oz/227 ml skimmed milk

1 teaspoon/5 ml bicarbonate of soda

1 teaspoon/5 ml cider vinegar

1 teaspoon/5 ml extra light olive oil with a dash of sesame oil

SYRUP

1 large Granny Smith apple, peeled and cored, but left whole

3 large red plums

8 fl oz/227 ml water

8 fl oz/227 ml cranberry juice

2 tablespoons/30 ml brown sugar

A 3-inch/8-cm cinnamon stick

8 whole cloves

⅛ teaspoon/0.6 ml nutmeg, freshly grated

4 allspice berries

2 tablespoons/30 ml arrowroot mixed with 4 table-spoons/60 ml water

FIRST PREPARE

■ Sift the flour into a bowl, make a well in the centre and pour in the lightly beaten egg, the yogurt and 6 fl oz/170 ml of the milk. Beat until smooth. The batter should be thick. Cover and let rest for 1 hour.

■ Cut the apple into four thick slices. The slices should look like flat doughnuts. Cut one plum in half and remove the stone.

NOW COOK

■ Put the water, cranberry juice, brown sugar, cin-namon stick, cloves, nutmeg and allspice berries into a saucepan and bring to a boil. Add the apple slices, the whole plums and the plum halves and poach for 2 minutes or until the fruit is soft.

■ Remove the apple slices and whole plums, leaving the two plum halves. Remove the skins from the whole plums and cut them in half.

■ Reduce the syrup by boiling to 8 fl oz/227 ml. Strain and transfer to a clean saucepan. Stir in the arrowroot paste and stir until thickened.

■ Mix the bicarbonate of soda and vinegar together and stir them into the batter.

■ Before you cook the pancakes, adjust the batter's consistency by adding the remaining milk (up to 2 fl oz/57 ml) until the batter runs smoothly off the ladle.

■ Heat an 8-inch/20-cm sauté pan and brush with oil. Ladle 2 fl oz/57 ml of the batter into the prepared pan and cook until bubbles appear and burst on the surface – about 1 minute. Turn the pancake over and cook another minute. Remove and cool on a wire rack. Repeat with the remaining batter. You need eight pancakes for this recipe.

■ Trim the pancakes into even circles (see *Helpful Hints*). Place one pancake on a serving plate and set a poached apple slice on top. Top with a second pancake, so that you have an apple sandwich. Top with a plum half and dribble with the syrup.

Helpful Hints and Observations

THE SPICED FRUIT SYRUP – Sugar and fat seem naturally made for each other: one begs for the other. When you try to separate them, it's difficult! One method, used here, is to develop an aromatic smoke screen of spices. I made up a simple syrup with only 2 tablespoons of brown sugar (a more complex flavour than white sugar) in place of the classic 12 tablespoons and none of the 12 tablespoons of butter! The spices do the trick but the syrup needs more flavour from the fruit than the brief poaching time would bring out. Therefore, I added an extra plum to the reduction process, giving me more body, colour and flavour in the syrup.

PERFECTLY TRIMMED PANCAKES – It's quite easy if you cut them with a 4-inch/10-cm round biscuit cutter.

About the Ingredients

ALLSPICE BERRIES – Although this sounds like a combination of several spices, the name comes from the fact that these berries are said to smell like a mix-ture of cloves, cinnamon and nutmeg. Allspice is the fruit of a slender evergreen tree native to Central and South America and the West Indies. The berries, each containing two kidney-shaped seeds, are harvested by hand while still green and then dried in the sun to a dark purple colour.

PLUMS – Do try to get fresh plums: the tinned ones just aren't big enough. We made this for the television show in the dead of winter, with plums that were available at the greengrocer's from South America! So it is possible to find fresh ones, even out of the normal plum season.

DUTCH PANCAKES

I've always had great fun with this dish. It began in Amsterdam, back in the early 1970s, when I ate it with gusto – not a side dish! Recently my recipe has changed, and when once you master the idea it's even more fun to fix – with much less risk!

This is basically a pancake and ham sandwich with glazed apples on top and a maple-flavoured custard sauce. I serve it as an unusual breakfast for a crowd. Everyone seems to have a good time!

Nutritional Profile

PER SERVING	CLASSIC	MINIMAX
Calories	1068	493
Fat (g)	60	10
Calories from fat	50%	19%
Cholesterol (mg)	580	128
Sodium (mg)	716	627
Fibre (g)	4	3

■ *Classic compared:* Dutch Pancakes

Time Estimate

Hands On									
Unsupervised									
Minutes	10	20	30	40	50	60	70	80	90

Cost Estimate

Low	Medium	Medium High	Celebration

Serves 2

INGREDIENTS

NOTE: This pancake recipe makes four pancakes, but you only need two for your finished dish. That leaves two pancakes for your children to try their hands with!

PANCAKE BATTER

1 whole egg

1 egg yolk

½ pint/284 ml skimmed milk

4 oz/113 g plain flour

¼ teaspoon/1.25 ml salt, freshly ground

¼ teaspoon/1.25 ml white pepper, freshly ground

1 tablespoon/15 ml extra light olive oil with a dash of sesame oil

SAUCE

2 fl oz/57 ml evaporated skimmed milk

2 fl oz/57 ml real maple syrup

1 tablespoon/15 ml cornflour

2 tablespoons/30 ml water

4 fl oz/113 ml strained yogurt (see page 210)

FILLING

2 oz/57 g back bacon, trimmed of fat

1 Granny Smith apple, peeled, cored and sliced

1 teaspoon/5 ml brown sugar for dusting

¼ teaspoon/1.25 ml ground cinnamon

FIRST PREPARE THE PANCAKES

■ In a small bowl, mix the whole egg, egg yolk and milk. Sift the flour, salt and pepper into a medium bowl and make a well in the centre. Pour the egg mixture into the well and gradually stir it together with the flour until fully incorporated with no lumps. Set the batter aside in a cool place to rest for 30 minutes. This will relax the starch cells and provide a more delicate pancake.

■ Heat a 10-inch/25-cm non-stick frying pan to medium. Pour the olive oil into the pan, coat well, then pour the oil into the pancake batter. Mix thoroughly. This will help make the pancake self-releasing.

■ Pour 4 fl oz/113 ml of pancake batter into the heated frying pan. Rotate the pan until the entire surface is covered.

■ When the edges of the pancake start curling up and the top looks waxy, flip the pancake over. Cook the other side until it's light brown – just a minute or two – and turn it out on to a dish. Finish cooking the rest of the pancakes.

NOW MAKE THE SAUCE

■ In a small saucepan, over medium heat, combine the evaporated skimmed milk and maple syrup. Cook until hot, but not boiling.

■ In a small bowl, dissolve the cornflour in the water. Stir into the milk mixture, bring to the boil and stir until the sauce has thickened. It will have the consistency of whipped honey. Remove from the heat and let it cool.

■ To finish the sauce, stir in the strained yogurt and return to lowest heat, stirring occasionally to keep the sauce from sticking.

TO ASSEMBLE

■ Put one pancake on an individual, flameproof serving plate. Place the back bacon on top of the pancake.

■ Arrange the grill pan 3 inches/8 cm from the heat source and grill the pancake until just brown, approximately 2½ minutes.

■ Remove from the grill, cover with another pancake and arrange the apple slices around the edge in two concentric circles: one circle around the outside edge and one in the middle. Extend the slices just over the edge of the pancake so the delicate edge doesn't burn.

■ Dust with a scattering of cinnamon, sprinkle with brown sugar and pop back under the grill until the apples are just brown on the edges and glazed.

■ Serve warm, with the sauce.

Helpful Hints and Observations

SKIMMED MILK – See page 203.

About the Ingredients

EVAPORATED SKIMMED MILK – See page 197.

MAPLE SYRUP – One of the sweet fruits of spring, when it is collected in the form of sap from holes drilled into maple trees, its unique flavour is the result of trace amounts of minerals, sugars and other substances in the sap: a combination that is very difficult to manufacture artificially. I use it as a personal 'signature' item that adds character to sweetened dishes and helps me to reduce the total sugars added.

WAFFLES WITH APPLE BUTTER

C*reating this recipe I faced the biggest gastronomic hurdle of my culinary life: could I find an alternative to waffles, dripping with butter and syrup, which would please a most discerning 11-year-old boy, Chris Cashman, otherwise known as 'The Waffle Master'? Let's just say that the only word uttered after 'The Waffle Master' tasted this recipe was 'Awesome!'*

Minimax Waffles with Apple Butter are a crisp, crunchy, wholesome food for a special breakfast. A variation on the apple butter can be made by combining it with a little strained yogurt. You'll be delighted with the resulting whipped cream-like mixture. And never forget the sweet pleasures of ripe, sliced fruit on a steaming waffle!

Nutritional Profile

PER SERVING	CLASSIC	MINIMAX
Calories	1069	460
Fat (g)	35	9
Calories from fat	29%	18%
Cholesterol (mg)	199	55
Sodium (mg)	916	412
Fibre (g)	3	4

■ *Classic compared:* Waffles with Syrup

Time Estimate

Hands On									
Unsupervised									
Minutes	10	20	30	40	50	60	70	80	90

Cost Estimate

Low	Medium	Medium High	Celebration

Serves 4

INGREDIENTS

APPLE BUTTER

3 sweet cooking apples, washed, cored and sliced

2 fl oz/57 ml clear, unsweetened apple juice

2 fl oz/57 ml water

2 tablespoons/30 ml dark (unsulphured) raisins

2 fl oz/57 ml brown sugar

⅛ teaspoon/0.6 ml ground cinnamon

Dash of ground cloves

Dash of ground allspice

¼ teaspoon/1.25 ml nutmeg, freshly grated

1 teaspoon/5 ml lemon rind, grated

WAFFLES

7 oz/200 g plain flour

1 tablespoon/15 ml baking powder

Pinch of salt

1 tablespoon/15 ml sugar

16 fl oz/455 ml milk

1 egg

2 tablespoons/30 ml extra light olive oil with a dash of sesame oil

3 egg whites

FIRST PREPARE THE APPLE BUTTER

■ Put the apples, apple juice, water and raisins in a saucepan and bring to the boil. Cover, reduce the heat and simmer until the apples are soft – about 20 minutes.

■ Press the fruit through a sieve, or process at high speed until smooth, then return to the saucepan. Continue to simmer, uncovered, on very low heat, or in a 300°F/150°C/Gas Mark 2 oven. Add the brown sugar, spices and lemon rind. Cook for another 30 minutes until very thick and a lovely dark brown.

■ Apple butter can be eaten right away or preserved by the usual bottling methods.

NOW COOK THE WAFFLES

■ In a medium-sized mixing bowl, stir together the flour, baking powder, salt and sugar. In another bowl combine the milk, whole egg and oil. Stir the wet ingredients into the dry ones and blend until smooth and creamy.

■ Just before cooking the waffles, in a copper bowl, beat the egg whites until they form soft peaks. Gently fold the beaten egg whites into the waffle batter, one-third at a time.

■ Pre-heat a waffle iron according to the manufacturer's directions, or until a drop of water sizzles and bounces when dropped on to the hot iron.

■ Brush the waffle iron lightly with oil, then pour in approximately 4 fl oz/113 ml batter per waffle square or enough to fill the entire waffle iron. Cook for 3 minutes and serve immediately with apple butter.

Helpful Hints and Observations

THE LIMP WAFFLE SOLUTION – If you are cooking a batch of waffles for the family, never stack them. Stacking causes waffles to go limp! Instead, pre-heat the oven to 300°F/150°C/Gas Mark 2 and slip them on to the racks, leaving the door slightly open. They will stay crisp for at least 30 minutes.

FRESH AND FRAGRANT – If you have the time, always use freshly ground spices – you will have a wonderfully fragrant experience.

IF YOU LIKE THE APPLE BUTTER – There is just enough volume in this recipe for you to make a small experimental batch. If you like it, simply multiply the amount and invite your friends to an apple butter production party, which is the way it is done in the Pennsylvania Dutch communities.

About the Ingredients

APPLES – Apples are the world's most common fruit. There are over 7,000 varieties, but only a few of these make it to our commercial markets. The best apple butter comes from firm-fleshed, slightly tart dessert apples such as Granny Smith or Jonathan (both imported) or the homegrown Worcester Pearmain, Laxton's Superb, or Cox's Orange Pippin, which are sweeter. Apples are at their peak of flavour in late summer and autumn, when they are being harvested.

ARNOLD BENNETT OMELETTE

There are very few classical exceptions to the rule 'savoury omelettes are solid in texture and sweet omelettes are fluffy', but having said this, I can fully endorse the Arnold Bennett Omelette as super! However, the method of egg yolk reduction that I've used here only works when you boost the basic one yolk with all the added seasonings.

Wholewheat rolls or wholewheat toast with a light margarine and a well-herbed green salad go very nicely.

Nutritional Profile

PER SERVING	CLASSIC	MINIMAX
Calories	239	182
Fat (g)	18	9
Calories from fat	67%	43%
Cholesterol (mg)	260	130
Sodium (mg)	501	786
Fibre (g)	0	1

■ *Classic compared:* Arnold Bennett Omelette

Time Estimate

Hands On									
Unsupervised									

Minutes 10 20 30 40 50 60 70 80 90

Cost Estimate

Low	Medium	Medium High	Celebration

Serves 2

INGREDIENTS

4½ oz/128 g smoked mackerel or other moist, tender, smoked fish fillet
Enough skimmed milk to cover the fish
3 tablespoons/45 ml sun-dried tomatoes
4 egg whites*
1 teaspoon/5 ml cold water
⅛ teaspoon/0.6 ml salt
1 egg yolk
¼ teaspoon/1.25 ml black pepper, freshly ground
1 teaspoon/5 ml fresh coriander leaves, finely chopped
¼ teaspoon/1.25 ml nutmeg, freshly grated
A good pinch of saffron threads or ¼ teaspoon/1.25 ml powdered saffron
2 tablespoons/30 ml spring onions, finely chopped
1 teaspoon/5 ml butter
1 tablespoon/15 ml mild Cheddar cheese, grated
1 tablespoon/15 ml fresh chives, finely chopped

The extra egg yolks can be frozen and added to the dog food. Dogs don't have a problem with cholesterol.

FIRST PREPARE

■ Cover the smoked fish in milk, soak for 1 hour, drain and pat dry. Remove the dark skin and flake the fish into a bowl.

■ Soak the dried tomatoes in boiling water for 10 minutes to soften them. Slice them thinly.

■ Whip the egg whites with the cold water and salt until they just peak.

■ Place the yolk in a 10-inch/25-cm diameter mixing bowl. Beat with the black pepper, coriander leaves, 1 tablespoon/15 ml of the sun-dried tomatoes, the nutmeg and saffron. This forms the essential flavour base; if you skimp on these flavours, the volume of the egg whites will turn the omelette into latex!

■ Combine the flaked fish with the chopped spring onions and the remaining sun-dried tomatoes.

■ Immediately before making the omelette, stir one-third of the beaten egg whites into the seasoned yolk mixture. You can make a thorough job of this so as to lighten the flavour base. Now pour the base into the remaining whites and fold together carefully; don't beat it – just fold until the yolk has evenly coloured the whites.

■ Pre-heat the grill and set the rack 4–5 inches/10–13 cm from the heat.

NOW COOK

■ Set an omelette pan over medium-high heat and, when hot, add the butter. Wait until the edges of the butter froth and brown. Add the egg mixture all at once and stir quickly, using a spatula and making a figure-of-eight motion. This helps to expose the eggs to the bottom heat.

Bang the pan on the stove top a couple of times to settle the mixture. Smooth the surface with a knife. Scatter the cheese and the onion/fish/tomato mixture over the top.

■ Slide the whole pan immediately under the pre-heated grill and cook until small, brown bubbles appear, the level has risen, the cheese has melted and the omelette is golden brown.

■ Loosen the edges and carefully ease the omelette out of the pan with a spatula on to a serving dish. Dust with finely chopped fresh chives and serve.

Helpful Hints and Observations

EGGS IN YOUR LIFE? – The problem with eggs is that they are perhaps the most perfect convenience food, an excellent source of protein, easily digested, extremely varied in use, universally enjoyed and reasonably inexpensive – but they have this problem with cholesterol. The American Heart Association has suggested, within its conservative guidelines, that we consume no more than three to four eggs per week, and then only if we are in good health and at no apparent risk of heart disease. If problems do exist, then it's no more than two, and some people I know, like my wife, Treena, are off them altogether with only an occasional 'reminder'. (We will not call it a 'treat' because that means that to avoid them is a continued denial that·can build up into a rebellion binge, and that can cause a great deal of harm.) This omelette is designed to meet your need for a pleasant reminder.

About the Ingredients

SMOKED MACKEREL – A moist, oily, smoked fish with a rich flavour, smoked mackerel may be too strong for some tastes. If you prefer something milder, substitute smoked trout, herring, or even salmon. Remember, smoked fish should smell smoky, not fishy. Select whole pieces that are more dry than slimy on the exterior.

SAFFRON – See page 61.

FU YUNG GAI *(Chinese Chicken Omelette)*

*A*re you a tofu fan yet? When I made this dish for the television programme, most of the people in our studio audience were quite hesitant! But once they had dabbed a bit of fresh ginger and oyster sauce behind their ears, they were ready for anything! Maybe all you'll need to do is taste this dish's unique combination of textures and flavours to become a true tofu connoisseur!

Nutritional Profile

PER SERVING	CLASSIC	MINIMAX
Calories	421	398
Fat (g)	30	10
Calories from fat	64%	23%
Cholesterol (mg)	562	189
Sodium (mg)	791	437
Fibre (g)	0.3	2

■ *Classic compared:* Fu Yung Gai

Time Estimate

Hands On		
Unsupervised		
Minutes	10 20 30 40 50 60 70 80 90	

Cost Estimate

Low	Medium	Medium High	Celebration

Serves 4

INGREDIENTS

OMELETTE

6 oz/170g boneless chicken breast, finely diced

4 teaspoons/20 ml lemon juice, freshly squeezed

4 teaspoons/20 ml rice wine vinegar

½ teaspoon/2.5 ml ginger root, freshly grated

2 spring onions, chopped

¼ teaspoon/1.25 ml white pepper, freshly ground

3 oz/85 g tofu, finely diced

1 teaspoon/5 ml extra light olive oil with a dash of sesame oil

½ oz/14 g butter

3 large eggs, beaten

1 tablespoon/15 ml fresh coriander leaves, chopped

1½ pints/900 ml steamed cooked rice

SAUCE

½ cup/113 ml clear homemade chicken stock (recipe page 210)

2 tablespoons/30 ml oyster sauce

2 teaspoons/10 ml lemon juice, freshly squeezed

1 teaspoon/5 ml arrowroot mixed with 1 teaspoon/5 ml water

FIRST PREPARE

■ Marinate the diced chicken in 3 teaspoons/15 ml of the lemon juice, 3 teaspoons/15 ml of the rice wine vinegar, the spring onions, ginger root and white pepper for 20 minutes. (Do try freshly grinding your pepper . . . it is a remarkable experience for your olfactory sense!) Lift out the chicken, drain and set aside.

■ Marinate the tofu for 30 minutes in the remaining lemon juice and rice wine vinegar. Lift out the tofu, drain and set aside.

NOW COOK

■ *The sauce:* Heat the chicken stock, oyster sauce and lemon juice in a small pan. Remove the pan from the heat, add the arrowroot paste, return to the heat and stir until thickened. Set aside and keep warm.

■ *The omelette:* Heat the olive oil in a non-stick pan and quickly fry the marinated diced chicken until white, about 1 to 2 minutes. Add the tofu pieces so the flavours can mingle. Because the pieces are the same size, the tofu will give you the feeling of a lot more chicken. Cook for about a minute, then remove the pan from the heat and turn the chicken and tofu out on to a plate.

■ Wipe the pan, add the butter and heat until it just begins to turn brown – this is the correct time to add the eggs! Pour the beaten eggs into the pan and stir quickly, spreading the eggs to cover the entire pan (stirring will bring the butter taste into the omelette).

■ When the eggs look fairly set, sprinkle the chicken and tofu on top in a vertical line down the centre of the pan. Fold over each side of the omelette.

■ *To Serve:* Heat a plate in your oven. Gently shake the omelette out of the pan on to the warmed plate so that the fold is on the bottom and the egg completely covers it. Pour your warm coating sauce over the top and dust with the chopped coriander. What colour! What aroma! Rice is the perfect accompaniment to sop up every drop!

About the Ingredients

TOFU – Did you know that for much of their history, Asian people didn't use butter or cheese? Soybean products have traditionally taken the place of dairy foods in their diet (soybean milk is quite similar to cow's milk).

If you're wondering where the connection to tofu is in all this, tofu is really soybean curd. Yes, I know, the thought of soybean curd as a substitute for meat or dairy products takes some getting used to. But tofu is inexpensive, high in protein, low in saturated fats – and definitely worth the effort!

Tofu is available in two basic textures: hard and soft. Pick the one that suits your fancy and you're off – on a new Minimax food adventure!

OYSTER SAUCE – Fu Yung Gai is really the dish for excitement! First tofu and now oyster sauce! Don't hesitate for even a moment: oyster sauce is dark, tangy, mysterious . . . well, almost inscrutable! You'll want to add it as a seasoning to all sorts of stir-fries and other dishes. Buy it in the bottle from Oriental foodstores or large supermarkets.

QUICHE KIRKLAND

$\mathcal{D}$epending, of course, upon how deep the quiche is, the nutrition risk often comes as much from the crust as from the filling.

In a classic butter-made crust there are about 21 grams of saturated fat, which means about 63% of calories derived from fat. That really isn't good news for pie fanciers (like me). However, here is an unusually tasty crust that goes a long way towards making this recipe an acceptable alternative: it's actually made from rice!

I always serve quiche with an attractive salad. See Helpful Hints *for the Split Salad recipe.*

Nutritional Profile

PER SERVING	CLASSIC	MINIMAX
Calories	464	195
Fat (g)	33	5
Calories from fat	63%	21%
Cholesterol (mg)	122	44
Sodium (mg)	637	607
Fibre (g)	1	2

■ *Classic compared:* Quiche Lorraine

Time Estimate

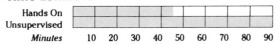

Hands On
Unsupervised
Minutes 10 20 30 40 50 60 70 80 90

Cost Estimate

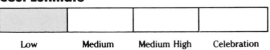

Low   Medium   Medium High   Celebration

Serves 6

INGREDIENTS

PARMESAN-RICE CRUST

16 fl oz/454 ml cooked long grain rice

½ teaspoon/2.5 ml salt

1 egg white, beaten

1 teaspoon/5 ml low-salt soy sauce

1 oz/28 g Parmesan cheese, freshly grated

Black pepper to taste, freshly ground

QUICHE FILLING

7 sun-dried tomato halves

4 fl oz/113 ml back bacon, all fat removed and matchstick-sliced

½ pint/284 ml mushrooms, thinly sliced

2 fl oz/57 ml sweet green pepper, diced

2 fl oz/57 ml sweet red pepper, diced

1 tablespoon/15 ml fresh thyme leaves

1 tablespoon/15 ml fresh basil leaves, chopped

¼ teaspoon/1.25 ml nutmeg, freshly grated

Black pepper to taste, freshly ground

1 oz/28 g Parmesan cheese, freshly grated

1 whole egg

4 egg whites

12 fl oz/340 ml skimmed milk

GARNISH

½ tablespoon/8 ml fresh basil, chopped

½ tablespoon/8 ml fresh parsley, chopped

Pinch of cayenne pepper

NOW COOK

■ *The Crust:* In a medium bowl, mix together all the ingredients. Press the mixture into a 9-inch/23-cm non-stick flan dish. Bake at 375°F/190°C/Gas Mark 5 for 25 minutes, until it looks dry and just golden-brown around the edges.

■ *The Filling:* Pre-heat the oven to 400°F/205°C/Gas Mark 6.

■ Soak the sun-dried tomatoes in warm water until plump – about 10 to 15 minutes. Drain and dice finely.

■ In a medium skillet, sauté the bacon, mushrooms, peppers and sun-dried tomatoes. Notice the great pink, red and green colours! Sprinkle with the thyme leaves, basil, nutmeg and black pepper. Cook the vegetables until they are just tender and their flavours blended – about 5 minutes.

■ Turn the cooked vegetables into a fine mesh strainer and drain off any excess liquids. Tip them into the cooked pie crust and sprinkle with half the Parmesan cheese.

■ In a medium bowl, beat together the egg yolk, egg whites and milk. Pour this custard on top of the vegetables. It should just cover them. Sprinkle with the remaining Parmesan cheese.

■ Bake at 400°F/205°C/Gas Mark 6 for 25 minutes, or until the custard is set.

■ *To Serve:* Sprinkle the completed quiche with fresh basil, parsley and cayenne pepper. Cut it into wedges and delight your guests!

Helpful Hints and Observations

SPLIT SALAD – One hidden source of fat is salad dressings. The split salad method allows the dressing flavour to marinate the vegetables while lowering the calorie count.

A mixed salad can be broken down into two kinds of components: hard and soft. For the hard vegetables, include celery, tomatoes, sweet onion, radishes and carrots. Place the finely sliced hard vegetables in a bowl, add a dressing and marinate in the refrigerator for at least 3 hours or even overnight. When you are ready to make the salad, pour off the excess dressing (which can be saved and re-used, providing it is kept under refrigeration), add the marinated hard vegetables to the fresh greens and toss.

This method substantially lowers fat and restricts the more liberal use of thin dressings for a zesty flavourful salad!

CHEESE . . . FRESHLY GRATED – I'm trying to reduce, but *never* eliminate, the fabulous taste of cheese which contains a high percentage of saturated fat, from some of my favourite dishes. I'm especially fond of the classic Parmesan cheese from Reggio Emilia, Italy, made from skimmed cows' milk (32% butterfat), mixed with rennet and cooked for 30 minutes, then drained and dried. For the best taste cheese should be grated as needed, and for this purpose, I use either the old-fashioned, hand-cranked, rotary Mouli from France, or the 'new' hand-held cheese stroker (as I call it).

STICKY FINGERS – When preparing the rice crust, it helps to have a small bowl of cold water to moisten your fingers and avoid stickiness.

FRENCH RAREBIT

*C*heese on toast? Well, not really! The Welsh make fine cheese and, like every cheese-producing area, they developed their own bread and cheese idea (Welsh Rarebit). A little beer, some mustard, a slice of toast. I've 'springboarded' on this classic to produce my own recipe.

This is really a snack food for the cold weather: a firm 'welcome home' when it's raw outside and the family has been burning energy. I've dropped the calories from 529 to 235 with only 6 grams of fat . . . so it's within the limit!

Nutritional Profile

PER SERVING	CLASSIC	MINIMAX
Calories	529	235
Fat (g)	39	6
Calories from fat	66%	24%
Cholesterol (mg)	170	19
Sodium (mg)	747	366
Fibre (g)	1	2

■ *Classic compared:* Welsh Rarebit

Time Estimate

Hands On Unsupervised									
Minutes	10	20	30	40	50	60	70	80	90

Cost Estimate

Low	Medium	Medium High	Celebration

Serves 6

INGREDIENTS

1½ lb/700 g yellow-skinned new potatoes
2 fl oz/57 ml skimmed milk
¼ teaspoon/1.25 ml white pepper, freshly ground
¼ teaspoon/1.25 ml nutmeg, freshly grated
2 tablespoons/30 ml white wine Worcestershire sauce
4 fl oz/113 ml de-alcoholized beer
1 teaspoon/5 ml dry mustard powder
4 oz/113 g mild Cheddar cheese (or another good grating cheese), finely grated
1 French baguette loaf (about 15 inches/40 cm long), sliced in half horizontally, doughy centre scooped out
Paprika
Fresh parsley, chopped

FIRST PREPARE

■ Bake the potatoes at 375°F/190°C/Gas Mark 5 for 1 hour. Wrap them in a towel and gently squeeze from all sides to break up the flesh, but take care not to rupture the skin. Spoon the potato out of the skin and into a medium-sized mixing bowl, and mash it well. Save the skins for use in Cynthia's Skins (see *Helpful Hints*).

NOW COOK

■ Return the hot potato to a warm saucepan over medium heat. Add the milk, white pepper and nutmeg and beat well to cream. (This is, by the way, the best way to make mashed potatoes. You may need ⅛ teaspoon/0.6 ml of salt, but you don't need added butter or fat.)

■ Now stir in the Worcestershire sauce, beer, dry mustard and finally 3 oz/85 g of the cheese – mix well and taste it!

■ Pour the cheese sauce into the hollowed-out baguette. Sprinkle with the remaining cheese and a little paprika.

■ Grill until dappled brown. Dust with parsley and cut it in front of the gang!

Helpful Hints and Observations

CYNTHIA'S SKINS – Cynthia is my Food Associate: she keeps tabs on how long everything takes to cook and how much it costs; and she hunts down the best suppliers for all the produce we need. While we were testing this recipe, she suggested an idea for using the leftover potato skins. We tried it, and it worked so well we named it after her!

Recipe: Brush the leftover potato skins with a little beaten egg white and put them on a baking sheet. Sprinkle them with cayenne pepper to taste, and about 2 tablespoons/30 ml of your favourite grated or crumbled cheese. Pop them under the grill for 4 minutes and serve.

About the Ingredients

WHITE PEPPER – Pepper was probably the earliest spice known to man. Wars have been fought over the pepper trade, and in England in the Middle Ages rents were levied for a time in pounds of peppercorns! Its value derived from its scarcity: the black pepper vine will only grow in rich soil in a moist tropical climate, while the demand for its berries is worldwide. Black pepper is the result of drying the red pepper berries, which then have a greenish-black, wrinkled surface. White pepper is produced from the same seed, but the berries are immersed in water for several weeks, then freed from the skin and the fleshy part of the fruit. White pepper is less pungent than black.

NUTMEG – The nutmeg tree produces a fruit from which both nutmeg and mace are extracted. Inside the fruit is a kernel protected by a bright red net-like 'mace', which dries to yellowish-brown. And the kernel contains a single glossy, brown, oily seed which is the nutmeg. Ground nutmeg is milder than mace, with a warm, sweet, highly spicy flavour.

WHITE WINE WORCESTERSHIRE SAUCE – 'Oh,' you say with a sigh, 'the yuppies of the world have finally triumphed!' 'Oh,' I reply, 'not entirely!' This white wine version was not created so that yuppies could nip at cool canapés while tinkling glasses at power parties. It was actually created by Lea & Perrins because they felt the public was becoming more health-conscious and needed a sauce to use with fish, chicken and pasta. 'Well,' you repeat, 'isn't that yuppy style?' 'OK,' I shrug, quite happy to be associated with young upwardly mobile professionals at the age of 57!

PEARS ROVER

My good friend Chef de Cuisine Thierry Rautureau, chef/owner of Rover's in Seattle, Washington, worked with me to develop this idea. We 'springboarded' off the famous French Bavarois dessert: a rich egg yolk and heavy cream custard with a wonderful texture and taste. Our dish begins by using strained yogurt in place of the cream! It's a good dessert for a hot summer evening.

Nutritional Profile

PER SERVING	CLASSIC	MINIMAX
Calories	299	225
Fat (g)	16	1
Calories from fat	47%	5%
Cholesterol (mg)	148	3
Sodium (mg)	39	94
Fibre (g)	1	7

■ *Classic compared:* Pears Rover

Time Estimate

Hands On Unsupervised		7 Hours	
Minutes	10 20 30 40 50	60 70 80 90	

Cost Estimate

Low	Medium	Medium High	Celebration

Serves 4

INGREDIENTS

4 ripe, sweet pears
2 egg whites
¼ teaspoon/1.25 ml +½ pint/284 ml water
Pinch of salt
1 envelope unflavoured gelatin
½ pint/284 ml strained non-fat yogurt (recipe page 210) mixed with 1 tablespoon/15 ml runny honey
12 fl oz/340 ml de-alcoholized white wine
Raspberry purée for garnish (optional)

FIRST PREPARE

■ Peel and core the pears, but leave them whole. Save the peel and cores. Cover the pears with water into which you've squeezed a few drops of lemon juice, to prevent browning.

■ In a large bowl, mix the egg whites with ¼ teaspoon/1.25 ml water and a pinch of salt (to help them hold their texture). Beat until just firm.

■ Sprinkle the gelatin on top of 2 fl oz/57 ml of the water and dissolve for 3 minutes. Individual granules will soften. Stir into the yogurt and honey.

■ Lightly grease four individual dessert moulds with oil.

NOW COOK

■ Put the pear peels and cores in 8 fl oz/227 ml of the water. Bring to the boil and reduce to 4 fl oz/113 ml. Mash and strain, saving the pear juice.

■ Add the wine to the whole pears along with the strained pear juice and gently poach the pears until tender, about 20 to 30 minutes.

■ Remove the pears, strain the liquid and cook the juice down until you have 2 fl oz/57 ml pear 'nectar'. Stir this into the strained yogurt.

■ Fold the whipped egg whites gently into the mixture.

■ Spoon 1 tablespoon/15 ml of yogurt mixture into each dessert mould.

■ Cut your perfectly poached pears into small pieces. Put a layer of diced pears into each mould. Top with a last layer of the yogurt mixture.

■ Put in the refrigerator to chill.

■ Unmould on to serving plates by submerging each mould in boiling water for a few seconds, then inverting it on a plate.

■ You can serve your Pears Rover encircled in a ring of bright red hearts! Simply beat some strained yogurt until thin. Pour a small amount in a ring around each individual serving. With an eye dropper, take some raspberry purée and squeeze small drops, evenly spaced, on top of the yogurt. Now take a toothpick or knife tip and drag it lightly through the centre of the raspberry dots. You'll create small heart shapes: a good-hearted garnish!

Helpful Hints and Observations

GELATIN – While preparing this recipe I really learned a lesson about gelatin and its qualities that I'd like to pass on here in detail. First of all, it's a natural protein found in young bones and connective tissues. The gelatin we use comes from pig skin (it's either that or gloves!).

One envelope of gelatin equals 1 tablespoon/15 ml. This will set 16 fl oz/454 ml of liquid. Some fruit will stop the setting process and should be pre-cooked: kiwi, papaya and pineapple, for example. *Essential hint*: Always sprinkle each envelope of gelatin on about 2 fl oz/57 ml cold water to soften it before adding to hot liquids. Stir rapidly and don't ever allow it to boil. The moment it boils its setting quality is seriously reduced. When the liquid is totally clear (no flecks left) it is ready to add to your recipe and have the desired effect.

PS Don't add too much unless you want to bounce the dessert on to your guests!

About the Ingredients

PEARS – Did you know this fruit is a member of the rose family, along with apples, peaches, plums and cherries? There are several thousand varieties known, but only about one hundred grown commercially. Among the best dessert pears are Conference, Doyenné du Comice and William's Bon Chrétien. Select pears that are just slightly soft. Pears are picked green and ripen off the tree.

Pears Rover,
Not a pair
of Rovers...

BREAD AND BUTTER PUDDING

$\mathcal{B}$read and Butter Pudding is a British standard with many regional and even family variations. It can be a humble affair or a special occasion dish. Unfortunately the extra eggs, fruit, nuts and cream which can be added to raise its status also tend to pile on the fat and calories. So I've tried hard to keep the ingredients modest while giving it a 'celebration' taste. See what you think for yourself!

Another big problem with desserts is that we insist upon whipped toppings, cream, or ice-cream as garnish. This simply increases the fat problem (and our waistlines) and sometimes hides the essential flavours and textures of an otherwise great idea. My suggestion is to leave this pudding alone. Let it be. The custard gives it built-in moisture.

Nutritional Profile

PER SERVING	CLASSIC	MINIMAX
Calories	600	191
Fat (g)	26	4
Calories from fat	38%	19%
Cholesterol (mg)	208	79
Sodium (mg)	564	159
Fibre (g)	5	3

■ *Classic compared:* Bread and Butter Pudding

Time Estimate

Hands On								
Unsupervised								

Minutes   10 20 30 40 50 60 70 80 90

Cost Estimate

Low   Medium   Medium High   Celebration

Serves 6

INGREDIENTS

8 tablespoons/120 ml raisins
4 tablespoons/60 ml wheatgerm
2 large eggs
2 tablespoons/30 ml brown sugar
1 pint/568 ml skimmed milk
Grated rind of 1 lemon
4 slices (1 oz/28 g each) wholewheat bread
4 slices (1 oz/28 g each) white bread
1 whole cinnamon stick, about 1½ inches/4 cm
long, or ½ teaspoon/2.5 ml powdered cinnamon

FIRST PREPARE

■ Wash the raisins and toss them with the
wheatgerm. Sprinkle half this mixture evenly into a
shallow, 1½-pint/850-ml capacity, ovenproof baking
or pie dish.

■ Make an egg custard by beating the eggs, 1
tablespoon/15 ml brown sugar, the milk and the
lemon rind together.

■ Leave the crusts on the bread and cut each slice in
half diagonally. Arrange the pieces in the baking dish
so that they overlap. Press them down to mould them
into the dish, then carefully pour on the egg custard
so that it soaks into the bread.

■ Grate the cinnamon stick and sprinkle it over
the top. I use a small coffee mill to powder it finely.

■ Finally, sprinkle on the remaining raisins and
brown sugar.

NOW COOK

■ Place the baking dish in a bain-marie (see *Helpful
Hints*) and bake uncovered in a 350°F/180°C/Gas Mark
4 oven for 30 to 35 minutes or until set.

■ Serve warm.

Helpful Hints and Observations

COATING THE RAISINS – I wanted to boost the nutritional value of the breads by adding the wheatgerm,
and found that it's better when 'stuck' to the damp
raisins by tossing them together.

BAIN-MARIE – This is simply a baking dish half-filled
with water into which the bread pudding dish can
fit. The water 'jacket' protects the egg custard from
curdling in the hot oven.

CRUSTS ON OR OFF? – The British upper classes have
traditionally cut the crusts off their bread. This might
have started as a means of cutting away mould, or
removing travel soil. Whatever the reason, it doesn't
make sense to throw out such good food, especially
since it helps to provide added texture.

BROWN OR WHITE BREAD? – For best nutrition,
wholewheat bread is the obvious choice. However,
it isn't as luscious as white. So we compromised and
went half and half, but tossed in the wheatgerm to
compensate.

About the Ingredients

WHEATGERM – The heart of the wheat berry, the
germinating centre for the wheat plant. The best
source of wheatgerm is in wholewheat products
such as bulgur or flour. Wheatgerm has a very
high oil content and can become rancid quickly. It
is best to purchase untoasted wheatgerm and keep it
refrigerated in an airtight container. Wheatgerm also
freezes well and can be bought in larger quantities
this way. Eat wheatgerm sprinkled on your breakfast
cereal or use it as a flour extender in any recipe for
making wholewheat bread. Try replacing half the flour
with wheatgerm when coating chicken.

JOYCE BROTHERS' COMFORT CUP

$\mathcal{D}$r Joyce Brothers has provided all of us with a great deal of good advice and comfort over the years. When she happened to be in town during one of our recording sessions, we created a dish that was comforting to her, based on a list of her favourite foods. The result: a very successful dessert for a smashing lady who, incidentally, is extremely interested in eating Minimax style.

Tall glasses with long spoons, or wide glass coupe dishes and short spoons! Your choice!

Nutritional Profile

PER SERVING	CLASSIC	MINIMAX
Calories	316	243
Fat (g)	19	0.3
Calories from fat	53%	1%
Cholesterol (mg)	65	0
Sodium (mg)	126	65
Fibre (g)	0.2	2

■ *Classic compared:* Rice Pudding

Time Estimate

Hands On									
Unsupervised					2 Hours				
Minutes	10	20	30	40	50	60	70	80	90

Cost Estimate

Low	Medium	Medium High	Celebration

INGREDIENTS

24 fl oz/680 ml + 2 tablespoons/30 ml mango nectar
1 tablespoon/15 ml cornflour
8 fl oz/227 ml uncooked short grain rice
24 fl oz/680 ml water
⅝ teaspoon/3 ml nutmeg, freshly ground
6 oz/170 g liquid egg substitute
2 oz/57 g castor sugar
4 oz/113 g dried mango slices, finely diced

FIRST PREPARE

■ Heat 8 fl oz/227 ml of the mango nectar, pour
it over the diced mango and soak for 2 hours.
Strain, reserving the mango pieces and soaking liquid
separately.

■ Stir the cornflour and 2 tablespoons/30 ml of the
mango nectar together to make a paste.

NOW COOK

■ Place the rice, 16 fl oz/454 ml of the water and 8 fl
oz/227 ml of the mango nectar in a pressure cooker.
Stir in ¼ teaspoon/1.25 ml of the nutmeg, put the lid
on and cook for 8 minutes from the time it begins to
steam. If you don't have a pressure cooker, put the
rice, 16 fl oz/424 ml of the water and 8 fl oz/227 ml
of the mango nectar in a saucepan, bring to the boil,
reduce the heat and simmer until the rice is cooked
through – about 25 minutes.

■ In a medium-sized saucepan, bring the remaining
water to the boil. Set a round copper bowl in the
saucepan, giving a double-boiler effect. Now pour in
the egg substitute, the remaining mango nectar and
the sugar. Beat until the consistency is thick and
creamy, like a custard.

■ Slowly whisk the cornflour paste into the mango
custard and add ⅛ teaspoon/0.6 ml of the nutmeg.

■ Spoon the cooked rice mixture into a large
measuring jug. Add the custard and half the soaked
and drained mango pieces.

■ *To Serve:* Divide the custard between six dessert
glasses. Top with the remaining mango pieces and 2
tablespoons/30 ml each of the reserved mango soaking
liquid. Sprinkle with the remaining nutmeg and enjoy!

Helpful Hints and Observations

COPPER AND ITS EFFECT ON EGG SUBSTITUTE
– I feel that a good 10-inch/25-cm copper bowl is
an essential Minimax kitchen tool because I use egg
whites so often to give added volume and texture –
without a gram of fat!

The reason why copper works so well with
liquid egg substitutes is because they are made
predominantly of egg white. In this recipe I used a
copper bowl over hot water as a double boiler, in
which I had the space to use a whisk, and it worked
wonderfully.

GRATED WHOLE NUTMEG – Don't miss the olfactory
(and taste) satisfaction that comes from grating whole
fresh nutmeg into your dishes! The little nut is quite
easily ground if you buy a small instrument that
looks a lot like a pepper grinder – just a twist, and
you'll be able to enjoy its full luxurious flavour. As
you'll see throughout this book, I use freshly grated
nutmeg often, even in my mashed potatoes!

About the Ingredients

MANGOES – Now here's a powerful fruit for your
Minimax A.C.T. (aroma, colour and texture): not
only do mangoes provide a gorgeous orange colour
for your dishes, but few fruits provide more vitamin
A per serving. In fact fresh mangoes provide 30% of
the Recommended Dietary Allowance of vitamin A,
along with the full allowance of vitamin C! Dried
mangoes will give you the same nutritional punch.
At the greengrocer's you'll know the ripe mango by
its colour: deep green with touches of yellow and red.
It should also yield lightly to the touch. Mango nectar
is available in tins.

GINGER PUMPKIN CUPS

This delicious dessert is the perfect accompaniment to the special Thanksgiving Turkey and Stuffing Pie that you'll find the recipes for on page 80.

But don't be restricted to enjoying Ginger Pumpkin Cups just one day a year – they're great any time!

good, aren't they? I saw them on graham kerr...

Nutritional Profile

PER SERVING	CLASSIC	MINIMAX
Calories	417	107
Fat (g)	18	2
Calories from fat	39%	13%
Cholesterol (mg)	99	18
Sodium (mg)	276	87
Fibre (g)	4	1

■ *Classic compared:* Pumpkin Pie

Time Estimate

Hands On / Unsupervised

Minutes   10   20   30   40   50   60   70   80   90

Cost Estimate

Low	Medium	Medium High	Celebration

Serves 12

INGREDIENTS

1 packet uncooked filo pastry
Extra light olive oil with a dash of sesame oil
2 fl oz/57 g brown sugar
8 fl oz/227 ml skimmed milk
1 envelope unflavoured gelatin
1 teaspoon/5 ml ground ginger
1 large egg yolk
A 16-oz/450-g tin solid-pack pumpkin
½ teaspoon/2.5 ml cinnamon, freshly grated
½ teaspoon/2.5 ml nutmeg, freshly grated
3 large egg whites
2 oz/57 g granulated sugar

FIRST PREPARE

■ Lay one sheet of filo pastry out flat on a pastry board and brush with oil. Cover with a second, third and fourth sheet, brushing each layer with oil.

■ Cut the layered pastry into twelve 4-inch/10-cm circles. Gently brush the top layer with oil.

■ Fit the layered filo dough circles, oiled-side down, into Yorkshire pudding tins to form cups. Gently brush them again with oil.

NOW COOK

■ Pre-heat the oven to 400°F/250°C/Gas Mark 6. Bake the filo cups in the pre-heated oven until browned – about 10 minutes. Remove from the tins and cool on a wire rack. These should be baked on the day itself as filo has a tendency to soften with time.

■ In a small saucepan, combine the brown sugar and 2 fl oz/57 ml of the milk. Sprinkle the gelatin and ginger evenly over the surface and let them soften for 5 minutes. Put the saucepan on low heat and cook, stirring constantly, for 5 to 6 minutes or until the gelatin and sugar dissolve. Remove from the heat.

■ In a small bowl, beat the egg yolk and remaining milk together. Slowly whisk in the hot gelatin mixture, then pour it back into the saucepan. Stir over the low heat for 2 to 3 minutes or until slightly thickened. Be careful not to let the mixture boil or it will curdle.

■ Transfer to a large bowl. Blend in the pumpkin, cinnamon and nutmeg. Cover and refrigerate for 20 to 30 minutes, stirring occasionally, until the mixture mounds slightly when dropped from a spoon.

■ In a large bowl, beat the egg whites at moderate speed until foamy. Slowly beat in the granulated sugar. Beat at moderately high speed until the whites hold soft peaks. Fold the egg whites into the pumpkin mixture and refrigerate for 30 minutes.

■ Not more than 1 hour ahead of serving time, spoon the ginger pumpkin filling into the filo cups (because of the pastry's tendency to soften). Refrigerate until ready to serve.

About the Ingredients

FILO PASTRY – This pastry is made by combining flour and water and kneading, resting and stretching it until it becomes tissue-thin. The result, when you use it in your cooking, is flaky and delicious. Fortunately, you do not have to make filo dough yourself. The thin sheets are available in packets, fresh or frozen, from many supermarkets or Greek foodstores (where it may be called phyllo). Don't be put off trying it – filo dough is so easy to use that you'll find yourself inventing many recipes to include it.

LONG WHITE CLOUD *(New Zealand Christmas Pudding)*

*C*hristmas Day in New Zealand can be really hot, with a temperature of 90°F/32°C on occasions. It is, after all, their summer. When Treena and I lived there (from 1958 to 1966) we had midwinter traditions in a midsummer climate. So we changed our Christmas Pudding to Long White Cloud, which is part of the English translation of the native Maori word for New Zealand, Aotearoa – the land of the long white cloud!

This recipe is a very lean edition of the British classic, which combines dried fruit with beef suet (the creamy fat that surrounds the kidney), brandy, heavy beer and eggs!

It is essential to let the pudding steam through on a very hot dish. We usually serve the apricot sauce warm, from a sauce boat at the table.

Nutritional Profile

PER SERVING	CLASSIC	MINIMAX
Calories	1189	245
Fat (g)	56	2
Calories from fat	43%	8%
Cholesterol (mg)	145	2
Sodium (mg)	483	86
Fibre (g)	7	4

■ *Classic compared:* Plum Pudding

Time Estimate

Hands On Unsupervised								
Minutes	10	20	30	40	50	60	70	80	90

10 Hours

Cost Estimate

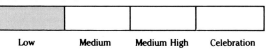

Low	Medium	Medium High	Celebration

Serves 12

INGREDIENTS

PUDDING

4 fl oz/113 ml minced dried apricots
4 fl oz/113 ml minced dried peaches
4 fl oz/113 ml minced raisins (I prefer the 'flame' variety)
4 fl oz/113 ml minced dried figs
A 16-oz/450-g tin plums in syrup
3 fl oz/85 ml sliced almonds
1 large Granny Smith apple, peeled, cored and finely chopped
2 tablespoons/30 ml molasses
½ teaspoon/2.5 ml cloves, freshly ground
½ teaspoon/2.5 ml mace, freshly ground
½ teaspoon/2.5 ml cinnamon, freshly ground
2 teaspoons/10 ml baking powder
2 oz/57 g plain flour
⅛ teaspoon/0.6 ml extra light olive oil with a dash of sesame oil

TOPPING

16 fl oz/450 ml frozen non-fat vanilla yogurt
Two 16-oz/450 g tins apricot halves
¼ teaspoon/1.25 ml nutmeg, freshly grated
1 teaspoon/5 ml arrowroot

TO COOK ON CHRISTMAS EVE

■ Combine the apricots, peaches, raisins and figs. It's really important to get them completely mixed up. Drain the tin of plums, reserving the syrup. Add the almonds and plums to the dried fruit.

■ Stir in the apples, molasses and the spices. Shape the mixture into a ball and put it on a board.

■ Sift the baking powder and flour together into a small bowl, then sift it again over the fruit mixture. Chop it all together with a broad knife or scraper, until it's thoroughly combined. Now drizzle in the reserved plum syrup, chopping as you go.

■ Scoop the pudding mixture into a slightly oiled bowl that will fit into the pan you use for steaming. Press it down lightly, allowing some room for the baking powder to expand.

■ Place greaseproof paper covered with a light cotton cloth over the top of the bowl. Tie this down with string. Now tie the tails of the cotton material over the top of the bowl to give you a handle!

■ Put the bowl in a large stockpot, or any heavy saucepan with a lid. Add water to reach halfway up the sides of the bowl. Drop a dozen marbles in the

water and put the lid on. Turn the heat to high and cook for 2 hours. If the water boils away, the marbles will start to clatter, giving you a noisy reminder to add more water!

■ Spoon the hot cooked pudding mixture into a lightly oiled 9½ × 5 inch/24 × 13 cm loaf tin. Press the mixture down into the pan, cover with clingfilm or foil and refrigerate overnight.

■ In another loaf tin of the same size, pack the frozen yogurt until it's a layer 1 inch/2.5 cm thick. Put the tin in the freezer. The pudding and its topping are now the same size.

BEFORE SERVING ON CHRISTMAS DAY

■ Drain the apricot syrup into a small bowl. Purée the apricots in a food processor or blender, reserving five halves for garnish. Pour the purée and syrup into a medium-sized saucepan set over medium heat. Stir in the nutmeg.

■ Make a paste of the arrowroot with 2 teaspoons/10 ml of the apricot syrup and stir it into the sauce. Bring to the boil, stirring until the sauce thickens. Remove from the heat.

■ The pudding must warm before serving. Heat a flameproof serving dish in a 475°F/240°C/Gas Mark 9 oven for 10 minutes. Remove it and put it on a baking rack on top of the stove burner on medium heat.

■ Unmould the pudding on to the hot serving dish. Unmould the frozen yogurt and place it on top of the pudding. Garnish or decorate with the reserved apricot halves.

■ *To serve:* Place a ½-inch/1.5-cm slice of the Long White Cloud on a plate. Dribble 2 tablespoons/30 ml of sauce on the side. Garnish with a small branch of holly (just don't eat the berries!).

Helpful Hints and Observations

DRIED FRUIT – Try to use unsulphured brands.

FROZEN YOGURT – You are more likely to find this in a tub than a block. Scoop it out while still frozen and pack it into the loaf-tin mould, pressing down hard to pop any air bubbles. Then put it in the deep freeze to get really hard. If you can't find frozen yogurt, freeze plain non-fat yogurt, with a stiffly beaten egg white and a few drops of vanilla essence blended in.

About the Ingredients

APRICOTS – Fresh, tinned, or dried, this golden fruit offers a bonus: carotene studies continue to link carotene to cancer prevention. Apricots also have lots of potassium and iron.

Long White Cloud
(New Zealand Christmas pudding) 187

NEW BOOK PUDDING

The classic recipe for Old Book Pudding, from one of my old television shows, was a real nutritional 'shocker'! This Minimax version brings you the same luscious flavour with a greatly diminished risk factor. But it's the 'toothpaste pump' idea that makes it truly memorable – see for yourself!

Nutritional Profile

PER SERVING	CLASSIC	MINIMAX
Calories	865	300
Fat (g)	76	7
Calories from fat	79%	20%
Cholesterol (mg)	199	1
Sodium (mg)	131	240
Fibre (g)	7	3

■ *Classic compared:* Old Book Pudding

Time Estimate

Hands On
Unsupervised

Minutes   10   20   30   40   50   60   70   80   90

Cost Estimate

Low   Medium   Medium High   Celebration

INGREDIENTS

PUDDING

6 fl oz/170 ml strained yogurt (recipe page 210)
2½ oz/70 g dry coconut macaroons, crumbled in
a food processor
8 tablespoons/120 ml raisin purée (see *Helpful Hints*)
4 drops almond essence
¼ teaspoon/1.25 ml ground cardamom
2 tablespoons/30 ml cocoa powder
1 tablespoon/15 ml almonds, finely chopped
6 egg whites
Pinch of salt

COCOA SAUCE

5 tablespoons/75 ml water
4 tablespoons/60 ml brown sugar
3 tablespoons/45 ml cocoa powder
1 tablespoon/15 ml arrowroot

GARNISH

Plain yogurt
Lime slices
Fresh mint leaves

NOW COOK

■ *The Pudding*: In a large bowl, stir together the
strained yogurt and the macaroon crumbs. Add the
raisin purée, almond essence, cardamom, cocoa powder and chopped almonds.

■ Beat the egg whites with a pinch of salt and a
drop or two of water to help them whip and retain
volume.

■ Gently fold one-third of the egg whites into the
yogurt mixture, then fold in the rest.

■ Put the mixture into a round mould (such as
a recycled 1-inch/2.5-cm diameter toothpaste pump,
see *Helpful Hints*) and freeze until solid, about 2 hours.

■ *The Sauce*: Pour the water into a small saucepan.
Over medium heat, add the brown sugar and cocoa
powder and stir until dissolved.

■ Take out 1 tablespoon/15 ml of the cocoa sauce
and mix it with the arrowroot to form a paste. Remove
the saucepan from the heat, add the arrowroot paste,
return the pan to the heat, and stir until the sauce has
thickened.

■ *To Serve*: Remove the pudding from the mould and
slice it into ½-inch/1.5-cm pieces. For each serving,
pour enough cocoa sauce on to a small plate to just
cover it. Spoon a little plain yogurt into a piping bag.
Pipe thin, straight lines across the cocoa sauce, about
1 inch/2.5 cm apart. Lightly drag a toothpick back and
forth, at right angles to the yogurt lines, to make a
'feathered' design. Lay some pudding slices on top
and garnish with the lime slices and mint leaves.

Helpful Hints and Observations

RAISIN PUREE – Put 3 oz/85 g raisins in 4 fl oz/113 ml
hot water, leave for 30 minutes, then place in a food
processor or blender and whiz until smooth.

TOOTHPASTE PUMP MOULD – To make this inno-
vative pudding mould, it's most helpful if you wait
until the toothpaste pump is empty! Then saw off the
'delivery end' and wash well. The plunger end can be
pushed down to expose the iced pudding so that it can
be cut off in neat discs.

About the Ingredients

MACAROONS – When fresh from the oven, these
biscuits are chewy coconut confections. You'll find
them at most good bakers' or pre-packaged at the
grocer's. Please note that we need them completely
dry for New Book Pudding. If they aren't dry enough to
crumble, you can bake them in a 200°F/95°C/Gas Mark
¼ oven.

COCOA POWDER – Imagine, for a moment, a tall tree
that bears red blossoms all year round – *Theobroma
cacao*, found in tropical America. The flowers ripen
into yellowish fruit. Cut the fruit open and there are
the seeds that are harvested to produce chocolate
and all its products. The seeds are roasted, cracked
to remove their hard shells, and then ground into a
thick paste called chocolate liquor. When the cocoa
butter is pressed out of the chocolate liquor, you are
left with cocoa powder. Keep cocoa powder in a cool,
dry place in a tightly closed container. It will probably
last about 6 months as long as no moisture is allowed
to make it lumpy or discoloured.

STEAMED MARMALADE PUDDING

$\mathcal{I}$ created this dish in 1987 on a visit to Scotland. It went down very well but has since been through several revisions to reduce the fat levels, and, as a result, the calories. It still has lots of appeal for a cold, blustery winter's day . . . or even a hot summer's evening with a cold fan running!

I always serve this at the table and cut it into four handsome wedges, or eight if the main course has been substantial. The sauce should bring you rave reviews!

Nutritional Profile

PER SERVING	CLASSIC	MINIMAX
Calories	523	241
Fat (g)	38	9
Calories from fat	65%	34%
Cholesterol (mg)	254	27
Sodium (mg)	213	196
Fibre (g)	5	3

■ *Classic compared:* Steamed Fruit Suet Pudding

Time Estimate

Hands On Unsupervised									
Minutes	10	20	30	40	50	60	70	80	90

Cost Estimate

Low	Medium	Medium High	Celebration

Serves 8

INGREDIENTS

PUDDING

1 teaspoon/5 ml + 6 tablespoons/90 ml margarine

4 tablespoons/60 ml Seville orange marmalade

2 oz/517 g brown sugar

1 egg, lightly beaten

1 teaspoon/5 ml vanilla essence

5 oz/140 g plain flour

1½ teaspoons/7.5 ml baking powder

6 fl oz/170 ml skimmed milk

4 fl oz/113 ml unsweetened frozen raspberries (do not thaw)

RASPBERRY AND ORANGE SAUCE

8 fl oz/227 ml unsweetened frozen raspberries (do not thaw)

2 fl oz/57 ml strained yogurt (recipe page 210)

2 fl oz/57 ml orange juice, freshly squeezed

NOW COOK

■ Lightly grease a 2½-pint/1.4-l capacity pudding basin with the 1 teaspoon/5 ml of margarine.

■ Spoon the orange marmalade into the bottom of the basin, smoothing it out evenly to cover about one-third of the inner surface. This will eventually be the cap on the pudding.

■ In a mixing bowl, cream together the brown sugar and the remaining margarine.

■ Beat in the egg and vanilla essence.

■ Sift the flour and baking powder into another large bowl. Now combine this with the pudding mixture. Pour in one-third of the milk, stir until completely combined, then repeat until all of the milk is added. Please don't overwork it. The fewer stirs, the better the eventual texture.

■ Carefully spoon one-third of the pudding mixture on top of the marmalade and sprinkle about eight raspberries on top of that. Repeat the layers, finishing with a layer of pudding mixture.

■ Cover the pudding basin with a sheet of greaseproof paper and a 14-inch/35-cm square pudding cloth. Place a rubber band over the lip of the basin, so that it holds the layers tight, and, finally, secure this with a piece of string. Now bring the opposite corners of the pudding cloth over the top of the basin and tie them together. This creates a marvellous handle for fishing the pudding basin out of the steamer.

■ Place the pudding basin in a large pan of boiling water. The water should come halfway up the sides of the pudding basin.

■ Cover and steam gently over medium heat on top of the stove for 1½ hours. Keep the water at a gentle boil.

■ Take out the pudding and leave it for 5 minutes before unmoulding. Then run a thin-bladed knife between the pudding and the basin. Put a plate on the top, hold it firmly in place and turn the basin upside down. The pudding should drop neatly on to the plate.

■ *Raspberry and Orange Sauce:* Push the raspberries through a fine sieve. Mix in the yogurt and orange juice and serve on the side.

Helpful Hints and Observations

FRESH vs FROZEN RASPBERRIES – I've used frozen raspberries for two reasons. The best (non-sugared) frozen varieties, in which each berry is individually frozen, are, in my opinion, better flavoured than early or late season fresh. Let me hasten to add that mid season fresh berries cannot be beaten. The second reason is that when added in their solid frozen form, they seem better able to retain their texture and flavour.

ONE-THIRD AT A TIME – I always add the dry and moist ingredients alternately and one-third at a time. It eliminates lumps and helps to keep the mixture light.

About the Ingredients

SEVILLE ORANGE MARMALADE – Marmalade became popular in Britain in the late nineteenth century, but it has been around for considerably longer. The Portuguese made a preserve called *marmelada* from quinces, and the British adopted the name to describe a preserve made from bitter oranges. Nowadays 'marmalade' means any 'jam' made with citrus fruit. I recommend Scottish Seville orange marmalade for this recipe. The Seville orange is a very sour Mediterranean orange that is considered the cream of the crop for marmalade. And then you'll have a few tablespoons left to serve with your toast at breakfast.

BLACKBERRY ZABAGLIONE

This dessert has lived for years in my memory, regardless of how often I try to beat it into submission!

Italian in origin, it is said that the first Zabaglione was invented by accident in the 17th century, by a chef who inadvertently poured wine into an egg custard. Well, in the 20th century, chefs purposely pour enough liquor into this dessert to create about a 40% alcohol content custard. For each egg yolk you add 1 oz/28 g brandy and 1 oz/28 g Marsala which, with the sugar, is like a superior egg nog.

But times have changed and now I've made a Zabaglione that has a great new taste and colour . . . and doesn't haunt my dreams!

Nutritional Profile

PER SERVING	CLASSIC	MINIMAX
Calories	296	169
Fat (g)	27	0
Calories from fat	83%	1%
Cholesterol (mg)	294	0
Sodium (mg)	30	87
Fibre (g)	0	3

■ *Classic compared:* Zabaglione

Time Estimate

Hands On									
Unsupervised									

Minutes 10 20 30 40 50 60 70 80 90

Cost Estimate

Low	Medium	Medium High	Celebration

Serves 6

INGREDIENTS

1 pint/568 ml frozen blackberries, thawed
12 fl oz/340 ml de-alcoholized white wine
3 tablespoons/45 ml real maple syrup
¼ teaspoon/1.25 ml almond essence
¼ teaspoon/1.25 ml vanilla essence
2 tablespoons/30 ml cornflour mixed with 2 fl
oz/57 ml de-alcoholized white wine
8 fl oz/227 ml water
8 fl oz/227 ml liquid egg substitute
4 oz/113 g castor sugar

FIRST PREPARE

■ Spoon 12 fl oz/340 ml of the blackberries into
six 6 oz/170 g wine glasses. They should be half
full.

■ Push the remaining blackberries through a sieve
to yield 8 tablespoons/120 ml of purée.

NOW COOK

■ In a saucepan, bring the de-alcoholized white
wine to the boil. Add the maple syrup, almond
and vanilla essences. Stir in the cornflour paste
until thickened.

■ In a medium-sized saucepan, bring the water to
the boil. Set a round copper bowl in the saucepan,
giving a double-boiler effect, and reduce the heat to
a simmer. Now combine the egg substitute and castor
sugar in the bowl and beat until the consistency is
thick and creamy, like a frothy pudding.

■ Slowly whisk the syrup mixture into the sweetened egg substitute. Add 6 tablespoons/90 ml of the
blackberry purée and beat well over heat to combine.

■ Pour the custard over the blackberries in the wine
glasses. Top with the remaining blackberry purée and
serve hot. (Wholewheat cookies are entirely optional!)

Helpful Hints and Observations

WHAT'S SO SPECIAL ABOUT COPPER? – See page 183.

About the Ingredients

ALMOND ESSENCE – An essence with a murky past.
You see, this delightful liquid flavouring is from the
oil of the bitter almond. (Did you know there were
two types of almonds: bitter and sweet?) And in its
concentrated form, almond oil contains a poisonous
substance called prussic acid. But don't worry. When
the oil is diluted with water and alcohol, it is trans-
formed into this quite harmless baking ingredient.

BLACKBERRIES – If you have the opportunity, and
it's a bright late summer day, do put on a straw hat,
wander down to your nearest blackberry patch and
pick plump, juicy berries straight off the brambles.
Failing this you can put on your straw hat and wander
off to a supermarket where frozen blackberries are
available.

CASTOR SUGAR – Castor sugar is extra fine granulated white sugar. Since the grains are so small, they
dissolve almost immediately when added to liquids.
Castor sugar is a lovely ingredient for desserts where
you want a very smooth texture. Granulated sugar
tastes exactly the same but will give a slightly grainy
result. 'Castor' is also the name given to a glass or
metal shaker used to dispense fine sugar at the table.
The dispenser has fine holes, hence the need for a
fine-grained sugar.

CARROT CAKE

This recipe is a perfect example of 'springboarding'. It comes from an in-flight meal experience had by Chef David Burke of the River Café in New York City. He made changes to suit his special needs by making a hot cream cheese soufflé topping. I subsequently made my own changes and added a spiced, creamy, apple butter topping.

I like to split the dish and serve half the cake hot with the topping and leave the rest of the cake for simple snacking. If you have twelve people to serve, just double the quantity of the sauce.

Nutritional Profile

PER SERVING	CLASSIC	MINIMAX
Calories	884	298
Fat (g)	51	5
Calories from fat	51%	15%
Cholesterol (mg)	305	36
Sodium (mg)	416	215
Fibre (g)	3	4

■ *Classic compared:* Carrot Cake with Cream Cheese Soufflé Topping

Time Estimate

Hands On / Unsupervised

Minutes 10 20 30 40 50 60 70 80 90

Cost Estimate

Low	Medium	Medium High	Celebration

Serves 12

INGREDIENTS

4 fl oz/113 ml raisins, preferably flame seedless
7 oz/200 g plain flour
5½oz/150 g wholewheat flour
2 teaspoons/10 ml bicarbonate of soda
1½ teaspoons/7.5 ml ground cinnamon
1 tablespoon/15 ml ground allspice
½ teaspoon/2.5 ml nutmeg, freshly ground
⅛ teaspoon/0.6 ml salt, freshly ground
6 oz/170 g brown sugar
3 tablespoons/45 ml extra light olive oil with a dash of sesame oil
2 eggs
6 fl oz/170 ml buttermilk
2 teaspoons/10 ml vanilla essence
12 fl oz/340 ml carrots, coarsely shredded
An 8-oz/227-g tin crushed, unsweetened pineapple
TOPPING
4 fl oz/113 ml apple butter (recipe page 169)
4 fl oz/113 ml strained yogurt (recipe page 210)
2 tablespoons/30 ml pure maple syrup

FIRST PREPARE

■ Put the raisins in a small bowl, cover with water, and soak until soft and plump – about 10 to 15 minutes. Then drain.
■ Pre-heat the oven to 350°F/180°C/Gas Mark 4.

NOW COOK

■ In a large bowl, combine the flours, bicarbonate of soda, cinnamon, allspice, nutmeg and salt. Stir well and set aside.
■ In a large bowl mix the brown sugar and oil. Add the eggs, one at a time, beating well with a wire whisk after each addition. Stir in the buttermilk and the vanilla essence.

■ Stir in the flour mixture. Add the carrots, raisins and pineapple.
■ Lightly grease an 11-inch/28-cm round cake tin. Pour in the batter and shake the tin to distribute it evenly. Place the tin on the middle shelf of the pre-heated oven and bake for 20 minutes. Turn out on a wire rack to cool.
■ *The Topping:* In a small bowl, mix the apple butter, strained yogurt and maple syrup.
■ Serve a wedge of the hot carrot cake with 3 tablespoons/45 ml of the topping spooned over it and garnish with a sprig of fresh mint.

Helpful Hints and Observations

APPLE BUTTER – I like to think that my apple butter is the best (certainly from a Minimax point of view) and if you like it you may want to use it in recipes of your own. I recommend making a large batch when Granny Smiths or other suitable apples (and good friends) are in prime season! Apple butter freezes very well in good freezer bags.

About the Ingredients

APPLES – See page 169.

CHEESECAKE WITH FIGS

$\mathcal{W}$ell of course, when it comes right down to it, cheesecake is the number one, knock down, drag out, temptation. We all know it's loaded . . . but what to do about it? Can anything compete? We've done our part but the real answer to the question is your own taste – combined with your own will to change! Have fun.

Any amount of fresh fruit served on the side is delicious. Fresh figs in season would be wonderful, but for my taste, fresh kiwi fruit peeled and cut in half lengthwise is the perfect garnish.

Nutritional Profile

PER SERVING	CLASSIC	MINIMAX
Calories	806	210
Fat (g)	62	3
Calories from fat	69%	11%
Cholesterol (mg)	290	28
Sodium (mg)	273	146
Fibre (g)	0	4

■ *Classic compared:* New York Cheesecake

Time Estimate

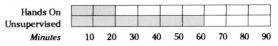

Cost Estimate

Serves 16

INGREDIENTS

4 fl oz/113 ml digestive biscuit crumbs

10 fl oz/300 ml dried white figs

2 fl oz/57 ml water

2 envelopes unflavoured gelatin

2 tablespoons/30 ml lemon juice, freshly squeezed

4 fl oz/113 ml evaporated skimmed milk or dried skimmed milk reconstituted at double strength

1 whole egg

3 oz/85 g light brown sugar

16 fl oz/450 ml low-fat cottage cheese

1 teaspoon/5 ml vanilla essence

5 kiwi fruit, peeled and cut in half lengthwise

FIRST PREPARE THE CRUST

■ Drop the crumbs and figs into a food processor. Blend until the ingredients are just sticking together. If you don't have an electronic assistant, you can chop the fruit to a pulp and stir the two together until moist and dough-like.

■ Press the mixture into the bottom, and halfway up the sides, of a lightly greased 9-inch/23-cm tin with a detachable base. A small bowl of cold water nearby will keep your hands 'non-stick'.

NOW PREPARE THE FILLING

■ Sprinkle the gelatin on to the water and stir gently. Add the lemon juice.

■ In a small saucepan, bring the milk to the boil, stirring constantly so that it doesn't stick to the bottom of the pan. Pour the milk into the softened gelatin.

■ Put the gelatin mixture into a blender. Add the egg, brown sugar, cottage cheese and vanilla. Blend until there are no lumps, but the texture still looks and feels somewhat 'grainy'.

■ Pour the filling into the crust. In order not to disturb the crust, you can pour it on to the rounded side of a wooden spoon held over the centre of the crust.

■ Chill for 1 to 2 hours.

■ Garnish with the kiwi fruit.

Helpful Hints and Observations

PRESSING IN THE CRUST – I've spent hours (in total) pressing biscuit crumbs into pie dishes. Let's face it – it's a crummy job! This recipe, which is entirely my own invention, makes the task almost easy, providing you have a small bowl of cold water handy to keep your fingers too moist to stick.

THE CRUST ITSELF: FAT OR FRUIT? – Where some amount of fat is absolutely essential, it can be a good idea to also raise the amount of dietary fibre since some fibres help to reduce the cholesterol-increasing properties of some fats. We moved away from the classic butter and the alternative margarine until we arrived at the high-fibre fig as a crust binder and the kiwi fruit as a garnish. The nutritional numbers changed and the taste improved.

EVAPORATED SKIMMED MILK – When humans first started drinking milk back in the dim recesses of civilization, the most common milk of all was mare's milk. 'The Mongols', wrote Marco Polo, 'are accustomed to drink every kind of milk', but though they had flocks of sheep and goats, it was mare's milk they preferred. (They used sheep's milk, disdainfully, to caulk their tents.)

If you balk slightly at the idea of mare's milk, evaporated skimmed milk must seem quite mundane. It is produced when cow's milk is evaporated in a vacuum to reduce its water content by 40–50%. You can get it sweetened or unsweetened. It has the consistency of cream.

About the Ingredients

FIGS – The early Egyptians heralded figs as a health tonic. The ancient Greeks celebrated figs as an antidote for *all* ailments. The first Olympic athletes wore figs as medals of honour ... well, you might not go that far, but figs are certainly worth a spot in your larder. Figs have the highest dietary fibre content of any common fruit, nut, or vegetable, along with a great deal of calcium and potassium. A great snack idea, perhaps, but watch the calories.

KIWI FRUIT – Who would have guessed that inside that egg-shaped, brown, furry object would be such a brilliantly green and tangy fruit? A great garnish for cheesecake, a lovely colour to add to your fruit salads, do try kiwis in many dishes. A ripe kiwi should be firm, just giving a little when squeezed. They are available year round, and will keep for months in your refrigerator.

MORAVIAN CAKE

*S*nacking cake: it raises all kinds of visions of hospitality. A great cup of coffee and a hunk of spicy cake! I replaced the classic lard with a good margarine. Other than that, the original was such good news I left it alone!

The cake is naturally moist but should be stored in a tightly lidded cake tin or a large sealable plastic bag. With a good cup of coffee you'll have all you need for your next get-together . . . have fun!

Nutritional Profile

PER SERVING	CLASSIC	MINIMAX
Calories	438	400
Fat (g)	9	6
Calories from fat	19%	13%
Cholesterol (mg)	8	0
Sodium (mg)	201	235
Fibre (g)	4	4

■ *Classic compared:* Milkless, Eggless, Butterless Cake

Time Estimate

Hands On	
Unsupervised	
Minutes	10 20 30 40 50 60 70 80 90

Cost Estimate

Low	Medium	Medium High	Celebration

Serves 8

INGREDIENTS

8 oz/227 g plain flour
½ teaspoon/2.5 ml baking powder
1 teaspoon/5 ml bicarbonate of soda combined with 1 tablespoon/15 ml warm water
1 oz/28 g sliced almonds
8 fl oz/227 ml water
8 oz/227 g dark brown sugar
8 oz/227 g seedless raisins
2½ oz/70 g margarine
1 teaspoon/5 ml cinnamon*
⅓ teaspoon/1.7 ml cloves*
¼ teaspoon/1.25 ml nutmeg*

*If possible, freshly grind the spices. You can grind the cinnamon and cloves in a coffee grinder or a blender. You'll need a 1-inch/2.5-cm stick of cinnamon and 6 cloves. The difference between these and the commercially ground produce is the fineness of the grind: I prefer roughly ground for this recipe.

NOW COOK

■ Pre-heat oven to 350°F/180°C/Gas Mark 4.

■ In a large bowl, sift together the flour and baking powder. You now have self-raising flour! Make a well in the flour and stir in the bicarbonate of soda mixture. Stir in the sliced almonds and set aside.

■ Pour the water into a high-sided saucepan on high heat. Mix in the brown sugar, raisins, margarine and spices. Bring to the boil.

■ Remove from the heat and pour into a bowl set in a larger bowl of iced water to cool the syrup.

■ Add the cooled, but still warm, syrup to the flour mixture all at once.

■ Pour the mixture into a 10-inch/25-cm shallow non-stick cake tin and spread it evenly. Pop it in the pre-heated oven and bake for 35 minutes or until the edges of the cake start to pull away from the sides of the tin. Turn out on to a rack and leave until completely cool. Then slice and serve – or if you want to keep it, hide it!

Helpful Hints and Observations

GETTING A RISE WITHOUT AN EGG – If you are watching your egg yolk consumption, this cake is good news. It relies upon a combination of baking powder and bicarbonate of soda for its texture. By adding the soda to the warm water and the powder to the flour, and then mixing them both together, you get the rise without the sometimes 'metallic' soda taste. Of course, the spices also help to control this side-effect.

BOILING THE SUGAR AND SPICE – Adding everything to cold water and then bringing it slowly to the boil really does help to infuse and combine all the flavours. You don't have to cool it quickly; it can be set aside to lose heat naturally. But if you are in the kind of hurry that faces me each day . . . the ice helps!

About the Ingredients

RAISINS – Raisins, like currants and sultanas, are produced by exposing ripe grapes to hot, dry air – either sunlight or an artificial source – so that their moisture is drawn out. It takes 4 lb/1.8 kg of grapes to produce 1 lb/450 g of dried fruit. Seedless raisins are produced in the United States and Mexico from the Thompson sultana grape, which is green when harvested. When exposed to sunlight its sugar caramelizes to give a purplish-brown colour to the raisin. A red raisin grape is grown in Afghanistan. This produces particularly large and luscious raisins, marketed as flame raisins – well worth looking out for.

CLOVES – If you're strolling in Zanzibar (or even the Moluccas) one day, and spot a tall, evergreen tree with smooth grey bark – climb to the tip of one of its branches, take a closer look at the buds of its purple-crimson flowers, and you will be looking at the beginning of cloves. I say the beginning because the flower buds are picked and then dried to bring cloves to your kitchen.

TADMILL MERINGUE GATEAU

$\mathcal{W}$hen one of my guests from the television studio audience tasted this dish, she said, 'I saw you make it, but I can't believe it tastes so good!' Truly, the original dessert from the Frogmill Inn was a luxurious-tasting confection: heaped full of whipped French custard and drenched in crème de caçao liqueur. But just as truly, this Minimax version has its own moments of luxury.

Any meringue monster like this must really come straight from the oven to the table. You can beat the meringue itself in less than 5 minutes, so it's not too much of a mid-dinner problem, providing everything else is done ahead of time.

Nutritional Profile

PER SERVING	CLASSIC	MINIMAX
Calories	427	215
Fat (g)	11	2
Calories from fat	24%	10%
Cholesterol (mg)	225	86
Sodium (mg)	162	126
Fibre (g)	1	0.3

■ *Classic compared:* Frogmill Meringue Gateau

Time Estimate

Hands On									
Unsupervised									
Minutes	10	20	30	40	50	60	70	80	90

Cost Estimate

Low	Medium	Medium High	Celebration

Serves 10

INGREDIENTS

SPONGE CAKE
4 eggs
4 oz/113 g castor sugar
2 oz/57 g plain flour
Pinch of salt, freshly ground

PASTRY CREAM
8 fl oz/227 ml strained yogurt (recipe page 210)
2 egg whites, beaten
2 tablespoons/30 ml maple syrup
½ teaspoon/2.5 ml almond essence
½ tablespoon/8 ml slivered almonds

MERINGUE
5 egg whites
Pinch of salt, freshly ground
8 oz/227 g castor sugar
¼ teaspoon/1.25 ml almond essence

SAUCE
2 tablespoons/30 ml maple syrup
2 tablespoons/30 ml unsweetened cocoa powder
1 tablespoon/15 ml water

FIRST PREPARE AND COOK

■ *The Sponge Cake:* Pre-heat the oven to 375°F/190°C/Gas Mark 5. In a medium mixing bowl placed over a saucepan containing lukewarm water, beat together the eggs and sugar until slightly thickened and light yellow in colour. Fold in the flour and salt, gently and slowly, until they are incorporated. Do not overbeat.

■ Pour the batter into a greased and floured 9-inch/23-cm cake tin. Tap the batter-filled tin on a hard surface to pop any air bubbles. Bake in the pre-heated oven for 25 minutes, or until a skewer inserted in the centre comes out clean.

■ When the cake is done, let it rest 5 minutes, then remove it from the tin and cool on a rack.

■ When the cake is completely cool, cut it horizontally into two layers.

■ *The Pastry Cream:* Mix all the ingredients together.

■ *The Meringue:* Make sure your bowl and beater are free of any fat residue of any kind or your egg whites will not stiffen properly. Beat the egg whites,

adding a pinch of salt and a drop of water. This will enhance the stiffening process. Start at a low speed and gradually increase to a higher speed. This will keep lightness in the finished meringue. Slowly stir in the sugar and almond essence. Beat until very stiff, or the meringue just holds to the back of a spoon. Be careful here because you can overbeat.

■ *The Sauce:* In a small saucepan over medium heat, stir together the maple syrup, cocoa powder and water.

NOW ASSEMBLE

■ Place the bottom layer of the sponge cake on an ovenproof serving plate. Dribble the cocoa sauce on top and let it soak in.

■ Spoon the pastry cream over the soaked sponge cake layer. Gently cover it with the other cake layer. Spoon the meringue over the top, spreading it completely down the sides. Make a nice design by dabbing the meringue with the back of a spoon to form small, graceful peaks.

■ Pop the completed meringue into a 500°F/260°C/Gas Mark 10 oven for just 2 minutes, until toasted light golden-brown.

Helpful Hints and Observations

A REVOLUTIONARY DESSERT – Every step in this recipe is a major change from the original. Just one glance at the nutritional analysis will give you the idea. I'm always sorry that restaurants don't try harder to make more desserts that are both visual celebrations and responsible offerings. If you like this recipe, why not make a copy and deliver it to your favourite establishment? Who knows ... we could start a revolution together!

About the Ingredients

EGG WHITES – What is this substance that transforms into glorious meringue? Mostly protein and water. Kept in a covered container and refrigerated, egg whites can be stored for about 4 days, or frozen for up to 6 months. (I can't think why you'd want to freeze egg whites, but there you go!) What about the leftover yolks? I recommend giving them to your dog. Dogs don't seem to have the same cholesterol problem as humans.

COCOA POWDER – See page 189.

CHAMPORODI GUAVA

This is a triumph of mind over coconut matter, possibly the most delicious milk pudding in the entire world. I invented it as a creative alternative to the classic coconut and chocolate chip rice dish that is a breakfast favourite in the Philippines.

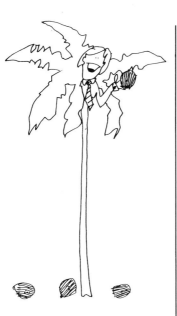

Nutritional Profile

PER SERVING	CLASSIC	MINIMAX
Calories	433	365
Fat (g)	31	8
Calories from fat	64%	20%
Cholesterol (mg)	9	3
Sodium (mg)	318	104
Fibre (g)	2	1

■ *Classic compared:* Champorodi

Time Estimate

Hands On								
Unsupervised								
Minutes 10 20 30 40 50 60 70 80 90								

Cost Estimate

Low	Medium	Medium High	Celebration

Serves 4

INGREDIENTS

1 whole fresh coconut
1 pint/568 ml skimmed milk
8 fl oz/227 ml uncooked short grain rice
1 tablespoon/15 ml brown sugar

SAUCE

1 tin (12 oz/340 g) guava nectar
1 tablespoon/15 ml arrowroot mixed with 1 table-spoon/15 ml water

FIRST PREPARE

■ Pierce the eyes of the coconut with a skewer and drain, saving the coconut juice.

■ Bake the emptied coconut in a 400°F/205°C/Gas Mark 6 oven for 20 minutes. This makes it easy to peel away the outer husk and the inner skin. Hit the coconut firmly with a hammer or mallet to crack it. Remove the coconut meat from the shell and peel off the inner skin. Shred the coconut meat in a food processor or, more slowly, with a very sharp knife.

NOW COOK

■ Combine ¾ pint/426 ml of the skimmed milk, the reserved coconut juice and the shredded coconut in a saucepan. Bring to the boil, then remove from the heat and allow the flavour to infuse for 20 minutes. Strain the infusion through muslin, squeezing out every last drop. Discard the fibre and cool the liquid until the heavier coconut 'cream' floats to the surface.

■ Put the rice in a baking dish. Remove ¼ pint/142 ml of the top surface coconut cream and set aside. Replace the cream with the rest of the skimmed milk, and pour this over the rice. Cover and bake at 350°F/180°C/Gas Mark 4 for 40 minutes.

■ *The Sauce*: In a saucepan, bring the guava nectar to the boil and reduce by half. Remove the saucepan from the heat, stir in the arrowroot paste, return to the heat and stir until thickened. Set aside. When the rice has finished baking, stir in the brown sugar and the reserved coconut cream.

■ Champorodi Guava can be served hot from the oven or chilled in small moulds. To chill, fill four small (4-oz/113-ml) moulds or timbales with the baked rice and place in the refrigerator to cool and set. Hot or cold, coat the servings with pink guava sauce – it is wonderfully delicious.

Helpful Hints and Observations

COCONUT MILK/CREAM – I must admit to being a coconut devotee. Now, how can this be, since most of us are clearly aware that this hairy masterpiece is actually crawling with saturated fat? It could actually be less dangerous to be hit by one than to eat it! Truthfully, the oil is highly saturated but that doesn't mean that the milk/cream is too – especially when we prepare it ourselves and it's used with moderation. Just glance at the nutritional analysis for a moment and you'll see that our dessert has only 2 grams of fat for each serving – only 7% of the total calories from fat. At that rate, the saturated nature of the fat doesn't really matter. So, coconut lovers of the world, take heart – by the time you've laboured to remove the flesh you'll probably have worked off the calories!

SKIMMED MILK – There is a constant problem when heating any skimmed milk . . . it catches easily and can burn before it boils. This is because there is no fat to grease the pan and protect the milk proteins. So? Well, watch it when bringing skimmed milk to the boil. Use a non-stick pan, a low to medium heat, and keep stirring from time to time with a flat ended spatula.

About the Ingredients

GUAVA NECTAR – The sweet juice from the small, fragrant, tropical guava. Originally from Mexico and Central America, guava is now harvested in New Zealand, Florida, Hawaii and South America. Guavas are about 4 inches/10 cm long, and oval-shaped; they have a skin that turns from green to yellow; the flesh can be white, pink, or red. Select guavas that are firm but slightly soft to the touch. Canned guava nectar is available at many supermarkets.

COCONUTS – One of the world's oldest food plants, originating in Polynesia and southern Asia. There are over 29 billion nuts produced each year. Coconuts are in season between October and December, and available year round on a limited basis. Don't be afraid to shake them while shopping. They should be full of juice and feel heavy.

CAPIROTADA

It's hard to believe that green peppers and onions can be part of a dessert, but here is a classic – this time served up without its incredibly high sugar content. This Mexican dish is often served during Lent, but frankly it doesn't seem to represent sacrifice! It has a wonderfully complex taste that doesn't need any whipped cream or ice-cream or custard. I've added a very sharp non-fat yogurt sauce that balances well with the sweet bread pudding – you'll only need a wee drop!

Although every nation has its own bread pudding recipe, this one definitely takes the prize for tasteful originality. Nothing other than the sharp side sauce is needed, but you could use bright Mexican-style dishes.

Nutritional Profile

PER SERVING	CLASSIC	MINIMAX
Calories	822	314
Fat (g)	25	8
Calories from fat	27%	23%
Cholesterol (mg)	37	3
Sodium (mg)	735	90
Fibre (g)	8	4

■ *Classic compared:* Capirotada

Time Estimate

Hands On Unsupervised									
Minutes	10	20	30	40	50	60	70	80	90

Cost Estimate

Low	Medium	Medium High	Celebration

Serves 8

INGREDIENTS

PUDDING

8 fl oz/227 ml low-fat cottage cheese; use lowest fat content available, but do not use 'no-fat'

6 fl oz/170 ml Minimax Seed Mix (see *About the Ingredients*), coarsely cracked in an electric coffee grinder

8 fl oz/227 ml raisins

2 small, sweet apples

2 lemon wedges

1 small uncut loaf of wholewheat bread

1 medium tomato, sliced

SYRUP

2 fl oz/57 ml sweet green pepper, de-seeded and chopped

2 fl oz/57 ml onion, peeled and chopped

4 fl oz/113 ml fresh coriander leaves, chopped

½ teaspoon/2.5 ml orange peel, grated

½ teaspoon/2.5 ml cinnamon stick, grated

1½ pints/850 ml water

8 fl oz/227 ml brown sugar

3 whole cloves

LEMON-YOGURT SAUCE

Juice and grated rind of 1 lemon

¾ pint/425 ml non-fat plain yogurt

Honey to taste

FIRST PREPARE THE PUDDING INGREDIENTS

■ Mix together the cottage cheese, 4 fl oz/113 ml of the seed mixture and the raisins. Set aside.

■ Wash, core and thinly slice the apples. Put them into cold water with the lemon wedges to prevent browning.

■ Cut the bread into ½-inch/1.5-cm cubes and toast for 10 minutes in a 350°F/180°C/Gas Mark 4 oven.

NOW COOK

■ Put all the ingredients for the syrup in a saucepan and cook for 30 minutes. Strain.

■ Layer half the bread cubes, cottage cheese mixture and apples in a 3-pint/1.7-l baking dish, finishing with the rest of the bread. Scatter the tomatoes and remaining seed mix on top.

■ Carefully pour the syrup over the Capirotada. Let the bread cubes soak up syrup from underneath. Don't drown them from the top.

■ Bake at 350°F/180°C/Gas Mark 4 for 1 hour. The Capirotada should be crisp on top, bubbling around the edges.

■ Combine the ingredients for the lemon-yogurt sauce and serve it on the side. Wait until your taste buds have a go at it! It's a marvellous thing when a nuance of green pepper comes through!

Helpful Hints and Observations

■ TEXTURE – This seems a good opportunity to tell you about the importance of texture in an overall 'soft' dish like this. Think for a moment about your breakfast cereal choices. Is crispness a factor for you? Do you like potato chips that crunch? This is texture at work in harmony with its sound as you chew! I've added seeds and nuts to this dish, not to get a crackle going, but to give some sharp, pointed relief to the otherwise plain 'landscape'! The seeds and nuts are only just broken by the small grinder. This allows for both texture and better assimilation of their nutrients. If left whole, they could whistle straight through without so much as passing the time of day with your ileum (small intestine).

■ ADDING THE SYRUP – You will note I've cautioned you to add the syrup so that the bread soaks it up from below. This is done to help the surface to crisp without burning and becoming caramelized.

About the Ingredients

MINIMAX SEED MIX – A very nutritious way of adding crunch to a meal. It's quite tasty and high in protein. Combine equal measures of sunflower seeds, unhulled sesame seeds, green pumpkin seeds and flaked almonds. Combine with half a measure of flax seeds. Seeds and nuts can be purchased in a variety of packages and a variety of processing. The more processed, the higher the price and the lower the nutritional value. Choose nuts and seeds that are firm and smooth. If they are in the shell they should be heavy for their size, indicating a meatier nut. Always avoid nuts and seeds with mould, even if it seems the mould wipes away easily. Because nuts and seeds have a high oil content, light will turn them rancid. To avoid this, store them in tightly covered dark glass or plastic jars.

SWEET GREEN PEPPERS – Wonderfully versatile and a great source of vitamin C, potassium and calcium. Select firm, smooth-skinned peppers.

CREPES SUZETTE TAKE II

The original Crêpes Suzette were made as a prop in a Paris stage show. I have always believed it to be No, No, Nanette, but I haven't been able to confirm this . . .

I named this version 'Take II' because of its obvious changes. It will, none the less, win you a standing ovation!

You can make the crêpes before dinner and cover them with a cloth. You can also make the sauce and then add the crêpes to warm up and finish – a classic dessert without fuss!

Nutritional Profile

PER SERVING	CLASSIC	MINIMAX
Calories	475	331
Fat (g)	26	7
Calories from fat	49%	18%
Cholesterol (mg)	260	111
Sodium (mg)	161	63
Fibre (g)	1	4

■ *Classic compared:* Crêpes Suzette

Time Estimate

Hands On Unsupervised									

Minutes 10 20 30 40 50 60 70 80 90

Cost Estimate

Low	Medium	Medium High	Celebration

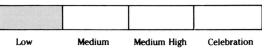

INGREDIENTS

CREPE BATTER

1 whole egg
1 egg yolk
8 fl oz/227 ml skimmed milk
4 oz/113 g plain flour
½ teaspoon/2.5 ml vanilla essence
Grated rind of 1 lemon
1 teaspoon/5 ml extra light olive oil with a dash of sesame oil

SYRUP

1 teaspoon/5 ml extra light olive oil with a dash of sesame oil
1 tablespoon/15 ml orange rind
4 fl oz/113 ml de-alcoholized white wine
8 fl oz/227 ml orange juice, freshly squeezed
2 tablespoons/30 ml lemon juice, freshly squeezed
2 tablespoons/30 ml brown sugar
1 tablespoon/15 ml cornflour mixed with 2 table-spoons/30 ml strained yogurt (recipe page 210)
4 oranges, divided into segments
1 teaspoon/5 ml fresh mint, chopped

FIRST PREPARE

■ *The Batter:* In a small bowl, mix the egg, egg yolk and milk. In another bowl, sift the flour and make a well in the centre. Pour the egg mixture into the well and gradually stir the flour and egg together until the flour is fully incorporated. Add the vanilla essence and the grated lemon rind. Set aside in a cool place and let rest for 30 minutes.

NOW COOK

■ *The Crêpes:* Heat the oil in an 8-inch/20-cm sauté pan, then pour it into the crêpe batter. This makes the crêpe self-releasing. Pour 2 fl oz/57 ml of the batter into the pan and swirl it to make a round thin crêpe. Toss so that the crêpe becomes slightly brown, approximately 1 minute on each side. Place the cooked crêpes on a plate and set aside, covered with a damp towel.

■ *The Syrup:* Heat the oil in a 10-inch/25-cm skillet. Add the orange rind and cook to extract the volatile oils – about 2 minutes. Add the wine and reduce until it is like syrup, dark in colour but not burnt.

■ Add 2 fl oz/57 ml of the orange juice, 1 table-spoon/15 ml at a time to keep the dark colour. Slowly add the remaining orange juice, the lemon juice and the brown sugar. Stir until dissolved.

■ Strain the syrup, removing the orange rind. Return the syrup to the skillet. Remove from the heat and slowly stir in the cornflour paste. Cook over low heat until the syrup is well combined and slightly thickened.

■ Place one cooked crêpe in the syrup and coat well. Using a spoon and fork, fold the crêpe in half and in half again, so the crêpe is now in the shape of a triangle. Move the triangular crêpe to the side of the pan. Repeat the coating and folding process with the rest of the crêpes. Spoon the segmented oranges and the mint into the syrup with the crêpes.

■ *To Serve:* Remove the crêpes to a warm plate and spoon the orange segments with syrup over the top.

About the Ingredients

ORANGES AND LEMONS – Such a common commodity at the greengrocer's, we forget the intensity that citrus fruits can add to our cooking. Low in calories, high in vitamin C, fresh and sweet, try experimenting with orange and lemon juice in other dishes. (Scallops and Prawns Vincent is a good example, see page 46.) All citrus fruits are ripened on the tree and ready to eat when you see them in the grocer's. Select citrus fruits with firm, thin skin. They should feel heavy in your hand.

TRIFLE WITH CRYSTALLIZED VIOLETS

𝒯his is no 'mere trifle': it is actually one of the best known of English desserts. Even the Italians call it Zuppa Inglese, or English Soup – doubtless because of the addition of sherry in the classic version.

I made this dessert as one large bowlful for at least six people. You may wish to assemble it and fill several small dessert dishes. I have always used crystallized violets to compete against the original's whipped cream.

Nutritional Profile

PER SERVING	CLASSIC	MINIMAX
Calories	634	434
Fat (g)	21	4
Calories from fat	30%	9%
Cholesterol (mg)	196	143
Sodium (mg)	202	119
Fibre (g)	9	6

■ *Classic compared:* Trifle

Time Estimate

Hands On	
Unsupervised	2 Hours
Minutes	10 20 30 40 50 60 70 80 90

Cost Estimate

Low	Medium	Medium High	Celebration

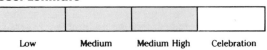

Serves 6

INGREDIENTS

SPONGE CAKE
4 eggs
6 oz/170 g sugar
4 oz/113 g plain flour, sifted

JELLY
1½ pints/910 ml fresh raspberries (frozen berries will work, but make sure they have no added sugar or syrup)
1¼ pints/680 ml cold water
2 flat tablespoons/30 ml brown sugar
2 packets unflavoured gelatin, softened in 4 fl oz/113 ml water for 5 minutes

CUSTARD
¾ pint/425 ml skimmed milk
1 vanilla pod or 1 teaspoon/5 ml vanilla essence
2 tablespoons/30 ml liquid egg substitute
3 tablespoons/45 ml runny honey
2 flat tablespoons/30 ml cornflour
2 packets unflavoured gelatin softened in 4 fl oz/113 ml water for 5 minutes

THE SPONGE CAKE

■ Beat the eggs and sugar together in a large bowl over warm water until the volume has doubled. Stir in the flour until fully incorporated. Pour into a greased and floured 9-inch/23-cm cake tin. Tap the tin on the counter to release any trapped bubbles. Bake in a pre-heated 375°F/190°C/Gas Mark 5 oven for 25 minutes. Turn out to cool on a rack.

■ When the sponge cake has cooled, cut it into 1-inch/2.5-cm cubes.

THE JELLY

■ In a medium saucepan combine 1¼ pints/710 ml of the raspberries with the water and brown sugar. Heat until boiling. Pour the contents through a sieve, catching the raspberry liquid in a bowl. Now capture the last essence of raspberry flavour by gently pressing the raspberries in the sieve to extract the juice. *Be gentle.* You don't want seeds in the raspberry juice. While the juice is still warm, stir in the softened gelatin mixture.

■ Pull out your loveliest large crystal bowl, or any bowl, but preferably one that you can see through. Put the sponge cake pieces and the remaining raspberries in the bowl and cover them with the warm raspberry juice. Press the sponge cake into the juice so that each piece is soaked. Put a plate on the surface to keep the cake submerged in the juice. Pop this into the refrigerator to cool and set.

THE CUSTARD

■ In a large saucepan, heat the skimmed milk and the vanilla pod (or vanilla essence). Turn the heat up and scald the milk.

■ In a small bowl, whisk together the egg substitute, honey and cornflour. Tip this mixture into the scalded milk, bring just to the boil and stir until it thickens. Add the softened gelatin to the custard. This gives it more 'holding power'. Let it cool.

TO ASSEMBLE

■ Take the bowl of soaked sponge cake out of the refrigerator. Pour the custard on top. Cover with clingfilm or foil and pop the trifle back into the refrigerator until set, approximately 30 minutes.

■ Your guests will never miss the traditional whipped cream when you dazzle them with crystallized violets scattered enchantingly over the top. You can find these in many cooking stores, or make your own! See *Helpful Hints.*

Helpful Hints and Observations

CRYSTALLIZED VIOLETS
4 oz/113 g castor sugar
4 drops peppermint extract
2 egg whites
About 20 large, fresh violet blossoms
A very small, clean paintbrush

Pre-heat the oven to 180°F/82°C/Gas Mark ¼ or lower, and line a baking sheet with foil. In a small bowl, rub the sugar and peppermint together with your thumb and forefinger. In another bowl, whip the egg whites to stiff peaks.

Paint each violet on both sides with a thin layer of egg white. Then dip the painted violets into the bowl of sugar and place them carefully on the lined baking sheet. When all the violets are painted, place them in the pre-heated oven for 1 hour. Leave the door slightly ajar to prevent any accumulation of moisture.

Remove carefully and cool completely before using. Store the crystallized violets in an airtight jar in a cool, dry place.

About the Ingredients

VANILLA PODS – These are the pod fruit of a vine that is a member of the orchid family. They are native to Central America and were used by the Aztecs in drink and food. There are three grades of vanilla: fine, woody and vanillon. Fine vanilla beans are very black and 8–10 inches/20–25 cm long. Often fine vanilla will have small crystals of sugar; they are actually drops of vanillin and are a sign of highest quality. Vanilla pods can be used up to ten times. After each use, make a notch in one side of the pod and keep it buried in a jar of sugar.

STOCKS AND STANDARDS

BEEF OR VEAL STOCK

1 lb/450 g de-fatted beef or veal bones
1 teaspoon/5 ml extra light olive oil with a dash
of sesame oil
1 onion, peeled and chopped
4 fl oz/113 ml celery tops
8 fl oz/227 ml carrots, peeled and chopped
1 bay leaf
2 sprigs thyme
4 sprigs parsley
6 peppercorns
2 cloves

■ Pre-heat the oven to 375°F/190°C/Gas Mark 5.

■ Place the beef or veal bones in a roasting tin
and cook for 25 minutes or until nicely browned.
This produces a richer flavour and deeper colour.

■ Sauté the vegetables in the olive oil, then add
the bones and the rest of the ingredients. Now pour
in enough water to cover the ingredients completely.
Maintain this water level by topping up as necessary.

■ Bring to the boil, removing any scum which rises
to the surface.

■ Lower the heat and simmer for 8 to 10 hours.

■ Strain. Set aside any you wish to use immediately
and refrigerate or freeze the rest.

CHICKEN OR TURKEY STOCK

1 teaspoon/5 ml extra light olive oil with a dash
of sesame oil
1 onion, peeled and chopped
4 fl oz/113 ml celery tops
8 fl oz/227 ml carrots, peeled and chopped
1 lb/450 g chicken or turkey bones
1 bay leaf
2 sprigs thyme
4 sprigs parsley
6 peppercorns
2 cloves

■ Sauté the vegetables in the olive oil to release
their flavours. Then add the bones and seasonings.

■ Cover with water and bring to the boil, removing
any scum which rises to the surface.

■ Lower the heat and simmer for 4 to 5 hours,
adding more water as needed to keep everything
covered.

■ Strain. Set aside any you wish to use immediately
and refrigerate or freeze the remaining portion.

FISH OR PRAWN STOCK

1 teaspoon/5 ml extra light olive oil with a dash
of sesame oil
1 onion, peeled and chopped
4 fl oz/113 ml celery tops
2 sprigs thyme
1 bay leaf
1 lb/450 g fish bones (no heads) or prawn shells
6 peppercorns
2 cloves

■ Gently fry the onion, celery, thyme and bay leaf
in the oil. Cook until the onion is translucent and the
flavours are released, being careful not to brown. This
will ensure a light-coloured stock.

■ Add the fish bones or prawn shells and cover
with water.

■ Add the peppercorns and cloves, bring to the
boil and simmer for 25 minutes.

■ Strain through a fine mesh sieve. This will keep
for up to a week in the refrigerator and 6 months in
the freezer.

STRAINED YOGURT

■ Put plain, non-fat yogurt (with no gelatin added)
into a coffee filter inside a strainer.

■ Place the strainer over a bowl and leave to stand
for at least 5 hours or overnight in the refrigerator.
The whey drains out, leaving you with a thick, creamy
yogurt cheese – an invaluable ingredient for many
recipes.

BOUQUET GARNI

To make a bouquet garni, cut a 4-inch/10-cm square
piece of muslin or cheesecloth, put the ingredients in
the centre and tie the four corners securely to form a
tight pouch. Hit the bouquet garni several times with
a mallet or the back of a knife to bruise the herbs and
spices, helping them to release their volatile oils.

Index